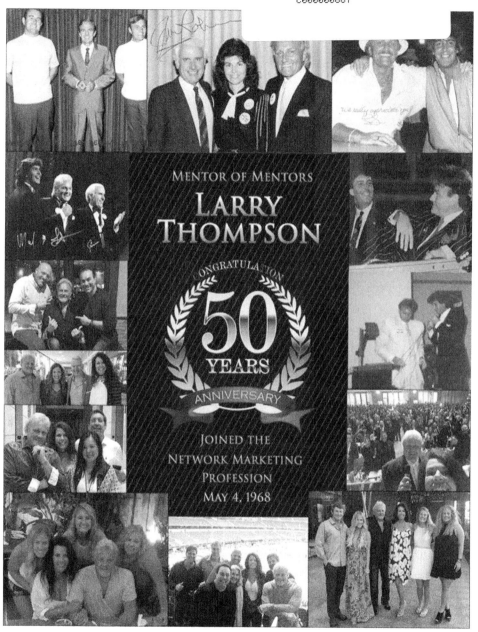

MENTOR OF MENTORS

LARRY THOMPSON

CONGRATULATION

50 YEARS

ANNIVERSARY

JOINED THE
NETWORK MARKETING
PROFESSION
MAY 4, 1968

JOIN

THE

Millionaire
Training™
BOOK CLUB

with Larry and Taylor Thompson

Join people from around the world every Friday at 12:00 CST, where Larry and Taylor provide free network marketing training to The Millionaire Training Book Club Members. You also will receive special offers exclusive only in The Millionaire Training Book Club.

Go to **TheMillionaireTraining.com** to register.

THE

Millionaire Training™

Golden Principles That Created the Top Network Marketers of Today

Larry Thompson

MANIFEST
PUBLISHING

To order copies in quantities of 500 or more, call 972.632.6364.

ISBN--13: 978-1-944913-69-4

ACKNOWLEDGMENTS

Thank you so much for purchasing this book. The information you're going to find within these pages has been transformational for me over the past 50 years of my life. I continue to find value from these concepts today, and there are countless numbers of others across America and around the world whose lives have been transformed just as mine has been by the very same principles you're about to discover.

Someone once said, "Long after I may have forgotten what you said, I will always remember how what you said made me feel." The way the following few people "made me feel" by something they did or something they said, helped me make a major transformation in my character.

This book is not about me; it's a compilation of the experiences of each of the contributors and how they used these principles and the philosophies to change their life for the better – whether they were a school teacher, a plumber or a salesperson.

There are so many people I want to thank and acknowledge, and the first two were both major mentors for me. What I learned from them has made this book possible. I met both of them on May 4, 1968, and while neither of them is still living, their names, their philosophies, and their legacies will live within me forever.

Bobby DePew and Jim Rohn

Bobby DePew and Jim Rohn, my very first two mentors, had such a major impact on my life that I cannot imagine where I would be today without them. I refer to Bobby as the original strategist and tactician of network marketing with his psychological, his strategic and tactical approach along with his teaching style that forever changed me.

And, Jim, because of his philosophical approach in what he taught and the example that he established for me to follow. I will never be the same as I once was because of who he was and how he was. Everything that I am today, I owe to both of these two gentlemen.

Today, each of us can reach out and touch the lives of others and change them in the process, in the same manner that Bobby and Jim's example impacted me.

Mark Hughes

Many, many years ago, a very young entrepreneur, Mark Hughes, invited me to play a key role with him in his newly formed company called Herbalife. Mark said to me, "I want you to take full responsibility for building my entire sales team."

I will forever be indebted to Mark for his faith and trust in me to do that because his distributors were his family, and without the platform he provided for me at Herbalife, I wouldn't have had the chance to be where I am today.

Lari - Leah

This special acknowledgement must go to my daughters, Lari and Leah. Together, we went through all of my growing years and becoming the person I am today. Many times, we missed birthdays, graduations and school events; yet, we continued to love and support each other through it all. Now, I am blessed to work with you in all the entrepreneurial businesses in which we've been involved. What a joyful life you have given me!

Tish Rochin

My sister, Tish, was the first distributor I sponsored in Herbalife, and she was the first distributor for our company in the state of Texas. I fondly remember Tish being at the front of the room the day *The Millionaire Training* was recorded in 1981. Mark and I always referred to her as "the lady truck driver," and her contribution to the success of Herbalife has been beyond question, immeasurable. She was the second distributor who became a Millionaire in Herbalife.

Dennis Dowdell

I want to acknowledge, Dennis Dowdell, who also was present the day we recorded *The Millionaire Training*. Dennis is a unique man who became a very, very good friend of mine and he was Distributor #86 in Herbalife. Time has intensified our friendship. His support over the years has always been appreciated, and now we're neighbors in Texas with four decades of special memories.

John Addy

Someone who has become a great supporting friend to me over the last decade is John Addy; his unwavering support, encouragement, wisdom and talent have helped make the world of technology work for me to the maximum extent possible. He turned out to be one of the missing corner pieces of the "success puzzle" by filling a very specialized need.

Carolyn Tarr, Vicki Tarr Sorg, Rolf Sorg and Carston Ledulé

In Europe 26 years ago, the combination of Vicki Tarr Sorg (who I sometimes refer to as my 'adopted daughter') and her mother, Carolyn Tarr, along with Rolf Sorg and Carsten Ledule', created a commitment to perpetuate the rise in popularity for network marketing in Europe. It was their commitment to perpetuate and share the principles and philosophies contained in the stories in this "success manual" that will help accelerate the growth of the industry throughout Europe for decades to come.

Ron Henley

Ron Henley has, for many years, been fascinated by the potential for opportunity to be found in network marketing. He has carefully recorded the history of the founders, the leaders, and the many companies that have come and gone, and that continue to emerge. His historical compilation allows us to better understand the evolution of our industry. A very close friend and confidante of Jim Rohn, Ron has emerged as the "museum curator" of network marketing. Ron and I both continue to grow because of our friendship and because of the presence we have on each other's lives.

Tonja Waring

I first met Tonja at one of her manifesting events and was immediately and profoundly impressed not only by the substance of her message, but also with how she delivered the message of *Getting Clear on What You Want.* I immediately knew that she had valuable skills that were parallel with my own. In addition to being the head of her own company, she serves as the editor and publisher of this book.

Tonja had been aware of *The Millionaire Training* even before we met and has used its concepts in building both her business and her life. She is multi-talented. I believe her marketing genius helped My Pillow become a dramatic success. In editing this book, she told me, "This book will have a greater effect on the lives of people than *Think and Grow Rich.*"

Taylor and I are proud to call her our friend.

John Fleming

John Fleming and I both joined the network marketing industry with Bestline Products. Even though, we were in different downlines, we had the same DNA profile that emanated from Bobby and Jim. I was so proud the day I heard that John Fleming brought networking marketing to Avon and later became president of Avon West.

Since then, we've worked on numerous projects together and our mutual respect is unparalleled, as there are so few who truly grasp the solid principles necessary to build an Avon or Herbalife. We have worked very closely together the last three years. In my opinion he is the premier authority on the gig economy. He has a vast understanding of who is in this enormous entrepreneurial playground and how they can prosper with the opportunity.

Taylor Thompson

Seldom does a person do well in life and business without someone at their side who has the keys to his or her heart and who at the same time possesses their own unique collection of skills and talents. My wife, Taylor Thompson, holds such keys, skills and talents.

First, the publication of this book would not be possible at all without Taylor. She was insistent with me that this message had to be made available for everyone to read, especially women. It was Taylor who did all the interviews and who remained focused on capturing the details of the many people involved to make certain the dream of completing the project became a reality and their contributions memorialized.

Taylor is much more than that. Taylor was successful before we ever met. For many years now, Taylor has digested and embodied the principles in not only *The Millionaire Training*, but also *The Six Pillars, The Four Generations of*

Network Marketing and so much more. She has stood beside me on stages around the world and delivered the heart and soul of this training that began with Bobby DePew and Jim Rohn so many years ago.

During *The Millionaire Training* four decades ago, I predicted the substantial impact women would have in network marketing. Today, 70% of people in network marketing are women. Because women and men assimilate and disseminate information differently, the same philosophies and concepts delivered by me (and now by Taylor) will have a greater impact in the future of our profession which is dominated by women.

I know of no other person than my wife, Taylor, who is better qualified to continue delivering these invaluable principles. Taylor is the founder of The SheNetwork and my training partner in the LT WealthBuilding Academy.

Taylor has blessed me immensely in her love and support through the years. I have no doubt she will continue to inspire and teach many entrepreneurs, especially women, these principles. I have the greatest confidence that the torch that was given to me by Bobby and Jim will burn brightly through Taylor for many years to come.

* * * * *

And, finally...it would be inappropriate to refer to this publication as merely 'a book' - implying that it's intended to educate or entertain those who read it. I believe it would be far more accurate to refer to its contents as a source of ideas and insights that have been used by many people around the world as a "success manual" to increase their wealth and enhance their personal life.

If that happened for ordinary working people like those who you will read about on these pages, it can happen for YOU – provided you not only read this book, but that you assimilate and internalize its truths to the extent that the contents become part of who and how you are. The good news is, you can do that!

Larry Thompson
September 5, 2020

CONTENTS

The Millionaire Training

Photos

Success Stories

LT WealthBuilding Academy

FOREWORD

by John Fleming

I felt honored when Larry Thompson asked me to provide a foreword for his book, *The Millionaire Training*. Larry and I started direct selling careers with the same company. We learned from the absolute best. A few, including Larry, went on to become legendary in their contributions. Larry's good friend, Mark Hughes, founder of Herbalife International, and Jim Rohn are names that many of us will never forget. Each of the three (Mark, Larry, and Jim) became known for the leadership, inspiration, teaching, coaching, and mentorship that became the foundation of what we know today as Herbalife. Mark was the charismatic founder and leader, Jim was the motivation and inspiration, and Larry, the teacher, coach, mentor, and builder.

Over 50 years ago, Larry Thompson found a way to reduce complexity to simplicity. Perhaps this is why Larry and I have become such good friends. My respect, appreciation, and enjoyment of our friendship probably have a lot to do with my background and way of thinking. I always wanted to become an architect. As a kid, I loved to draw buildings, not things or people. I chose my college based solely upon the relationship of the college with the legendary architect Ludwig Mies van der Rohe, the founder of the school of architecture at the Illinois Institute of Technology. Mies was an influencer in the world-renown Bauhaus School of Design founded in Germany in 1919 by architect Walter Gropius.

I worked in the office of Mies van der Rohe while he was still living, and the impact of a "less is more" philosophy, applied to architecture, changed my entire way of thinking about everything else I would do in life. I also learned to understand that good design is only meaningful when it leads to good construction. The pyramids in Egypt, the Parthenon in Athens, Greece, and many other structures that remain standing, in whole or part, throughout the world are evidence of the lasting effect of great design. Yet, as amazing as the designs are, they would not have lasting influence were they not built in a way that stood the test of time.

To this day, we do not understand precisely how the pyramids or other ancient structures I have mentioned were constructed. How could anyone have possibly built some of those structures more than 2,000 years ago? These thoughts relative to my love and respect for architectural history relate to how I think about Larry. I view Larry as one of the great builders of the direct selling business model. His business-building construction techniques are legendary.

The stories herein are amazing … stories that need to be told! Each one is an incredible example of how the direct selling model was used to accomplish extraordinary success. Most of the stories are about those who built their businesses as independent contractors. Some are about how personal efforts have contributed to the growth of other significant direct selling companies. Foundational to each story is an encounter with Larry Thompson and the adoption of his principles. His approach to how we can adopt behaviors and duplicate behaviors in others remain legendary teaching concepts. His ideas remain as relevant today as at any time in the past, perhaps even more relevant.

As this book goes to press, the direct selling channel of distribution, which is often recognized by such other labels as Network Marketing, Social Selling, Social Entrepreneurship, or Social Commerce, is at an inflection point. The business model's attributes are being refined, and often redefined, to better position opportunities that will resonate in a marketplace that has grown to embrace technology and simplification in how we work and live. I call this new frontier the gig economy because of the enormous opportunities it offers, the incredible use of technology, and the simplicity associated with gig income-earning opportunities.

The opportunity to earn $500 to $1,500 per month, in ways that offer flexibility and freedom in how the work is done, has attracted an estimated 50 million-plus Americans to gig opportunities. The current world changes may accelerate this growth. There always will be some people who will earn a lot more than the income range we have mentioned, and their leadership can make it possible for more people to experience what they desire.

Direct selling companies are a part of the gig economy, and the opportunity to thrive has, perhaps, never been greater. However, new opportunities also require the development of, and adherence to, foundational principles that enable the building of lasting structures. I am not surprised that Larry has an excellent vision for what the future holds. The pyramids still stand, and so do the basic principles Larry has advocated over many years. How the principles are used and supported by technology has changed.

The stories on the following pages are the beginning. These stories are testimonies. They are also building blocks. Read them carefully as times are changing, and the future is always faster than we think. In fact, we are in the future! The stories are not about the present and past; they are about what the future holds. Will there be modifications? Of course. It is my pleasure to have been able to share a few words before you read some of the greatest stories ever told, relative to direct selling!

John Fleming

John T. Fleming is a student and advocate of the direct selling channel of distribution. His many years of involvement with the direct selling business model has been through actual participation as a direct seller, as an officer and pace-setter within one of the world's largest direct selling companies, as well as Publisher and Editor-in-Chief of Direct Selling News, Researcher, Consultant, Speaker, and Writer. Acknowledgment of John's accomplishments, advocacy, and understanding of the direct selling business model is best summarized by the three most distinguished awards he has received: the Direct Selling Education Foundation's Circle of Honor award in 1997, and induction into the Direct Selling Association Hall of Fame and recipient of the first Direct Selling News Lifetime Achievement Award, both in 2016. You can read more of his story at www.johntfleming.info. John is currently the Project Lead on the Ultimate Gig Research Project and co-author of Ultimate Gig, www.ultimategigbook.com.

A LOOK AT HISTORY

by Ron Henley,
Network Marketing Historian

The date is February 21, 1981. It is a bright, sunny morning in Los Angeles, California and we find ourselves at the Bonaventure Hotel. We're there for the first and only event of its kind, an event called, *The Millionaire Training*.

Forty-eight hours before the event begins, sensing the enormous value of what was about to be shared, Mark Hughes decides to record what is said. A man is hired to record the event and is paid $150 to capture the audio. He duct tapes a microphone to the center seat in the front row and turns on the recorder.

It's time to get started and Doug Stuntz walks up in front of the room. The boisterous room goes quiet as he gets everyone's attention. After a brief introduction, a 35-year-old, excited Larry Thompson takes the stage.

Once too shy to stand up in front of his classroom and give an oral book report, he is a walking example of everything he is about to share. He brings everything he has to the small and enthralled crowd.

Four hours later, he has given what has been called, "One of the greatest business speeches of all time." With zero edits, the now world famous *The Millionaire Training* audio cassettes are distributed to the field and the rest, as the saying goes, is history.

Speaking of history, where did Larry Thompson learn all that he shared that day? Who did he learn it from? That, my friends, is a fascinating story. One I am honored to share with you.

Larry learned all he shared that day from some of the original founders of the network marketing profession. What he shared came from a unique set of circumstances that had begun decades earlier. Circumstances that gave Larry Thompson credentials that few on the planet have.

To better understand *The Millionaire Training*, we must go back to the place it all started:

1934: Carl Rehnborg starts selling a vitamin and mineral supplement. He names his new company, California Vitamins, Inc.

1939. At a cost of $69.56, Rehnborg renames California Vitamins, Inc. to Nutrilite Products, Inc. At this point, it was still a direct sales company.

1943-1944: Having too many customers to personally service, Rehnborg asks people in key areas to buy a little extra product and service a customer base. He agrees to pay a commission and later, overrides, to these key people, loosely creating the business model that becomes network marketing.

1945: Sensing the huge opportunity of the supplement business, two men named Lee S. Mytinger and William S.

Casselberry make a deal with Rehnborg to become Nutrilite National Master Distributors.

Here's where things get COOL.

1948: Rich Schnackenberg joins Nutrilite and develops the core foundations that finish out the business model started by Rehnborg while building the largest known team in the company.

1949: Neil Maaskant joins the Schnackenberg organization in Nutrilite. Knowing his cousin, Jay Van Andel, was always looking for a good opportunity, he tells Jay, and his partner, Richard DeVos, about the opportunity.

Jay Van Andel and Richard DeVos (future founders of Amway) join the Schnackenberg organization in Nutrilite, but after only selling a single order of product, they completely lose interest in the business.

A few weeks later, Maaskant talks Van Andel and DeVos into attending a Nutrilite company event in Chicago where they hear Rehnborg, Schnackenberg, and other leaders speak.

The event rekindles their interest and the two men go to work. Over the next decade, they build a thriving organization of over 2,000 distributors.

About this time, the FDA really goes after Mytinger and Casselberry for many infractions including false advertising and bogus product claims.

Rich Schnackenberg tries to warn the two men and advises against their strategies to no avail. Frustrated by all of this, Schnackenberg tries to buy controlling interest in Nutrilite but Rehnborg would not sell. Rich maintains his distributorship but stops actively building.

1953: Dr. J. B. Jones, a direct student of Napoleon Hill, tours the country giving lectures on Hill's *Laws of Success*.

Seeing the promise of food supplements, he starts a company that couples the philosophy of abundance with vitamins and christens his new company Abundavita.

Dr. Jones, having watched and admired Rich Schnackenberg from a distance, and knowing of his current frustrations with Nutrilite, recruits him as Executive Vice President of Training for Abundavita. Reluctantly, Schnackenberg resigns his position with Nutrilite. Excited about joining a success philosophy with selling food supplements, he throws himself into this new enterprise.

Within months, the new company is thriving. While giving a lecture on Napoleon Hill's success philosophy in Long Beach, California, Dr. Jones recruits a pants presser named J. Earl Shoaff.

Shoaff and Schnackenberg become best friends and, under Schnackenberg's watchful eye, Shoaff works his way up to Executive Vice President of Sales in less than a year. Dr. Jones promises the two men lucrative stock options once the company hits $1 Million per month in sales so they throw their heart and soul into it.

1955: The two men cross the country building Abundavita until, one night, in October, they find themselves in Pensacola, Florida. There, a 25-year-old Sears stock clerk, Jim Rohn, blown away by what he had heard the two men share, joins the company. He borrows $200 from his parents to get started.

About this time, Shoaff and Schnackenberg are left in charge of the company as Dr. Jones begins an around-the-world vacation spanning a year and a half. The company explodes under the two men and they quickly hit their $1 Million per month sales goal and sales kept climbing.

1957: Upon his return, Dr. Jones' ego could not handle the fact that Shoaff and Schnackenberg had tripled the company without him. Jones not only reneges on the stock deal he made with the two men, he cuts their pay. They resign on the spot.

Frustrated beyond belief, they ponder on everything that has happened to them while considering their next move. After much discussion, Schnackenberg convinced Shoaff that they should try to buy controlling interest in Nutrilite. They made their proposal, but, again, they could not get Rehnborg to sell.

The men meet in Schnackenberg's living room and decide to start their own food supplement company from scratch. In July, the Nutri-Bio Corporation is born. They flip a coin to decide who would become President and Shoaff won the toss. Schnackenberg would be Executive Vice President.

Jim Rohn, along with a huge chunk of Abundavita distributors, leave to join Nutri-Bio. It was here that Shoaff and Schnackenberg absolutely thrived. Jim Rohn, under the direct mentorship of the two men also thrived.

So many legends and icons of the profession got their start in Nutri-Bio, such as:

- Jim Rohn (who had come on in Abundavita)
- William E (Bill) Bailey
- Robert "Bobby" DePew
- William Penn Patrick
- Zig Ziglar

Both Shoaff and Schnackenberg become multi-millionaires while helping create unheard of fortunes for their distributor base. Nutri-Bio begins outselling Abundavita,

Nutrilite, and every other food supplement company in business at the time.

1959: Van Andel and DeVos, also frustrated, leave Nutrilite, and with many of their top earners, begin their own company called The American Way (Amway) selling liquid soap called Frisk.

1961: When Shoaff and Schnackenberg decide to expand Nutri-Bio into Canada, they hand pick Jim Rohn to be Executive Vice President of the Canadian Division. At 31 years old, the huge bump in pay along with lucrative stock options make Jim a multimillionaire with a net worth of $2.3 Million.

1963: Nutri-Bio folds. Schnackenberg and Rohn decide to launch a new supplement company called Bio-Lite but are shut down before they can launch. Rohn, realizing the value of all he had learned, gives his first public speech at the Beverly Hills Hotel which starts a speaking career on the side.

1964: Shoaff wants completely out of the food supplement business and starts Ovation Cosmetics, Schnackenberg comes on as Executive Vice President. The company is still in business today.

1964: William Penn Patrick starts Holiday Magic Cosmetics. Bill Bailey and Bobby DePew come on as executives with Bailey becoming the first president of the company. Zig Ziglar joins and quickly becomes one of the top earners in the company. It was at this time that a sewing machine salesman named Glenn W. Turner joins and becomes a top earner.

1966: After a disagreement with Penn Patrick, Bill Bailey resigns from Holiday Magic and starts Bestline Products selling a biodegradable soap called Zif. Bobby DePew joins as Vice President of the new venture. Larry Huff joins.

1967: Glenn Turner leaves Holiday Magic and starts his own company called Koscot Cosmetics. He also later starts a motivation company called Dare to Be Great!

1968: Bobby DePew invites Jim Rohn to a Bestline meeting in San Jose, California. Mike Fuller invites a co-worker named Larry Thompson to that same meeting where both men join the company that night.

1969: John Fleming (future president of Avon West and gig economy expert) joins Bestline Products and is introduced to the network marketing business model.

1972: Les Brown joins Bestline Products. He's at the Neil House Hotel in Columbus, Ohio. There for another meeting, he hears Bill Bailey's voice through the walls and decides to check it out. Bill introduces Jim Rohn and Les is blown away and joins the company.

All of this is filtering down into that fateful day of *The Millionaire Training*. Here's where it really starts to tighten up.

1978: A suit salesman named Mark Hughes joins a supplement company called Slender Now. It is in this company where Mark attends his first Jim Rohn seminar.

1979: A pivotal year. Slender Now goes out of business. Larry Huff starts a new company called Golden Youth that markets supplements and a piece of exercise equipment called a Slim Gym. Huff invites Larry Thompson to take a look. Mark Hughes is there, too. Mark and Larry Thompson meet and both men join the company that night. Mark quickly becomes a top earner and Thompson becomes Vice President, so the two men form a solid friendship.

Within a few months, Golden Youth folds and Mark decides to start his own company. Thompson, needing a break, and missing his family, moves back to Texas to be closer to them. Mark is serious about starting this new company and wants Larry to be a part of it. Larry is hesitant to jump back in but gladly consults with Mark about products, marketing, compensation plan, etc. Jim Rohn was also consulting with Mark offering his guidance from the beginning, too.

1980: Mark launches Herbalife International. Selling products from the trunk of his car, the company does $24,000 in sales their first month. $48,000 the second month. By May, Mark and Larry shake hands on a deal for Larry to officially become part of Herbalife, but it's not until October 7th that he actually does so.

Mark wanted to make him vice president of the company right away, and just like Jim Rohn had done in Bestline, Larry said, "No, they're not going to accept me unless I build a team." So, he went to work building a team. On January 4, 1981, Larry became the official Executive Vice President of Herbalife International.

Six weeks later, on February 21, 1981, Larry hits the stage and delivers *The Millionaire Training*. It was a culmination of all Larry had learned over the previous 13 years.

Here's a simplified view:

Rich Schnackenberg started it ALL and is the man this entire profession can be directly traced back to and he was an avid student of Napoleon Hill, Orison Swett Marden, Wallace Wattles, Dale Carnegie, George S. Clason, James Allen, and more.

Rich Schnackenberg poured into Earl Shoaff.

Both men poured into Jim Rohn, Bill Bailey, Bobby DePew, William Penn Patrick, Zig Ziglar.

Jim Rohn, Bill Bailey, and Bobby DePew poured into Larry Thompson.

Jim Rohn and Larry Thompson poured into Mark Hughes.

The same ideology that created the legends and icons of this profession, the same ideology that had been poured into Larry Thompson is what he shared that day in *The Millionaire Training*.

The people in this book are all products of what was shared and captured that day. Some were there in person. Most of us were given the audio and wore out more cassettes than you can count. All that Larry had, he poured into us. Now, with this book, let all of us pour into you.

You are holding a time machine in your hands that reveals every secret, every nuance, every foundational principle that created, sustains, and will build and maintain this profession forevermore.

The 2nd edition of *The Millionaire Training* is being written at this very moment by YOU. It's being written by what you do with all that you learn here. It's being written by the people who use the knowledge in this book to change lives.

Let me share an insight with you that can make all the difference with your mindset and your attitude. Remember this as you read, study, and implement what you learn in this book:

We are all part California Vitamin Company.

We are all part Nutrilite.

We are all part Abundavita.

We are all part Nutri-Bio.

We are all part Amway.

We are all part Ovation.

We are all part Mary Kay.

We are all part Bestline.

We are all part Holiday Magic.

We are all part Koscot.

We are all part Dare To Be Great.

We are all part Slender Now.

We are all part Golden Youth.

We are all part Herbalife.

And so many more.

Past.

Present.

FUTURE.

Just as much as we are all part of the companies that came before us. Just as much as we are all part of the founders of this profession. So are we ALL a part of *The Millionaire Training*!

The DNA from the very beginning.

The DNA from *The Millionaire Training*.

Is in our blood.

In our hearts.

In our minds.

A treasured few like Larry Thompson are still around.

Most have gone away.

But the lessons they taught.

The skills they sharpened.

The attitudes they forged.

The hope they brought.

The lives they forever changed.

The legends and icons they created.

Are within us ALL!

The failures taught us what not to do.

The successes taught us what to do.

We carry all of that force with us.

To invest in today.

To invest in our better future.

As individuals.

As leaders.

As companies.

We all stand on the shoulders of giants.

Together, we can pay it forward.

ACCOLADES

I got my hands on Larry's *The Millionaire Training* tapes and wore those tapes out. Those became my original training as far as understanding the concepts, basics, and fundamentals, and how to build a business. I would listen over and over again and take notes which kept me in the game. I would run the ads and do the briefings, month after month, person after person.

It wasn't easy, though; I was often crying at night with no idea what to do. I had all this product, and nobody was signing up to join, but I just kept doing it. I stayed in the game and did it over and over and over again. A few simple disciplines done consistently would eventually equal multiple rewards. *See full story on page 161.*

Jeff Roberti
#1 Distributor, Juice Plus+

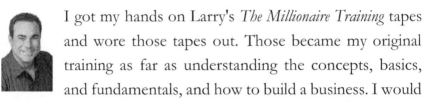

Nearly 40 years later, *The Millionaire Training* is just as relevant and useful today for building a business as it was back then. The tools and concepts Larry taught us never change. You could take the Herbalife distributor kit with Larry's *The Millionaire Training*, drop it on an island somewhere, and the person who found it could build a business. I'm grateful Larry believed in me and encouraged me to spread my wings and move to Texas. He took me, a lady truck driver, and helped me build a business that has flourished beyond my wildest dreams. *See full story on page 170.*

Tish Rochin
Chairman's Club, Herbalife International

 My story is probably a lot different than many of those who join network marketing. I've never had any other job. I started in the network marketing industry at the age of 19 and built it into a career. One of the key takeaways I got from *The Millionaire Training* was to Employ Yourself. I know this wasn't as big of a challenge for me as it was for some coming from other industries because I've never known anything different. So many people want to be their own boss, but they are terrible at it. If you start with Larry's methods as the foundation of your business, you'll have the right mindset to build a successful business. *See full story on page 179.*

Trey Herron
Chairman's Club, Herbalife

 Through the years, Larry has been a great advisor and a constant inspiration. He helped give me the confidence I needed to build myself up and make my business what it is today. His ability to see the big picture and evaluate things from the outside helped open me up to new possibilities and the chance to see growth I didn't dream possible. He truly is the best promoter I have ever met in my life and a true master at sales strategies. When I signed my contract with him back in 2011, he told me we were going to hit a billion a year in sales by 2018. He always was a little faster than me (it

took until 2019), but he wasn't far off. And now, he's telling me we're going to hit $2 billion a year in the next two years. I believe him. *See full story on page 187.*

Rolf Sorg
Founder, PM International

 I was basically on my own and in a place where I didn't have a support system; so, *The Millionaire Training* tapes became my support system. I would listen to them over and over again. And some of the concepts that were on there and what I learned and what I applied made a huge difference. So, as an example, when Larry talked about when he went to buy his Cadillac Eldorado. Larry and *The Millionaire Training* taught me that you put your intention out there, you work hard, you have a great attitude and you just keep going forward with it. It was a persistence and consistency that I could see. I thought, *You know, I might not have the skill, but I do have persistence going for me!*

Larry said, "What you lack in skill, make up in numbers." So, I believed that if I just kept going, I could do like this guy. And he was so down to earth. That's what I loved the most about listening to Larry. *See full story on page 193.*

Karla Ingolio
President's Team, Herbalife International

 If you keep it simple, *The Millionaire Training* is remarkably as relevant today as when it came out in 1981. Whether you sell skincare, weight loss, hair care, services, remote controls, whatever your company is, it doesn't matter. It doesn't matter what your compensation plan is. Follow *The Millionaire Training*, because it's proven it works for over 40 years. These concepts are not something Larry just came up with yesterday. You've got somebody with 50 years' of experience in the network marketing industry.

No matter what company you're with, stay focused on *The Millionaire Training*. I'm not saying don't get involved with your company, don't go to your corporate events and all that. But ultimately, I believe you've got to keep it simple. Right now, I can go on Facebook or Instagram, and there's 50 people offering training. The funny part is though, all of them put together don't have the experience Larry has. Larry has been doing network marketing longer than these people are old. It's easy to get hooked by the latest, greatest shiny object, or the fanciest, newest trainer, or the guy that got lucky one time in a deal but never can do it again. Larry's concepts are constant. These are things that are not going to change another 50 years from now. We'll all be gone, but they'll still be going. If you follow the simple basics, no matter what your company is, you're going to be successful. *See full story on page 204.*

Jeff Weisberg
Top Earner and Entrepreneur

 We may have switched to another company that happened to be better for us timing-wise, but we applied every single principle we had learned from Larry. We didn't add to it or take away from it; we simply did what Larry taught us, and then suddenly, we had

success. Fortunately, or unfortunately, depending on how you look at things, we've had to change companies several times, but each time we made a switch, we did the same things. We would take Larry's principles and teachings and do it again in another company with different products.

It didn't matter because it worked every time. Rick and I have been working together for 30-something years, and that's because we got educated by the best and applied what he told us to do. Nothing has been perfect along the way, but we've never doubted a single second how we should go about doing things. You see that it works, and you just do it over and over again. That's the bottom line. *See full story on page 218.*

Rick & Michelle Teague
Top 10 Distributor, Modere

 In a lot of ways, it was that initial devastation of Herbalife that built the network marking industry to where it is today. Many of the Herbalife distributors who left, went on to different companies that now make up this industry.

One of the critical things that stuck with me from Larry's principles is a mantra passed on to him from Jim Rohn. You read about it in *The Millionaire Training* – for things to change, you have to change. There's a natural tendency to point fingers outside of yourself, but if you accept the fact that you're the one in charge, you're embracing the philosophy that everything you could ever want can come your way. *See full story on page 231.*

Jay Bennett
Top Field Executive, Isagenix

I never had a problem with listening to *The Millionaire Training* over and over and over. I never ever had a problem with that. Some people, they'll listen to that and never again will they listen to it. It's like they just don't get it. It's because of denial, because of arrogance, because of lack of teachability, or because they really didn't listen that first time. I'll tell you what, all my key people, they've all metabolized it. It's their foundation, too.

If you are a new distributor, plug into to the support system, plug into the closed LT WealthBuilding Academy group we have with Larry and Taylor Thompson. It's an incredible learning environment, that becomes part of your breakfast in the morning. *See full story on page 241.*

Jack and Julie Silva
President's Team, Herbalife International

 I would listen to *The Millionaire Training* over and over until I eventually lost track of the set. Well, years later, when the internet first came about, I heard about eBay and started stalking their site to see if I could find myself another set of the *The Millionaire Training* tapes. It took me a while, and I ended up paying five times what they initially cost me to buy them new! I am not sure why the seller wanted to let these tapes go, but I'm so grateful he did because I attribute them to part of my success. *See full story on page 246.*

Lisa Grossmann
Top Rank Distributor, Pruvit

Larry Thompson is solely responsible for *The One Thing That Changed Everything* in my life. Listening to *The Millionaire Training* tapes gave me the inspiration and belief that I could succeed in any business. What Larry instilled in me was something more valuable than any college master's degree. He gave me the ability to know my audience, language, and behavior. He helped me to develop an *Unshakeable Belief System* that would be crucial later in life no matter what challenges I would face. *See full story on page 255.*

Frank Mulcahy
Top Earner, LegalShield

When Larry comes out on stage, it is a magical moment. There were compelling things Larry said that day, that I still use in my business 36 years later. The number one being the mantra he had learned and passed on to us, "For things to change, you have to change. For things to get better, you have to get better."

It was the first time that I had heard those types of words articulated by someone. And, Larry's a stranger to me. He's an executive in this big company that I joined, and I'm just a total nobody. I'm just a kid out there in the audience, but that message was crucial not only for my career but for my life. *See full story on page 264.*

John Solleder
Senior Platinum, Immunotec

The principles in *The Millionaire Training*, are universal, they are timeless. I was just a young man when I started. Larry was so good at every aspect of what his mentors taught him of breaking it down, simplifying it. When a distributor calls me today, and they want to talk about why they're not where they want to be, I point to those principles. There's nothing outside of it. There are new shiny objects, but there's only one shiny object that Larry taught me, and that is we get paid to recruit and sell. What do I do every day? I recruit and sell. *See full story on page 273.*

Dan McCormick
Top Global Distributor, Nu Skin

While Jim Rohn and I were riding along one day and the conversation turned to Larry Thompson, he got really quiet. He was on the passenger side, and he kind of turned toward the window. Then he turned back around and caught me in the corner of his eye, and said, "You know, when Larry Thompson was in his prime, nobody could touch him." What Jim meant was, when Larry gets in the groove, when he gets in that sweet spot and he taps into this eternal wisdom of the ages (which he is so perfect at doing), there's not anybody on this planet who could touch him as a speaker and trainer.

Ron Henley
Chief Historian of Network Marketing
Worked with Jim Rohn

I learned my most valuable skills from Larry during my time at Herbalife and was able to take them with me everywhere I went and be successful. The concepts I learned from *The Millionaire Training* are timeless, and the beautiful part is you can teach those same skills to others and replicate them throughout your entire organization. If you're consistent and persistent, you'll build yourself a nice army that duplicates into a massive sales force which in turn allows you to **achieve** what at one time may have seemed unimaginable. *See full story on page 289.*

Dan Stammen
Co-Owner, WorldVentures Holdings

 There's no question that Larry's concept of talking with 10 people a day was vital. I was not going to let my team or myself have a negative Mental Projector or a Disease of Attitude. Things are going to grow no matter what, so eliminate what's bad. To take care of a rose bush, you have to water it, and you don't allow the weeds of negativity to grow. Those concepts have never left me, even 37 years later.

I relied so much on Larry's teachings during this time of transition at Herbalife. Larry would often come to Dallas to lead trainings, and if I knew he was coming, I would drive my old beat-up car three-and-a-half hours to listen to a two-hour training. I'd take my notes, drive back to Austin, and hold my own meeting where maybe three people would show up, but I would just go after it and teach those three people. *See full story on page 307.*

Dan Waldron
Chairman's Club, Herbalife

If someone handed out badges for being Larry Thompson's number one fan, I'd be the first in line. I can't think of anyone else who has added as much value to this industry as Larry has. It's an honor to be a forever student of his, and that I'm able to call him a friend. *See full story on page 316.*

Ray Higdon
Founder, The Rank Makers

 Most of the training today is all based on marketing training, not network marketing training. Marketing training is evolving constantly, changing day-to-day and not the foundation. It all changes on things that we have no control over like apps that come and go.

Network marketing training is about people and how people relate to each other through sharing stories and wanting to help each other. That never changes. *See full story on page 320.*

Taylor Thompson
Founder, The SheNetwork®

THE
Millionaire
Training™

On February 21, 1981, Larry Thompson, the mastermind behind the Herbalife International success story, was recorded presenting the 1st official Herbalife International Training Seminar at the Bonaventure Hotel in Los Angeles, California, USA. At the time, Herbalife was doing less than a $1,000,000 a month. Four years later, it was producing more than $100,000,000 per month...

The Millionaire Training, a four-hour recording, was a distillation of 15 years' worth of applied information, tactics, and psychology that Larry mastered from mentors and peers, Bobby DePew and Jim Rohn, who are considered the original strategists and personal development cornerstones of the network marketing industry. Larry was very fortunate to learn directly from the source and to be able to share with you.

Keep in mind that there was no YouTube, Facebook, or any other training that an individual could access online like they can today that taught how to employ yourself, build a team, and essentially become successful.

The Millionaire Training has been, and still is, the ultimate full-immersion training for ambitious entrepreneurs, regardless of what company, products or services they represent.

There is no telling how many lives and companies it has positively affected since then. For perspective, *The Wall Street Journal* called Larry "The Original Architect of Wealth Building."

Long-haired Hippie
Construction Worker

You want to know what this is all about? I'm going to share some ideas with you here that have helped many of us over the years (especially me), become successful. And, success is always relative to where you are and where you've been.

It's an exciting day for me. Since my first meeting at Herbalife and being involved with it, this is a training class that Mark Hughes (Herbalife founder) and I talked about since Day One. We're real excited about this – to be able to share some of the things with you, aside from our product line, aside from our marketing system, a very important part to make your business work.

I really appreciate those of you who have taken the time to be here who are not a part of Herbalife. You're certainly welcome to take some notes here today, and if this can benefit you and your business or your job or your profession or career, you're certainly welcome to some of these ideas. We're going to be talking about Herbalife primarily, and you should be able to use some of these concepts in all areas of your life.

You know, when I was sitting in the back of the room earlier, and I saw all the people out here and I could feel the excitement. Well, it made me a little humble to come up and share some of these things with you.

The things that I'm going to share with you today are things that are a part of my life. They're a part of me. They're not things that I developed. They're things that were shared with me about 13 years ago that made sense to me, and I applied some of these things to my life, and it started making a significant change in it. My background prior to network marketing was strictly construction work. That's all I'd ever known in my life. Construction work. That was it.

Back then, I lived in a small city up north near San Jose, California. Do you know where Livermore, California is? It's just a small city. I lived up there and went to school up there. I grew up doing construction work because my dad did construction work and my brothers did, and a couple of my cousins, and so we kind of had our own built-in crew there.

I started doing construction at 13 years old in the summers in between school, and I liked it. Quite honestly, I never thought about doing anything different than construction work. That's the only thing I ever thought about. It wasn't necessarily a goal or anything. It was just what I grew up with it. I was going to do it, and that's how it was going to be.

I do remember this, though. I remember my income goal. I did have an income goal back then. My goal was to earn $25,000.00 a year. Not a month, a year. That was 1968. I knew back then, and I said to myself, *if I can just get to $25,000.00 a year, I'm going to have it made.*

That's the only real goal as I understood it at that point.

Now it is springtime, and we're getting ready to go into our spring season, and I know what will be happening. I will be getting ready to come right out of the rainy season, like I had all the other previous years. It was around this time that I was fortunate enough to get exposed to a different kind of opportunity, and I never will forget that. I'd like to take a couple minutes here and share that with you.

It was my first exposure into the direct sales industry as we have here in Herbalife. A good friend of mine had found a little part-time business, and he got ahold of me one night to tell me about it.

His name was Mike Fuller. And, like me, Mike Fuller was also a construction worker. I really respected him because Mike was different than most of the construction workers I knew. He had a couple of homes, and he had a few dollars put aside, so I respected him besides liking him. I respected him a lot.

He called me one night. It was on a Monday night. I never will forget this. He was *very* excited (and Mike was not that kind of a person). He started telling me about this opportunity he'd found, and how he thought he could make some real serious money. He thought that it would fit me like a glove. Besides that, he sounded like he was walking three feet off the ground. That's how he sounded that night. And, he got my interest way up.

Even though he had gotten my interest up, I was hesitant. He had called me at 6:30 at night, and he wanted me to go over to the Hyatt House Hotel in San Jose and be there at 8:00 pm, which was a good 45 minutes away. I wasn't hesitant because of his excitement or because I didn't believe in him; I already knew I was going. I was hesitant because I didn't want to go to a meeting if my hair wasn't right. So, I said, "Well, you call me back in 10 minutes."

I was excited because of his excitement. And, I was curious about anything that could get Mike going like that. But, I had really long hair and a beard to match it. (I was looking pretty good, though! I got to share that with you!) And, so I did check in the mirror to see if my hair was right and if not, to see if I could get it going. I decided I looked okay and could go.

He called me back and I said, "Okay, I'm coming."

I was really excited about it. At first, I was nervous and everything, but I was excited because I'd never been to a business meeting before! I'm going over there and really jetting around because I have no idea what I'm going to see.

I'm more into the getting ready and what's going to take place than that opportunity he's talking about. Because it was a business meeting, I didn't know what to wear, so I just put on my best beads. Yes, I was that kind of guy!

I wanted to look the best I could. I went to the Hyatt House Hotel and I never will forget walking in. (By the way, I'd ever been in a hotel before. That's the truth! I'd been to a few motels before, but never a hotel. There is a difference.) My hair was down to the middle of my back, and you know, I was walking just right, doing everything I could to look my best. If you're going to go there, you might as well do it with style.

When I walked in there, I know the people thought they were hallucinating. That's the first time they'd ever seen anybody like me in there – a long-haired hippie. And, I won't ever forget it.

First of all, when I came into the room and sat down, everybody left. You know what I mean? Today, if somebody like me who looked so different walked in, nobody would think anything about it. Back then you didn't necessarily want to be the person sitting next to me, right?

And so, everybody moved away; that didn't bother me at all because I'm into everything that's happening around me. And I no sooner got there than the meeting started. The presenters got me excited that night. I never really thought that anything at all was going to develop from me going there. But they got me excited by some of the things they shared.

When it was all over, Mike's sponsor walked up to me and he looked at me and he said, "You don't want to do this, do you?" shaking his head no.

When I said, "Yes, I do," he didn't know if he wanted me to sign up or not. Well, I got started the next day. That first week, I had some incredible things happen to me. I got off to a good start because of Mike and his sponsor. Right away I got into a training class that was kind of like this, and they really got my attention.

In the first week, I earned $600.00 working part-time. I was just a babbling idiot after that, because I didn't think it was possible. I'd never made $600.00 working full-time in a week, let alone part-time. So, it was really something for me.

I remember what happened the end of that day. It was a Friday. It was five days after I signed up, and a gentleman who I used to work with came up to me to say hello. I wanted to recruit this guy. We used to work together doing cement work. So, I was drawing the marketing plan out in the cement there and telling about how you could do all this and you can do that, and he looked at me and said, "If it's so good, what are you doing here working in construction? Why aren't you doing this full-time?" I thought about it.

"By golly, you got a point!" And, I quit! I did! That impressed him. I got him into my business. And I left, I did. I left my tools and everything right there and I told them, "I'm not coming back." About two hours later I thought, *Hmmmm. What'd I do now?*

You get all excited and do all these crazy things. *What if $600.00 isn't going to come in next week? What's going to happen to my family?* The most important thing that happened to me was that I got off to a really good start. I started thinking, *maybe this could really work out for me after all.*

After becoming full-time, the first couple months to 90 days were very positive for me. Then, I went through some transitions personally, and that's when these concepts that I'm going to share with you today came into play.

You see, when things are moving, when things are going well, you can do anything, and it'll work. But what happens when you stub your toe a little bit? What happens when you get a little confused? What happens then? When you're not sure of the direction you're going in. That's when concepts like this will come into play.

You Have to Drive a Cadillac

I was taking Mike's sponsor up north, driving across the San Mateo Bridge to get to the San Francisco Airport, and I had this black Ford.

Let me explain my car to you. I had this black '62 Ford, and it just wasn't normal – it was really low! I had lowered it to the ground so I'd be looking good driving down the road. However, there were a couple of problems with this car. Just a couple.

One problem was, it, didn't have an emergency brake, which was no big deal - only it didn't go into park either. So, when I stopped, I had a problem with it rolling backwards. I fixed that problem with a little cement rock I made, and I kept it behind the seat. When I stopped, if I was kind of going downhill, I just eased up on it, and put the rock on the ground so I could roll up on it. I got so good at it that nobody could tell that I was even doing it.

The second problem was it had burnt valves in it. So, it sounded like bloop, bloop, bloop all the time. Even though, I started making all this money and stuff, I was concerned. I didn't want to spend money because what if my success didn't last? What if it was a fluke? That was the truth of the matter.

I remember as I was taking Mike's sponsor across to the San Mateo Bridge, he looked at me and he said, "I don't want to ever ride in this dirty, blankity blank blank Ford again. Go buy yourself a Cadillac!"

He had a Cadillac, and he kept telling all his people, "You have to buy a Cadillac. If you're going to be in business, as soon as you start making the money, start showing the money here. Start showing people that you really believe in what you're doing. And that just didn't compute to me at all, but it was exciting!

I replied, "Okay, but listen, you don't understand. I can't afford a Cadillac yet."

He looked me square in the eyes and said, "Let me tell you something, Larry. You can't afford *not* to have a Cadillac."

"That makes sense to me!"

I came right back across the San Mateo Bridge. The Cadillac dealership used to be Buchanan Smith. Now, it's Lou

Doty. I told myself, *I'm going to go get me a Cadillac* - never believing in a million years that it was going to happen.

First of all, when I pulled in the driveway, you have got to understand, I had my big, tall boots on and I had my hair down. I've got my beads and my little shades and, you know, they don't like to see me coming in in there, at all!

Of course, because my car is so low, it scrapes as I go across the driveway pulling into the dealership. I can see them through the window, and they're just having a ball with this whole deal. First thing is, I want to be as cool as I can be, and wouldn't you know it? I forgot to put the cement block down. My car starts taking off. I'm walking real slow and cool after it, until it started beating me. That was the first deal that happened.

The second deal that happened? I went inside, and nobody would wait on me. You know what I mean? NO ONE. I kept on walking around acting all cool. I kept waiting and nobody showed up – finally it was getting obvious. I'd been there for 15 minutes and I kept doing as much as I could to get some kind of attention to me.

Either they drew straws, or they got the rookie salesman to come out and wait on me. I'm not sure. They were all just having a ball with this deal, and finally this guy came out and says, "Can I help you?"

"Yeah. I want an Eldorado."

You would never believe how I said it. (I said it *real* good, *very* arrogantly. Mike's sponsor told me to be assertive and I was.) The salesman got very nervous because he could sense this was a real deal. So, he says, "Well, let me get my, let me get my manager."

Off he went to get his manager, and out came Gil Wilson. Now Gil Wilson and I have become real good friends since this, but Gil is the epitome of a Cadillac salesman. Black suit with the thin stripe, right? The little bitty, skinny tie. Black horn-rimmed glasses with the grey temples. Know what I'm talking about? That's Gil Wilson, a really nice guy.

Gil Wilson came out to me and he says, "Yes, can I help you out with something, here? What can I do for you?"

I told him what I told the other salesman, "Yeah. I want an Eldorado."

This was in 1968 and the Eldorados were very rare – they only came out in '67, and there were very few Eldorados around, maybe only three. I had to have something that was different, so I wanted an Eldorado.

He told me, "Well, we don't have any Eldorados available,"

I asked, "What about this green one?"

It was a forest green Eldorado with a kind of beige top, and I'm telling you, it was beautiful! It just really got me when I saw it, because when I drove up, the sun was shining on it, and it was just gorgeous.

"Oh, that one's sold."

"Well, what's it doing here if it's sold?" (I couldn't even believe I said that! I was really getting on with it that day. Feeling my oats!)

"The gentleman's supposed to come out and pick it up. He's supposed to come and pick it up on Monday."

Well this is Friday. So, I persist, "Well, I need an Eldorado. I need it today." Without missing a beat, I told him, "I've got a very important business meeting I have to go to tonight, and I need an Eldorado."

"I can't sell you that one today, but if he doesn't pick it up, you can have it on Monday."

"Monday will not work at all."

"Listen, come with me." He took me to the back where they were unloading the new cars off the truck. There was a gold Eldorado.

I don't know if you've seen the cars when they come off the trucks. They don't have hubcaps on them, and they're real ugly. They've got that stuff on them to protect them. It was a real ugly deal. I didn't like it at all.

I told him straight up, "I don't like that one."

"But you've either got to take this one, or you have got to wait until Monday."

"Okay. Let's go back and talk."

He took me back into his office, what I really call "the confession booth." You know what I'm talking about. When you go in there to buy something, you got to confess all your sins before they let you buy it. Gil wrote down a few figures on a piece of paper, and he slid it over to me.

I looked at it, and I said, "I'll take it!"

He couldn't believe it, right? Truth is, neither could I! You have no idea what I was going through there. I was having so much fun, and I had no idea what the end result was going to be. Then he said, "Okay. If that's acceptable to you, then we'll get the paperwork going."

"Okay! But, before we do the paperwork, I've got to be assured the car can be ready by 4:30 pm *today*. Can you get that car ready, because if you can't, well, I've got to know right now."

"Oh, I assure you, Mr. Thompson," (He calls me *Mister* Thompson now.) "We can have that car ready."

"Okay. Now, hold it. Can the papers be ready by 4:30? Because if not, I'm going down the road here to Smith Cadillac."

He looked at me and said, "I get your point." And, he started writing.

I went home.

I had about 45 minutes to kill. He was going to call me back to make sure everything was going to be taken care of, and I got cleared on the whole thing. Honestly, I never thought it was going to happen. I was surprised when he called me at 4:00 pm and said, "Mr. Thompson, come and get your car."

I let out a scream that you wouldn't even believe. I smoked it back to the dealership. I don't even remember how I got there. I do remember I drove my Ford right up in front, right there, and I left it; I didn't even try to hide the rock. I just got out and put the rock there.

When I looked up and saw the sun shining on my new Cadillac, it looks good! I can't even believe how good this thing looks. It looks much better than the green one, maybe because I knew it was going to be mine. I said, "Okay, let's get on with it. I got to get going on this thing."

I was nervous that I was going to change my mind, and I wanted to get out of there with my car. He told me, "Well, it's going to take about 45 minutes, there's one other client ahead of us here and my girl's working on the paperwork. It's going to take about another 45 minutes."

"I don't have 45 minutes! Can I just sign it and you fill out the paperwork and send me my copies?"

He said, "Well, of course I can."

"Okay. Let me do that."

I'm really going for this thing. I sign at the bottom knowing full well he can put any figures in there he wants! I thought to myself, *Well, that's all right. At least I'm going to have a Cadillac for 90 days!* You know what I mean? For 90 days I knew I was going to look really, really good!

So, I did that and now by this time (this is the truth) everybody in this whole agency is getting into this thing. The salesmen are into it, the mechanics keep coming out, some of them got their wives and a couple of girlfriends there, they can't believe this deal is going on!

We go out there and Gil Wilson is plenty excited about this whole thing now. He is really excited about it. He's explaining everything to me, how it works and everything, and I said, "Listen, I haven't got time for that, I've just got to get going."

"Well, listen," he told me, "in the glove box is the operator's manual. That explains everything to you."

Meanwhile, I'm pushing every button. I can't believe it. The seat goes every which way. I mean, this is just really unbelievable to me, this Cadillac is – well, until you experience something like that, you've never experienced it, you'll never understand that.

I'm pushing all the buttons and going back and forth, AM and FM radio, and I can even hear the dust on the needle on the station on my stereo – I'm convinced of that. And everything is perfect.

Finally, I said, "I have got to go." I started that baby up. It's backed in, and for those of you who live up north, you know it's a real long driveway out there. I adjusted the seat, got my mirror set on this one over here, got the mirror set over here, pulled the steering wheel down, brought it out, feels good. I said to myself, *This is it!*

As I started to leave, I told Gil, "Thank you very much, Mr. Wilson." Then, I buzzed up my power window and eased out of the parking lot.

Just as I turn, I'm doing two or three miles an hour, and I look up and there's Mr. Wilson kind of trotting alongside of me, and I thought, *Golly, what a friendly salesman, you know?* So, I gave it one of these deals where I kind of wave.

Then, I got that baby up to about 10 miles an hour and I can't believe it – I look up and there's Mr. Wilson, you know, still trotting alongside my Eldorado.

Finally, I look over, and see that I've got the boy's tie caught in the window! I slam on my brakes and he goes, "Oop!" with a friendly wave. I buzz down the window. Unbelievable. True story. True story.

If I can do it, you can do it.

About a year later, I was living out in Oklahoma, and I wanted to get another Cadillac. I called up Mr. Wilson and I was ready to tell him what I wanted and everything. The plan was to have my folks drive it out. I wasn't sure he was going to remember me at all when I called him. But, he certainly did!

I share this story with you for several reasons. Number one, I enjoy telling it, as you can tell, but also to give you an idea about where I've come from, what's happened to me, and what has taken place in my life. I think more importantly, to share with you that if I can do something like this and make the significant changes in my life that I've made, then you can, too.

It really doesn't make any difference about our ages, and it doesn't make any difference about our business background or education level. What makes a difference is about how we feel about ourselves and our opportunity.

I encourage you all to take really good notes as we go over this and hopefully it'll have the impact on you that it's had for a lot of us.

The One Variable is You

It is easier to make a lot of money and be successful than it is to make a living. It's difficult to make a living. Do you understand? It is not an easy factor making a living. It is an easier thing becoming successful, but it is not easier unless you know a few things. You've got to be aware of those few key factors that make a difference, and I'm going to go over them with you.

There are three parts to our direct sales business, and they are easy to master.

Of course, the products. I am not going to talk about the products. You need to master your products. You also need to master the second part of your business, the marketing.

Both of these are real simple.

Take an afternoon of two, three, or four hours and master the products and the marketing system, that's really simple. The third part of your business is the one that we are going to talk about today. This is the one that you need to work on and that's the YOU part. That is the only variable in any business.

If there's one person succeeding in your company with the products and there are 99 failing, then we know that the products are working.

If there is one person succeeding in your company with the marketing structure, and there are 99 failing, then we know that the marketing structure is working.

The variable is not the products or the marketing structure. The variable is the individual. That can only mean one thing…YOU are the only variable to your success.

What is the day of the month today? Is today the 21st of the month? There are people right here in this room who have already earned over $5,000 this month. There are also people in this room who have earned only $500 this month. Now, it's the same 21 days, it's the same product, and it's the same marketing system. Okay?

What causes one person to earn 10 times more money than another person? What causes that? It's not the product and it's not the marketing structure because those are identical. It's the person sitting in your seat, right?

It's not 10 times the contacts.

It's not 10 times the time.

It's not 10 times the experience.

That is not the factor. If that was the factor, I wouldn't be here today. Do you understand that? Because I didn't have any of those things when I started.

I didn't have them. It's within you. It's how you feel about the products. It's how you feel about the marketing structure, but most importantly it's about how you feel about your own personal financial future – it's about how you feel about you. I know that if I can do this, you can do this.

You got involved in your company because you were looking for something to change in your life. All of us have different reasons for becoming involved in our company, but we are all looking for something to change and improve.

Well, I'll give you a formula here, a real easy formula that I use that I personally got from Jim Rohn:

For things to change, you have got to change.

For things to get better, you have got to get better.

I'll tell you what the rest of this year is going to be like: exactly like the first part of this year unless you do something differently, and that is not only talking financially. Today's training can help you create enough self-value to start the positive changes in your life. It's about family, relationships, your spiritual life, your mental and physical health.

We're talking about in all areas of your life, not just money. If you don't like the way your personal life is going, I'll tell you what it's going to look like the rest of the year. It's going to look just like the first part of the year - it's going to.

If you don't like how your spiritual life is going, it's going to be just like it is.

If you don't like the way your family life is going, it's going to be just like this, okay? It's not going to change.

For things to get better, you've got to get better. For things to change you've got to change. It's a very simple formula.

Almost everybody I have ever met in my life, wants to have an above average income. Having an above average income is very simple: you've got to be willing to become an above average person. You've got to be willing to have an above average attitude, an above average handshake, an above average desire, an above average willingness, and above average excitement.

You become *above average* and you get an *above average* income. You've never met anybody with an above average income that isn't above average. See?

You've got to be willing to become above average.

You've got to be willing to *invest more time working on you* than on your job.

You've got to be willing to *invest more time working on you* than on your products.

You've got to be willing to *invest more time working on you* than on your marketing.

You've got to be willing to do that sort of thing because that's the real factor here. The first part we are going to do here is talk about the concepts of how to build up an organization. I will give you some notes on how to build an organization and I'm going to do a lot of abbreviating, but you'll get it down.

Now, how to build an organization? The same things apply on how to make a retail sale. The same things would apply no matter what you do. When you get the concepts down, they apply to everything.

The first thing is that if you're going to build an organization, you've got to know what type of people to look for, who to look for.

Dissatisfied People

Who do we want to look for? We have a lot of schoolteachers in Herbalife and a lot of people say, *Boy, I better go get me some schoolteachers*, right?

Well, we have a lot of doctors in Herbalife; let's go get some doctors.

We have a lot of professional people; let's go get some professional people.

We've got construction workers, accountants, we've got all types of people here. What type of people do I look for? What type of people am I'm going for?

I'm going to give you a common denominator that we all have here in the room and the common denominator that all of us have – it has nothing to do with our backgrounds at all. It has nothing to do with our experiences. There's one thing that we have in common in this room, and this is the type of person that you're looking for: We're looking for dissatisfied people.

Dissatisfied. See, it sounds a little strange, right? Dissatisfied. That's right! That's what, we've got in common. All of us in this room were dissatisfied with something.

We came to Herbalife hoping that Herbalife would change that for us, and I'm going to give you some categories here, and I encourage you to take note of these.

Financial Dissatisfaction

Of course, money, right? Show me someone who is dissatisfied with their income, and I'll show you somebody that you need to be talking to, okay?

There's two parts to recruiting and you need to separate these two parts and that's what we do when we recruit, make no mistake about it.

We recruit. Don't you ever shy away from the word *recruit*. The most successful organizations in the world are the biggest recruiters in the world. Some of you in this room are familiar with the different colleges and universities and institutions out there, IBM, General Motors, Xerox; all the major corporations send their recruiters out to get the most talented people who can to go to work for their organizations, right?

That's what we do, also.

We send you out to get the most talented people you can find and one thing that we're looking for beside dissatisfaction in an individual - we're looking for one key factor also and that's called a *nice person.*

You ever notice that about Herbalife? You've got to be a nice person. If someone isn't a nice person, let's say they are really arrogant, they generally don't last long here because they just don't fit around our group of nice people.

There are a lot of nice people here, and it really matters to me when someone comes and looks at our business or our product line and when they leave, they say, I tell you one thing, those Herbalife people are nice people. That matters to me. I like them and that's the kind of feeling I want to have, and I know that's the kind of feeling you want and that's what we have.

Okay, two parts to it as we said earlier. One part is going out there and prospecting. Prospecting is the formal term in the industry. That's just finding somebody to talk to and that is all that is.

The second part is inviting them or what would that be called? Talking to them, right?

So, if you were going to sell a product, the first thing you would need to do is prospect; you would need to find someone to talk to about your products, right? Then you would need to do what? Talk to them. Two separate things.

So, we're looking for dissatisfied people and the first thing we've got to do is find somebody who we sense is dissatisfied, and then we're going to talk to them, okay?

But, what could they be dissatisfied with? How about income? I would say that initially, probably 60 or 70 percent of the people in our company come to look at Herbalife because of this, and we have an opportunity to make money here.

Doug Stunts stood up here and he told you, which is a fact, that he made more money last month than he earned in a whole year teaching school and that's a phenomenal success story, right? It's a very big one.

But when you take into consideration it's been less than a year that it's taken him to learn the talents to be able to do that, that is really phenomenal and that's the kind of thing that we need to pay attention to.

We don't have to accept things the way they are seen.

There's only been about a half a dozen things that I have ever learned in my life that have made the majority of the difference in my life. Not just from income, I'm talking about personally, a half a dozen things that made 80 percent of the difference.

See, the nice thing is you could have more than you have now. You can only have what you are, right? But you can have more than what you are now, because you can become more than what you are right now.

That's what's exciting. Don't ever let people tell you there is no opportunity left. There's plenty of opportunity. In 1950 there were 16,000 millionaires in this country. There are over 600,000 millionaires in this country today, right now, so don't you buy the "there is no opportunity" story. Don't you buy this "you better get something safe and secure" story.

You don't want to go for that story at all because that is all you're going to get. Go for opportunity and remember the 600,000 millionaires and all the millionaires that will be created this year. This is the first year (1981) that more than half of all the millionaires are going to be women.

There is going to be something for everybody here. When we are talking about income here, we don't need to be talking about those kinds of incomes. Listen, we started talking about making $5,000, $7,000, $15,000, $20,000 a month - you don't need to be talking about that kind of money.

Let me tell you what is exciting to most people: $300, $400 or $500 a month. If you would have shown me a way before I got started in the direct sales field, how I could have $300 left over at the end of the month free and clear, I would have been completely satisfied because I liked my job. I enjoyed the people I worked with. I was happy there.

The only thing that I wasn't pleased with was my income, and it never occurred to me that I could change it. You know that?

It never dawned on me that I could do something about it. I didn't know that I could. I thought that's the way it was because everybody I knew was that way. Everybody always had just enough money to get by. They did. I'm not making money out to be like it's everything because money is not everything – unless you don't have enough. You think about that for a minute.

What happens when you don't have enough? What does money become?

Everything.

Money becomes everything when you don't have enough. So, we need to face the facts here today. We need to tell ourselves the truth. What will get a lot of people excited? Three, four, or five hundred dollars a month.

When March is over, if you've got $400 left in your bank account to do with as you please, to buy clothes, to go out someplace, to go away on a trip, to spend on your home, to give to somebody, (whatever you want to do with it) free and clear, that would be something for the majority of the people in this country.

And now have another $400 left in your bank account at the end of April, and now have it at the end of May, and now have that at the end of June. You understand? That's a lot of money.

If a person has $100 free and clear at the end of each month, and now they go to $400 free and clear each month, it's not just an additional $300, they actually get to have 3X the lifestyle. That's a big difference! They have 3X the amount of entertainment they can experience. They have 3X the quality of vacation. They have 3X the quality of everything extra.

That's very important to understand – $300 or $400 is a lot of extra money per month. You do not need to be talking about "fortunes" to everybody. It's important to understand that just a few hundred dollars extra is a lot to most people.

That doesn't mean that people aren't making large sums, because people are doing that.

If you show me someone who is dissatisfied with their income, that is someone that you need to put down and be talking to. So, dissatisfaction. Here is another area: Career.

Career Dissatisfaction

Their career is a life path that they are on, not necessarily by choice. It's what they've known. It's who they've been. What they are educated to do. And, now they are dissatisfied with it. They are not doing what they enjoy, or their company doesn't allow them the freedom and flexibility to enjoy their income. Maybe they've been a stay-at-home dad or mom, and now they want to get into a career. Where do they go? Where do they begin?

At Herbalife, we are an equal-opportunity career changer. Our top distributor in the company is Geri, she used to teach school and used to be a checker at Market Basket.

We don't have two marketing systems here, one for men and one for women. We don't say that if you are a man and when you become a Supervisor you get 50%. But, if you are a woman you get 48%, do we?

We don't say that men have to do $4,000 in one month to move up, but women have to do $4,200. We don't have any of that, do we?

We don't say if you are a man on your royalty override bonus you get 5%, but if you are a woman you only get 4-1/2%. See? It's an equal deal here. It's equal compensation as equal does. We have a chance for a woman to step up here and create a career of her own if she wants to do that. I'll use my sister as a good example.

My sister, Tish Rochin, was looking for a career. My sister got started in Herbalife in December of last year with a kit. Her very first month, she took that kit and she earned $560 working part-time. She was living in a brand-new state, had only been there a few months. She didn't know anybody at all, but she got started. She was excited about the product because she lost 10 pounds on it, and she started telling people about the product. That made her $560 working part-time in December. And, she was loving her new career.

I'll tell you who doesn't believe it most of all. My sister doesn't believe it. She used to drive a truck. That's the truth. She was a truck driver! She's loving this whole thing. She's sitting back there. She's got a few hundred dollars in her pocket and she's looking really good, you know. She's doing really good. Now you know that a person can start right where they are and go wherever they want to go.

Let's talk about men. Put them in a separate category. Most men want a career. They get going out there and all of a sudden, they find themselves wanting something more or something different. I never would have gotten out of construction work if I hadn't learned of the opportunity from Mike Fuller.

I know I still would be there working construction and never know the difference, okay? I'd have been happy because I wouldn't have known the difference. I would be unhappy now knowing the difference, and being back there, but I wouldn't have been any less happy if I didn't know the difference.

But now that I know the difference, it's a world of difference. You understand? When you have choices, knowing things, becoming aware of things gives you more options for you to exercise.

I would love to get 50 men in a room with one thing in common: their age. I'd like them to be about 35 years old. I'd like to ask these 50 men one question, "So, gentlemen, you're now 35 years old. In another 30 years, you are going to be 65, and you're going to be retiring. My question to you is this: Do you want to be doing the same thing that you are doing now for another 30 years?"

If they were to answer us truthfully, what do you think the majority of them would say? They would say no.

And, if we followed them until they were 65, what do you think would happen? We'd find out that the majority of them were doing exactly what they were doing at age 35. Let me ask you this, "How come?"

Why would a person do something for 30 years that they don't want to do? Security? The answer is: They have little choice.

A 35-year-old man generally has a family and a lifestyle to a certain level, right? He does not want to take a chance and jeopardize what he has to start something brand new, even though he knows he wants another career. He tells himself, *Oh I won't be doing this until I'm 65*, but then 36, 37, and 38 rolls around with no change. Before he knows it, he is 62, 63, 64, 65 and he is doing the same thing he had no intention of doing.

But you see, he gets to 60, 61, 62 and you know what he says? "Well, it hasn't been the best job in the world, but I'll tell you right now it's certainly provided a lot of security for my family, good insurance, good retirement, right?"

You know what that's called? Justification.

He is justifying to himself and to his family why he did something for 30 years he didn't want to do. Now, I'm not putting that down. Do not misunderstand that at all. I'm saying he has got to justify because if he can't justify it, he's got to go to the local bridge and he's got to jump.

So, they've got to justify it, but I am also saying this: You take that man at 35 years old, and you give him an opportunity that he can work at his own pace. He doesn't have to jeopardize his job. He doesn't have to jeopardize his family. He can go at his own pace, his own rate. He can find his own space.

If he believes in what he is doing and believes in himself enough to try, I'm telling you, you better get out of his way because he will take advantage of it. So, when we are looking for dissatisfied people, I need you to understand the issue here, it's not just about money at all, not whatsoever.

Let's talk about another area here, it's called Challenge.

Challenge Dissatisfaction

Some people are just flat-out bored. Some people are making a decent income, some have got a decent career, but they are bored. Lack of challenge is a terrible deal to have. There's nothing that does it for the human spirit like the thrill of challenge.

When a person is challenged, they walk differently, they talk differently, they act differently, you get up in the morning differently.

Everything is different.

The way you talk to your lady, the way you talk to your man, the way you talk to your children, the way you talk to your employees and to your coworkers, it is different. Do you understand? When you've got a challenge in front of you, it doesn't make any difference if it's cold or it's rainy. It doesn't make any difference if it is hot. It doesn't make a difference if your tire blew out on the freeway. If you've got a challenge you've got something more important in front of you. You've got something more important than coming home and eating a little bit and turning on the television and going to sleep at 10:00 every night.

Sometimes it's money and career, but sometimes it's boredom or lack of fun.

Fun Dissatisfaction

Here's another one. This is important: This is called fun.

Show me someone who is dissatisfied with the fun in their life. Let me tell you, fun is really something. I mean, that – people enjoy fun right? I mean, fun is something. You can't even say the word fun without smiling. Try it. Say, *fun*. Am I right?

See? You kind of smiled when you said *fun*. You can't even get it out of your mouth without smiling, right? It doesn't happen. I mean everybody enjoys having fun. They do.

But we've all been in this situation before; we're sitting there and there's going to be a big party coming up in three weeks. And we are talking, and someone says, "I'm telling you in three weeks, we are going to have some fun!"

What happened to this time in between? I mean are we only reserved for fun in three weeks at this party? Is that the only time we can have fun? Or, can we have fun going to work and can we have fun taking rejection?

Can we have fun with disappointment?

See, can we do that deal? I mean listen, if fun is such a good deal, it seems like we should be able to capitalize on it as much as we can. Doesn't that make sense to you?

So, you know, the party deal, "In three weeks we're going to have fun," right?

In two weeks, "We're going to have fun at this party…"

One week, "Oh boy, one more week and we're going to have a ball!"

Saturday night comes around and guess what? It's a big bummer, right?

You can't just say okay, it's 8:00 pm on Saturday night, three weeks later now we are going to have some fun. It doesn't work that way, right?

Fun is either part of your life, or it's not a part of your life.

What causes people to not have fun? Lack of money. Lack of career. Lack of challenge. Boredom.

You've got these things going, and you're going to have fun no matter what happens to you. You are going to have fun because you now have the capacity for life. You've got the capacity to have fun. You can only have as much fun as you have the capacity to enjoy it, see?

You're only going to have as much fun as you are entitled to have according to your personal growth and your personal awareness. That is the only amount of fun that you can have.

So, you show me someone who is dissatisfied, and I will show you someone that you need to put down on your list. So, you get the idea of what we are looking for?

Identifying Dissatisfied People

If you are going to build an organization, you now know who to look for – dissatisfied people. Now, you can come up with a lot more categories than I've got here, can't you? I mean just go to work and write your list. Who is dissatisfied?

Now, if you find someone who is completely satisfied, you don't want to invite them at all, right? It would be a waste of your time. And when you find someone like that, do me a favor, take a picture of them and get a description so we can pass it around and say, "If you find one like this, don't invite them. They are completely satisfied."

I don't think you are going to find them too easily.

Okay, who to look for, now, we got that one done. We are going to put together a list of names of who? Dissatisfied people.

Let me give you some categories here. Let's break this list up into categories. If you are going to be developing up the organization, you are going to need a list to reference. If you are going to be developing customers, you are going to need a list. Here's the list.

How about friends? Make a list of the friends you have who you feel might be dissatisfied with one of these areas. The point here is not if they want to become part of your organization. The point here is not if they would like to be a Supervisor. The point is not if they want to be involved in the direct sales industry. That is not the point.

What is the point? If they are dissatisfied, they go on the list.

You say, *Well, I don't think they are going to want to do it because they don't have any time.*

That is not the point here, right? The point is if you feel like they are dissatisfied they go on the list.

Now, let's put another one down here. How about relatives? Okay, how many relatives do you have who you feel might be dissatisfied with one or more areas of their life? Write them down.

How about neighbors? How about coworkers? How about clubs, organizations? How about your church group? How about old high school friends, college friends?

How about anything? Just start to think here.

Friends, relatives, neighbors, coworkers.

I Shouldn't Make Money Off My Friends

Now, let me share something with you about friends. I have had people say, *I don't want to recruit my friends. I don't want to sell to my friends. I feel funny making money off my friends.*

How many of you have ever heard that statement, right? I've heard it. I've heard it a lot. However, rather than avoiding sharing this opportunity with your friends, you want to look at this from a different perspective.

Let's say you have a dress shop and one of your friends comes in to visit you. You haven't seen her for a while, and when she comes in, you're all excited and you're talking and catching up. You talk a little gossip and everything's going on getting everybody caught up again, and then she says, "I've got to buy a dress here. That's the real reason I came in."

She goes over and, on the hanger, she sees the perfect dress for her – the right color, the right cut, right collar, everything is right. She tries it on, and it takes five years off her age, she looks at the price tag, she can't believe it. She says, "I'll take it."

And you, as the owner of the shop say, "Hey listen, I wish you would go down the street and buy it at Bullocks."

"I'm confused," she says. "Why would I go down there and buy it? Is it less down there?"

"No, as a matter of fact, it probably costs a little more down there than you would pay here."

"Well, why would I go down there?"

You explain, "Well, Mary. I feel uncomfortable making money off my friends."

Now, if your friend has that dress shop and she has invested her time and energy and money into that dress shop, is she entitled to make a profit off anybody that walks in there and wants those goods?

The answer is, *yes*.

The only way you are entitled to make a profit is if you provide goods or services. It is immoral if you provide goods or services and don't make a profit from it. I'll tell you who expects you to make a profit on it, anybody and everybody who walks in your dress shop expects you to make a profit.

You are entitled to make a profit.

You need to get your thinking straight here.

You've got the finest quality products in the world to share with people. These are the finest quality products and you are hesitant to share them with your friends and relatives and neighbors and coworkers? If that is you, you need to evaluate you, not the products and the opportunity. You need to evaluate your thinking. Do you see that?

Get the point here where it belongs: if you are hesitant to talk to friends, relatives and coworkers about the opportunity, then you need to face the real issue here. You need to look at your thinking here and get it straight.

Now, it's not important if you still feel like that after you do it. The point is to do it any way you can. Do you understand? If you still say, "I don't want to talk to my friends, relatives or neighbors," then go talk to people you don't know yet, go put flyers out, run ads, do anything, talk to strangers on the street, knock people down, do anything you have to do. But you need to think about this one here. Get your list made. Does this make sense to you?

Get a list put together of 100 people. You might say, "I don't know 100 people."

Of course, you know 100 people! If you divide it into categories, you won't come up with 10 people if you think, *Well, I don't want to put John down because he doesn't have the experience for this*, and, *No, I don't want to put Uncle Joe. No, no, no, no. Not him, he doesn't have the time for this deal at all.* Right?

You see what I mean? If you start doing that, you can't come up with even 10 names. Your job here is not to think if it would be for them. Your job is not to think if they would like it. Your job is not to think if they wouldn't like it.

Your only job here is to think if they are dissatisfied or not.

Remember there are two parts: **Finding someone to talk to**. What's the second part? **Talking to them**! Your job is to talk to them. You think that they don't have the time? You don't know that. That's up to them! See what I'm saying?

Okay, now, we've got who to look for, dissatisfied people. We have put them on a list of names. Now, the next thing we get to do before we talk to anybody is, we've got to get our attitude straight.

Get a Gold Mine Attitude

Before you talk to anybody, you've got to get our attitude straight.

There are three areas to your attitude that you need to go to work on before you talk to anyone. We all go through periods of time when we need to do this, me included.

When you go to talk to somebody and you know your attitude is not quite the way you'd like it to be, don't talk to them. You're just not quite as positive, you're not quite this, you're not quite that, the answer is don't talk to them until you get your attitude straight. That's all.

This is simple. Don't go out there and deliberately set yourself up for a fall. Don't do that deal. Don't botch your delivery, there's no need calling him, he's not going to want to do it. You're right, save a phone call, right?

We communicate with feelings, we don't communicate with words.

I used to be afraid of dogs. I really was. I am not afraid of dogs anymore. I got my fear of dogs down by going to a few training classes. That's true. Because animals communicate with feelings, not with words.

I want you to picture this. Picture a house that's set back off the street a little bit with a little picket fence about waist high with a long sidewalk like the old houses used to have, right? When you walk right up that little sidewalk, there's the front door. You have got to go in there, but on the gate the sign reads, Beware of Vicious Dog.

It doesn't say Beware of Dog. It doesn't say Beware of Bad Dog, it says *Vicious* Dog and you know, that's a whole different deal right there. It makes you look at it twice!

But you've got to go up and you say to yourself, *Okay, I'm going to do this.* And, as soon as you get there, that dog runs up and he's giving you his teeth and his snarls and he's gnarly. He's doing all that stuff. You say to yourself, *I have to go, I'm not afraid of you dog, oh what a nice pretty dog you are.* And, you start to go in there, and you're afraid of what's going to happen.

You know he's going to get you. He's going to get you, right? That's what's going to happen.

But as soon as you run back outside the fence, here comes this little four-year-old girl, she's never seen that dog before at all, and she decides she's going to walk up that same sidewalk as you do and as she walks up there, the dog licks her heels all the way up – the same vicious dog.

How come he doesn't growl and snarl at her? Because the dog can feel it, right? She's not a threat. The dog can sense it. So can people.

Have you ever talked to someone and no matter what they said, you just sensed that they were lying to you? That's communicating with feelings. If you sense something's not right (it doesn't have to be lying, it could be anything), you automatically don't trust it. You sense something's not quite right, because we communicate with feelings. That's the same thing that happens when you go to talk to people about your products, your business opportunity when you don't feel good about them.

You need to get your thinking straight first or they're going to pick it up, and that simply doesn't work. I had a lady come in once and she said, "I need some help."

I told her, "I'll do anything I can to help you."

"Well I can't get anybody at all to look at this opportunity."

I agreed, "You're absolutely right. What else can I help you with?"

"Oh, you didn't understand, I can't get anybody I talk to, to look at this…" blah-blah-blah and she went on and on and gave me the whole list of people she had talked to that day. Twenty-seven people and da-da-da and she said, "I can't get anybody to look at this opportunity."

"I agree with you," I told her, "Is there anything else I can help you with?"

"Are you making fun of me?"

"I'm not making fun of you at all," I said, "You just told me you couldn't get them to look. We don't have anything else to discuss about that, you're right. You can't get them to look at all. Can I help you with another project?"

As long as she's thinking that way, what is she doing when she picks up the phone? She's communicating it to them because just like the dog, she's going to show her products while thinking they're not going to want to buy. They're not going to buy, right? So, you see, she's right! This thing is not fallible, and I'm not telling you anything here that you don't already know.

There's going to be very few steps that I'm going to share with you that you don't already know. It might give you another viewpoint, but there's going to be very little you don't already know. Here's the attitude you've got to have before you talk to anyone about your opportunity.

You Need the Gold Mine Attitude

That's what you need, the gold mine attitude. I'm going to share a story with you here, and I want you to kind of go along with me on this story. Get into this story, and if I talk to you about the wind blowing, I want you to feel the wind blowing in your face. I tell you a perfect time for this story, Sunday morning. That's the best.

Sunday mornings are different, did you ever notice that Sundays have a different feeling than Mondays and Saturdays and Fridays? Sundays are different. Every day of the week has a different feel to it. Even if you didn't know what day of the week it is, you could almost tell what day it is by just seeing a few people and watching stuff.

Sundays are special, and I want you to think about waking up real early. I know we've all experienced this sometime, even if we don't like to wake up early, but I want you to think about waking up real early in the morning. Maybe 5:30 am. For some reason, you have no idea why you're awake. You look at your clock and see it's 5:30 am, and you can't believe this for a minute. But you feel so alive, so alert. Instantly, you're on just like that and you can't believe it.

The sun is shining outside, you can see it. You get dressed and you go out there and you start to make yourself some orange juice or something. Everyone in the house is asleep and it's real quiet, and you're kind of glad they're asleep because you're enjoying this so much.

You decide to walk outside and there's just that slight chill in the air, but it's going to be warm and you can tell it. The birds are chirping, you can hear them and there's hardly any traffic.

It's one of the clearest days that you've seen in a long, long time. And you're just enjoying it and you decide, *Heck, I'm going to go for a drive and head up to the mountains*. You get in your car and you start driving up into the mountains. You've got your arm out the window and wind's blowing, and it just feels so refreshing.

You get out to the foothills, you're driving around and finally all of a sudden, you start driving on one of your favorite roads, just a few houses on it. Driving around, you look up and there's a road off the right that you've seen before and you thought about taking before but never have. But, today you're going to do it and see where that road goes.

You start driving up this road and every now and then, you can catch a glimpse of the valley down below. And then, the road comes up here and you can see that there hasn't been anybody driving up here in years because there's no tracks. There is grass all over the road, and you get up on a little flat plateau there and you park your car.

You lean against your car, and you're looking at one of the most magnificent views that you've ever seen in your life and you can't believe that something this beautiful exists. As you're standing there enjoying it all, you look over to the right and there's something over there that's different, you're not quite sure what it is, but you decide to go investigate.

The closer you get to it, the more intriguing it becomes and if you get a few feet away, your suspicions are confirmed here. It looks like it's the mouth of a cave that's been covered up with brush. You quickly start pulling all the brush off and find it's a big cave and it goes for 10 feet and then turns to the right just a little bit, and the sun is shining right in on it.

It looks like it's a safe cave, so you decide to venture in, and you begin to get really nervous. As you are walking in, you have no idea what's to the right. As soon as you get there, you look to the right, and what do you think you see?

Gold coins from floor to ceiling! Wall-to-wall gold coins!

There is no telling how long they've been there. After you bite one and make sure it's real, next thing you do is look over your shoulder to make sure no one's following you, right?

For me, I'm going to get my car as close to the cave as I can, and I guarantee you when I go home it's going to be so loaded with gold coins it will be like my low riding Ford. If it is dark, the headlights would be shining up in trees, right? That baby is going to be loaded!

You get back home. Now, your wife or husband is awake and says, "Where have you been? It's 10:30 am, I've been worried. I've been worried to death about you."

You say, "Open the garage door quick!"

They get the garage door open and you pull the car in. "Where'd you get this?"

"I don't have time. Help me unload it," and they certainly do, right? You say, "Load that baby into the basement, I'll be back!"

This time, you go get a pickup truck and a U-Haul trailer. You're going to need a shovel, right? You stop by the local hardware store. You don't even go down to 'Pick and Save' to get it at 40% off. No, no... you go to the local hardware store and pay retail, right?

New shovel. And you get out there and you load that baby up and you still can't believe your good fortune! You go and unload that one.

You come back for a third load. But when you come back for your third load, something's not quite right. You're not sure what it is. So, when you leave, you take a stick and just put a mark on the ground. When you come back for your fourth load, you've got the answer. What you were thinking all along is true.

There's more gold now than when you started!

You discover every coin you take out, two coins comes in its place, and the first thing you do is get very excited. The second thing you do is realize you've got to have some help, right? Or, it's going to be out the mouth of the cave and the whole world's going to know about it.

So, who is the first person you want to help you? Are you going to run an ad? Are you going to go to the local unemployment office? Are you going to hang some fliers at the shopping center? What are you going to do?

Well, I'll tell you what I would want to do. I'm going to go get my brother, Johnny, right? I have to go over and get him. He has to help me load this gold up, right?

Now, I go over to Johnny and he's watching the Super Bowl. It's the last minute and a half of the first half. It's tied, and they're going for the score. Am I going to sit there and wait for it to get over? Or, am I going to turn the television off and say listen to this? What's more important, right?

You see, that's the gold mine attitude.

I know there's not a gold mine like that which exists in this country, but I'll tell you what, I would not trade what I've got in Herbalife for a gold mine like that. I wouldn't do it.

See Herbalife has got the vault door open and we're saying take all the gold you want. You can take it all. Everything you want. Come on in. You need some help? Get some helpers who can come and get it. Need some more? Get some more helpers. Get out and then get a couple more. Come and get all you want.

Just don't push, don't shove and don't be greedy.

The more gold that we take out, the more gold there is for everybody. There's more gold in the Herbalife vault now than there was a year ago, and the more people that come to the vault and take out the gold, the more gold there is for everybody else.

Now that's the attitude you need when you share this opportunity with people. You need the goldmine attitude. Okay?

And, here's a second thing you need to do. You need to get excited and enthusiastic, and if you've got a gold mine, you have no problem getting excited and enthusiastic – none whatsoever.

I'll tell you what, if you go over to your brother Johnny's house and said, "Come with me and dig the gold,"

And he replies, "No, I want to finish the game,"

Would you wait and say, "Please, oh please, oh please?" Would you think, *nobody wants to help me dig the gold. I'm going to go back home. Nobody wants to help. I'm finished.* Would you think that?

Are you going to call up wife and say, "Nobody wants to go with me. This is not for me."

If you said that, you know what she is going tell you. She is going to tell you, "Hit it!" right?

She is going to say, "Get somebody right now," or, "You stay here and I'll go get the gold!"

You see you have to be excited and enthusiastic about this whole thing. Now I'm talking about genuine excitement. I'm not talking about phony excitement. I'm talking about real, sincere excitement is what you've got to have.

You know you can come to one of these meetings and you'll get excited. You go to one of our meetings in any of our offices and you can't hardly even talk to a customer and not get excited. People can get you easily excited about this offer.

Things can get you excited, right? But I'm talking about real sincere, deep excitement that comes from within, and the only way I know to get that is with the facts.

That's the only way I know to get it. You've been at that gold mine. You've seen it and you've bitten into it. You've seen that every coin you take out, two more come back in, and if someone says, "I'm not going to go with you," you're not going to feel bad at all. You know better, and that's the same thing here.

People are going to spray rain on your parade. You bet your life they are. People are going to tell you you're crazy. People say, "Oh no, another one of those deals. Oh no, oh no." They're going to pull that deal on you. Makes no difference what they do. It only makes a difference what YOU do. I'm telling you right now, you can go out there and you can talk to people, and the most important thing is that it makes no difference if the people you talk to buy your story. What makes a difference is if you buy their story.

It makes no difference if the people you talk to buy your story. What makes a difference is if you buy their story.

They're going to dump on you. They're going to tell you how bad your products are. They're going to tell you how bad your opportunity is. They're going to tell you how foolish you are.

They're entitled to say what they want to say. You're entitled to believe what you want to believe. Well the greatest stories of all, the greatest teacher of all, some 2,000 years ago had to develop His organization.

He had His, not Top 10, but His Top 12 that He spent three years training and teaching. And finally, the time came, you know what the story is, the time came for Him to send them out into the cities, and they were going to go out in the cities two-by-two. Remember the story?

And they were all excited. They were jazzed up. They were excited. They were going to go out and they were going to tell this story to everybody. They were going to convert the whole world over to their story.

The greatest teacher of all saw that there was something there and He said, "Before you go fellas, there's one thing I need to share with you. When you go out into those cities, not every home is going to be of your accord, and when you leave the home shake every grain of sand from your shoes."

Now, I thought about that one for a long time. What does it mean? *Shake every grain of sand from your shoes.* And I think I understand it. If you have a grain of sand in your shoe, one grain of sand won't necessarily hurt you unless it stays there over a prolonged period of time and it will start a little irritation.

As a matter of fact, you can probably leave one grain of sand in your shoe for some time and never shake it out. But if you've got two grains of sand in your shoe, now it's a little bit uncomfortable and you need to give it some attention, and if you leave it there it becomes increasingly more of a hindrance.

And if you get three grains of sand in your shoe and you don't do anything about it, the next thing you know you have a blister. And if you don't pay any attention to it then, the next thing you know, it's infected. The next thing you know, you have to have your foot amputated and it could kill you.

Is that the truth? From one grain of sand? Remember, it was important enough for Him to mention just before they left. And you know what that means to me? When you go out there, you think every person's going to be of your accord. They're not. And what that means is it makes no difference if they buy your story. What makes a difference is when you leave them that you don't buy any part of their story. And the reason you're not going to do that is because you've got the facts. You've got the facts.

So, your excitement and your enthusiasm are *genuine.* Genuine excitement. Genuine enthusiasm. Don't let anybody sell you their bill of goods at all. If you do, you deserve what you get. Period! Over and out, you deserve it. If it's not genuine excitement and enthusiasm with sincerity, it'll get you.

As I said earlier, you can come to meetings and you can get excited. You can. You can do it. You can read a book and get excited. You can listen to a tape and get excited.

If there's one book that you can read in Los Angeles to teach you how to be excited, there's a thousand books you can read in Los Angeles that teach you how to be more excited and more enthusiastic.

If there's one course you can take for $25 or $2,500, there has to be a hundred courses you can take that would teach you how to be more excited and more enthusiastic. They teach you things you wouldn't believe. Actually, you would believe it because you've gone through them, too.

They teach you things like this: When you wake up in the morning, one of the first things you want to do is you want to yell as loud as you can, beat yourself on the chest and run to the bathroom. They claim you have to go anyway, so you might as well run, right?

Heck, I tried that. I got in there and felt foolish. I didn't have to go, you know. There are others that teach you that if you feel a little introverted to wear red underwear. That's right; they said you need to just wear red underwear. They think of it as the same concept as tying a string around your finger. If you need to get yourself worked up, just pull those babies out and look at them. Right? Oh yeah, more excited and more enthusiasm.

I tried that. That doesn't work either.

If you want to get excited and enthusiastic, don't wear any underwear and that'll get the adrenalin flowing right now, okay?

Look here. You know what this is here? Up and down, up and down. You know what that is? That's a new distributor's psyche. That's what it is. New distributor's psyche. Up and down, up and down.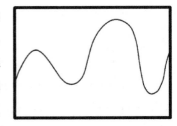

Let me tell you what happens to a new person when they come and look at our business. They get really excited when someone invites them down to see the opportunity, right? They get kind of excited down here when they come, and they see it.

They really are thinking exactly like I was thinking over 13 years ago, *Well, you know, it's really not for me and you know, it's going to be for others, but not for me.*

Yet, they get there and they say, "Hey, this product sounds good." They start seeing a few of the people and say to themselves, *That guy's not any different from me*, or *She's not any different from me. Maybe I can do this thing.*

They say everybody's into health and nutrition. So, let's say it's a couple and they get all excited and they let you know they are going to start off with that senior consultant's merchandising pack. Let me start out right now. I'm going to go on this deal, okay?

And then, they get home and they're all excited and you're talking to them that night and they get home and the husband and wife is heading home and say to one another, "Hey, this is really something. We're going to go in on this. We should not be spending $285 but we can get it back; we'll use our vacation money. We got it, we're okay. Maybe this thing will work out well." And, they're all excited that night and they stay up a couple hours extra talking about it.

Next morning something real interesting happens – they both wake up before the alarm clock goes off and they're lying there perfectly still not talking to each other and not moving, looking straight up at the ceiling and they got this strange feeling inside their stomach. They don't know if they got the flu or they're in love again, right? You know the feeling.

And it's neither one; it's their $285, right? And they're scared. He doesn't want to say anything to her because he's afraid if he does, she's going to say, "I told you so."

She doesn't want to say anything to him because she's afraid if she does, he's going to say, "I told you so."

And, no one is saying anything but the next couple days the kids get yelled at a lot and the dog gets kicked, nothing's going smoothly there until finally, he comes home from work and he says, "Honey, it's Tuesday night and John's going to the meeting tonight. Let's go, it's going to be something." She perks up and they get ready. They're heading down to the meeting and they start talking now.

They went here, they were up here, down here and now they're up here, right? They're up here; that's where they are and he says, "You know something, honey. I didn't want to say anything about it; I've just been sick you know. I haven't been myself the last couple days because I started thinking what are we doing in this business? We don't know anything about sales; we don't have any experience. I'm thinking all I am is a plumber. I need to be doing this stuff here and the money we spent? I could have bought you new clothes, and I could have done a lot of things."

"But I'm telling you, I've got a good feeling about this Herbalife thing and John's excited about it too, – he said he thinks he could do something like this, and he knows a couple people who want to do it. I think we got something going; this is really something."

She says, "You know, I've been experiencing the same thing, and I feel good about Herbalife, too. I think this is something."

They go down there that night and start shaking hands and say, "Hi, my name is Bob, and this is my wife, Mary." They are going on and on introducing themselves to people.

Five minutes to 8:00, John hasn't shown up yet.

Two minutes to 8:00, and they're all looking like their dog just died...

Seven minutes *after* 8:00 and they're convinced that John is not coming and they slip out the back door, going home.

Whoa, way down here, right? And you know the conversation on the way home?

Bob says, "You know, maybe this business isn't for us after all. We don't have any sales experience, no business experience, and you know, if it was a different time of year, maybe it'd be better, maybe we made a mistake. Well let's try and get our money back anyway, okay?"

Things rock along for about a week and then all of a sudden, Bob talks to Frank. Frank says he's coming, he's going to meet them at his house next Thursday night and they're all going over together and he's really excited about this, alright?

So, here comes Frank, right on time and they get Frank down to the meeting – all three of them go down to the meeting together and they're all excited and Frank sees it and he says, "This is the best thing I've ever seen in my life! You can't miss with a product line like that and the people around here if they're willing to help you the way it all seems, this thing is, this is wonderful."

Frank says, "Listen, you can forget about building an organization, you can retire off of me alone!"

Got it? Whoa, way up here! They take Frank home and they go out for a drink, right? And here's the conversation, "We've been up and we've been down in this business, but I just feel so good about Herbalife; I know it's the best thing that's ever happened to us and maybe in another six months I'll be full time and the two of us can work together and we can do all the things we ever wanted; we can fix up the family room, we can get the new car and we can have this and this is so good; I'm just so excited about Herbalife!"

Frank backs out… WHOA! Then what? "You know it's the wrong time of year and we haven't had any experience in this before," right?

How many have experienced that? It's going to get you. This is what happens, okay? But let me point out something – do you think this is only reserved for new distributors, or do you think old distributors go through this?

You bet your life they do!

You think I go through this? Absolutely.

The difference is – if I invite somebody and they don't show, do I get disappointed? Yes. But not for two or three days – I'm disappointed for maybe two or three minutes. You just have to start hacking away at the time. This is not going to switch for you overnight. You have to hack away at it and instead of two or three days, it's going to be two and a half days and it's going to be one and a half days – you're going to start moving on it. You're not going to go from two days of disappointment to two minutes of disappointment – you've got to be a little bit better at it today than you were yesterday.

You've got to be able to control your attitude just a little bit more today than you did yesterday.

You've got to be a little bit more excited today than you were yesterday.

You've got to be a little bit more sincere today than you were yesterday.

You've got to be a little bit more effective today than you were yesterday.

You don't go from here to here.

You do it a little bit at a time.

Never let a day go by that you stay the same, because I'm going to tell you something, you're either going up or you're going down – you don't stay the same and if you're not going up, check the gauge, it's heading down – you have no choice in this matter at all.

And the only way I know to control this is with the facts. That's how I keep my attitude up is with the facts. You've got to get excited and you've got to be enthusiastic, but sincere excitement through that only comes from the facts.

Here's something else you've got to have in your attitude – deadly serious. You say, "Hold it, how am I going to be excited, enthusiastic and deadly serious at the same time?"

Here is a scale that we all fit on. Up here's delirious excitement, down here's deadly serious. Everybody fits in there some place. Now if you're the type of personality that's always so enthusiastic about something, no one's going to want to look at your products or your opportunity because nothing can be that good, right?

If you're the type of personality that's so deadly serious, nobody's going to look at it because it's too grim, right? You've got to blend in here. Of course, you want to – someone says you're excited about this, you don't have to tell them this, your attitude does – you bet your life I'm excited, but I'm serious about it, too.

"This is the finest opportunity I've ever seen." That's got to come across in your attitude. It does. You'll see somebody come in here and they'll go right to the top right now. It's because they're able to handle that. They feel strongly about the product, they feel strongly about the marketing, they feel strongly about themselves – it's not their talents – it really isn't – it's how they feel about it. Does this make sense to you?

Deadly serious in your attitude. You bet your life you're deadly serious. You'd be deadly serious about any opportunity that you have. Don't be deadly serious about skating by – don't be deadly serious about Friday coming and it's a weekend.

You be deadly serious about your financial future and your personal future at all times and don't let anybody do anything that would detract you from that. Period. Especially if they're people close to you.

The people close to you are ones that get you – sometimes. They say, "Oh, I support you 100 percent in this business – anything you want to do is fine with me, I'm here to support you – go to it."

And then they'll turn right around and say, "Hey, why don't you come on over Saturday and help me out?"

You tell them, "Oh, I'm going to my business meeting."

They can't hold their tongue, "Oh, you're going to *another* meeting?"

That's called arrows of the tongue – *unintentional* – it doesn't mean they don't love you; it doesn't mean they don't care – but that's called arrows of the tongue, okay? It's sharp and it's piercing and after a while, you've got to understand the facts – that's the only thing that you're going to get by with here. You can't get to the top and be successful without the fact.

Death of a Salesman

What Can Hold You Back in Your Profession?

Let's talk about what is the *death of a salesman*? Or, we also can call this the death of someone in their own business, or we can call this the death of someone in their own profession.

There are certain things that hold people back, and we're going to talk about that. I will note this: no matter if you're in the sales profession, or if you're in the acting profession, or if you're a lawyer or a doctor or an Indian Chief, it really doesn't make any difference. There's one thing that is important here: We are all salesmen.

If we're going to be successful in life, we all have to learn to be salesmen. Let me rephrase that... we already know how to be salesmen. All of us do. However, the majority of us don't know it.

The best salesmen in the world are kids. Right? Have you ever noticed that? Have you ever seen a kid like that? Little five-year-old kid says, "Daddy, Daddy, can I have an ice cream?"

"Absolutely not. We're going to eat two hours,"

"Oh, Daddy, Daddy, can I have ice cream, please?" the kid goes on.

"Absolutely not. If you say that one more time, you're going to get it," the dad says just a little more tense this time.

Fifteen minutes later, the kid's licking on his ice cream, right? Kids know just how to take it so far, right, and get what they want. So, kids are the best ones.

Next to kids are women. Women are the best salesmen in the world. Uh, there's been very few things, ladies, that you've ever wanted from your man, but you haven't gotten unless you'd given up on it. Okay? Uh, that's really, really something.

The most important thing about sales is remember this: Salesman has an S in the middle. It means plural - more than one time, right? You can't just sell one time and now you have got the thing figured out and handled.

I'll relate this to relationships.

Men, you can't make one big sale to the lady of your dreams and expect that it's over. It's got to be every day that it has to take place. And ladies, the same thing goes for you, right? You don't make one big sale for your man and then it's all over, right? It's a continual situation, every single day. And you need to understand something about the salesmen profession, the most honorable profession in the world today. And, it is the most professional profession in the world today.

Everyone says, "Well, yeah, I'll tell you what the backbone to America is. It's the farmer, right?" Let the farmer stop producing food for 30 days. And, very little is going to happen.

So, you might say, "Well, the backbone is the legal industry." Let's shut down the legal system, the lawyers and the judges for 30 days. Again, nothing much happens. Let the medical professions shutdown for 30 days and nothing much happens.

A salesman stops selling for 30 days, and it stops everything. So, it is the most highly respected profession in the world. It's also the most highly paid profession in the world, too. It is salesmen, not doctors who make the most money. It's not lawyers, right? It's salesman who make more money than anybody else. And I'm talking about true salesmen, not someone that you walked down to the department store and they have a little badge that says, *salesperson*.

And, I'm just using the word *salesman* here. Ladies, please understand. Salesman is easier to say than salesperson, right? Just because someone has a tag here that says salesperson doesn't mean that they are a true sales professional. They might just be an order taker.

True professional salesmen are the highest paid individuals in the world and the highest paid in the sales field is in what industry? The direct sales industry. They make more money than anybody else in the world, so you've come to the right place for opportunity. You know you also come with the right credentials.

You know what you need to take advantage of this? Nothing.

You need desire and willingness. You need burning desire. It takes three things to succeed. I encourage you to write these down.

Burning Desire

It takes a burning desire to improve yourself financially. See, I don't care if a person is earning $500 a month or $5,000 a month. They could be a financial failure or a financial success either way. The key is, are they succeeding in their goals? Are they getting what they want for them and their family?

Regardless if it is $500 or $5,000, isn't that the important thing?

Somebody says, "Oh yeah, I'm making real good money. The question is *compared to what?* Right? Don't compare it to someone earning less or more than you. You need to be comparing it to, *Are you succeeding in your goals for you and your family?* And, if not, the question has got to be asked, "Why not?"

It isn't because you don't have the experience and it isn't because you don't have the time. It's none of those things. The real issue is just you.

So, death of a salesman... When I'm talking about salesmen, we're going to talk about how important it is, and we're going to talk about what some killers are, and that you need to understand how important the sales profession is.

Sometimes we think badly of salespeople, right? Because you've gotten a lemon; you got stuck with something, so you blame the salesperson. But what you need to do is turn that around.

Think of any object that you have in your home that you like – your clothes, car stereo, bed, plants, anything that you have that means a lot to you. I want you to notice that you bought that from a salesperson. Understand? And you think well of them, you think of them as someone who's nice and a good salesperson makes you feel good about it because they continually sell you on it, and that's not negative.

I mean, they're telling you, what they're telling you is the truth, right? But they're continually making you feel good about it.

Here's what a salesman is:

A salesman is a mind maker-upper.

That's what a salesman is. A mind maker-upper. And because the mind fluctuates, the salesman has to do what? Continue to make it up, right? Remember I said in a relationship, you can't just make one big sale and you got it, because the mind fluctuates. If you want to know why relationships don't do what they want, it's because the mind fluctuates. You have to continually make the mind up here. You have to continually work on it. Okay?

Now, I'm going to talk about the death to the salesman. Death of someone being in business for themselves, deaths of any type of professional individual. I have to tell a story here. Maybe that'll help out.

We've all known somebody like this, maybe the guy at the gas station, right? He keeps the gas station going. He keeps everything going, all the customers happy. He keeps everything moving, everything going and uh, he's the best mechanic. He treats everybody nice and you say, "I don't understand why Bill does not go out there and get in business for himself. He is just so talented. He would do just wonderful for himself; he's made a fortune for his boss. Why doesn't Bill get into business for himself? We've all seen that.

Bill finally gets into business for himself. He lasts six months, goes bankrupt working in his own place. He ends up going back to his old job and while he's gone, his boss's business has gone down the tubes. Right? He's so glad to get back there now; he gets back there, and he fixes up his boss's business and it takes off like crazy, right?

We've all experienced something like that. Well, what happened? What's the difference here? Is it because Bill doesn't have the talent it takes? Bill has some things that he was lacking in his character that showed up when he was his own boss. It was to his advantage when he had a boss, but it was a detriment when he didn't have a boss, and I'm going to go over those with you, okay?

Let's talk about habits.

Habits

We all have habits. Everything we do is a habit. The way we talk is a habit. The way we walk is a habit. The way we relate to others is a habit. The way we eat is a habit. The way we drive is a habit. Everything we do is the result of a habit that we have.

Our success in life, or failure in life, or mediocrity in life is a result of our habits in life, not anything else. It's based on our habits. So, if we want to change that, then we need to go to work on our habits. That's the thing that we need to go to work on and zero in on.

A bad habit – you hear the thing that a bad habit is hard to break, right? We've all heard that but let me tell you what else is hard to break. A good habit.

A habit is a habit.

The fact that it's good or bad happens to be that it's relative to the individual in the situation, right? Bill had some habits that were good while he was working for someone else. But when he got into business for himself, he fell right on his face, a result of bad habits.

So, a habit is a habit, and the only way that you can do anything with a habit, the only way that you can change a habit is you got to replace it with another habit. That's all. You change it with another one. You have got to make that the predominant issue here, and then you can alter it.

I'm going to talk to you about a couple of habits here that will get you in trouble being in business for yourself. One is lying to yourself.

Even the most honest people in the world have a tendency to lie to themselves. You will tell yourself a lie. Don't lie to yourself. Tell yourself the truth.

That is very easy to do when you get into this business. You find yourself doing well, then the next thing you do, you find yourself going full-time. You get out there full-time, and you do great here for about two months and then you start going downhill.

Takes about two months after being full-time for it to start catching up with you. I'll tell you what happens. You have only so much time when you're part-time to make it work, and you've got your momentum going and it's working for you and you say, "Okay, my income is up. I feel stable with this thing," and your decision to go full-time is accurate. And then, that momentum keeps carrying you for about another month or two months.

What happens in your business today is not a result of what you do today. It's a result of what you did yesterday. What happens in your business in the month of March has nothing to do with what you do in March. It has to do with what you did in February, right? And without noticing, you've changed a couple of habits in March and all your business keeps going up in production, keeps climbing, your income goes up, your sales go up because of what you did in February. You say, "I'm doing the right thing now because I changed this over here. And look what's happened."

But, it has nothing to do with what you're doing now in March, it's because of what you did over here in February. So, when a person gets in this business and goes full-time, their decision is accurate, but then they change a couple of things that they have been doing. And, it takes a couple months to figure out that what they have changed is not going to produce the kind of results they had in February.

And because their production keeps climbing, they think, *This is what I need to do*. And the next month it starts falling off and then they start doing footwork again. They don't know what to do. They start working on solving the wrong problem.

There's only one thing you need to do.

Basics

It's called *Back to Basics*. And write that down, *Basics*. You've got to do the basics. For those of you who are sports fans, you understand this. How many follow basketball very closely at all? I didn't use to follow basketball. But, I started to watch and now I know that basketball is very exciting, and I had no idea it was exciting at all until I got into it. I really, really like basketball now.

In basketball, because it is so fast, you can go along and just keep hitting points and everything is hitting it. Then, all of a sudden, you can go along, and the team can't make any points at all! It can be three minutes, four minutes, five minutes, and they put no points on the board.

Now, if they're scoring a lot of points, they know what to do. They keep doing the same thing, right? But what do you do when you're not scoring a lot of points? It's very simple. You go back to the basics.

You keep doing the basics over and over and over and over again. You stick to the basics. It's called the hot hand in basketball and sports.

So, all of a sudden, you're going along and you're scoring no points at all. Three, four or five minutes, no points in. All of a sudden, someone gets a hot hand. But, what do you do when you don't have a hot hand? Basics. Basics. Basics.

Keep doing the basics (and there's only a handful of basics here.) We're going to come down to it.

Now, one of them is lying to yourself. Don't lie to yourself. Lie to me. Lie to your sponsor, lie to your spouse. Lie to your neighbor, but don't lie to yourself. Tell yourself the truth. Have the ability to see it as it is and call it as it is.

You don't have to work a lot in this business. It's the easiest business I've ever seen in my life, okay? I've been in a lot of businesses and made a lot of money in a lot of businesses, but I'd say I've never done anything like this. This is the easiest thing I've ever done in my life! Maybe I shouldn't be telling you that. I'm hesitant to say that, but it is easy.

When my sister can start and 90 days later, have a royalty check of $2,010.88 her third month, that's unheard of, okay? That is unheard of, so it's an easy business to do, but don't lie to yourself about what you're doing.

Tell yourself the truth. All you need is eight hours a day, five days a week, every single week for three months straight, and you'll never have to worry about your financial future again.

When I first went full-time, I was told, "All you have to do, Larry, is work half as hard here, as you did in construction work and you'll be wealthy quick." And I said, let me at it. Half as hard? I'll work twice as hard, right? It didn't work that way at all because of habits. Understand? Habits.

One of them is lying to yourself... "Oh, I know what's coming! I got it going now, I've got it coming in now," right? Well, where is it? It is the only thing you have to ask yourself, "Where's the production today?"

Some people get so engrossed putting projects together, brochures together, big schemes, booklets, everything else together, that they don't produce today! They don't make one sale today. They don't recruit one person today. They don't really seriously talk to anybody about the product or the opportunity today.

I'll tell you how to make $5,000 a month in his business. I'll tell you how to do it and it'll take 90 days, if you will do two things:

Number One: Sell the product at every opportune moment.

That doesn't mean that you go out here and go door-to-door. It doesn't mean you get party plans. It doesn't mean you have to go to office buildings. It doesn't mean that. Sell the product at every opportune moment. Wear your LOSE WEIGHT NOW, ASK ME HOW! button, open your ears, open your eyes, pay attention, and sell the product at every opportune moment.

Number Two: Sponsor 10 people a month.

I've told this to some of you before, and I'll tell you this again, "There's not a person that's heard this before, who did it, who is making less than $5,000 a month. Period, over and out. That's what I told my sister to do, and that's exactly what she's doing. That's something. That's all she's doing is those two things. Sell the product at every opportune moment and sponsor 10 people a month.

That doesn't mean 11 in March, nine in April! Sponsor 10 people every month. And sell the product at every opportune moment. You can do that and $5,000 a month is yours. It's waiting for you, but don't lie to yourself here. OK?

Who did you talk to TODAY about the product? Who did you talk to TODAY about the opportunity? Don't tell me about what's going to happen next week with all these big plans you have. Don't you do that! What did you do TODAY that made a significant difference in your financial future? What was it TODAY?

You are the only one that's got to have the answer to that question, but tell yourself the truth on it, okay?

I'm going to give you a problem here, but I'm going to give you a solution to it. Procrastination.

Procrastination. I don't know how to spell it.
I was going to look it up this morning, but
I thought I'd do it on Monday.

I just want to see if you're awake. Okay, procrastination. How many of you are procrastinators? All of us have procrastinated. All of us. There's not a person in the world who is not a procrastinator in some area. Procrastination.

Procrastination took me awhile to understand and I had to relate it, but there were a couple of things that really got to me. I didn't think I was going to be able to make it. Even though I was making money and stuff, it wasn't secure money to me. See, it wasn't any of that stuff because I didn't think that I was going to be able to get it put together. And procrastination was one part of it, and it took construction work to get me back to understanding procrastination.

I couldn't understand it. Some things I just keep putting off and off and off and off, and other things I'd do right now, and I just didn't have any handle on why I did that. I didn't understand it. Let me share a story with you about procrastination.

The Fried Bologna Sandwich

We're in the nutritional business, but I'm going to tell you right now my favorite sandwich in the whole world, and I love sandwiches. I mean I don't just like sandwiches, I love them, just love them. And my favorite sandwich in the whole world is a fried bologna sandwich. Any of you ever had a fried bologna sandwich? Let me tell you - you never had one in the world like I can make it. Sometimes I will prepare a fried bologna sandwich, and you'll never believe it. You'll never be the same again in your life over this.

When I did construction work, you know what I had every day for lunch? Fried bologna sandwich. It's got to be prepared, right? It's got to be eaten, right? It's so good. You have no idea. And I'd been in sales about a year, and I was having tough times. I was making money and everything, but I was having some rough times because I wasn't secure as I said. I was nervous about it all the time.

It was a day that I planned to be off. It was in March and I wanted to do some work on my deck. I was building a deck out there and I've been piddling around with it and I was going to take a day and really get on with it. I was there by myself and I never will forget it. I didn't want to eat anything in the morning at all, because I don't like to get all bogged down. And I had it figured out where I could do X amount of work and stop about 1:00, rest a little bit, and prepare a fried bologna sandwich and eat it leisurely at 2:00. It was going to be so good.

And I kept working, right? Finally, I got down and it was time to eat my fried bologna sandwich. I prepared it and all of a sudden, I'm eating this fried bologna sandwich. (And it had been a while since I'd had one because I hadn't been doing construction work for some time.) And for some reason, this fried bologna sandwich didn't taste nearly as good to me is I felt like it should, and that was bothering me.

I'd trained myself enough by now to pay attention to things that didn't feel quite right; to analyze them and figure it out and change it. And for whatever reason, I couldn't figure it out. And then it got me. I understood it. You know what it was? I don't like the crust. Terrible, right? I don't like eating the crust, but you also can't throw the crust away because there are starving kids in India, right? (You know how your Mother put you through that deal, right?)

So, you can't throw the crust away. And so, what do you do? I looked at the sandwich. I started over here in this corner and I started eating in the middle and it was ending up that I was going to have this big piece of crust left at the end. You know, it's dry, it's terrible tasting; nothing good about that deal at all, and then it hit me.

I figured it out, and I related that to *procrastination.* I said to myself, *I know how to do it now - make the whole sandwich taste good from start to finish.* You know what you do?

Eat the crust first. You get on with the crust! You eat little pieces of the crust at a time until it's all gone. You don't mind eating the crust because you know you'll get down to the last bite, which is the heart, right? The good stuff is in the heart of the sandwich. Everything is there, in the maximum! Whatever you have on your sandwich, it's all in the middle of the good stuff, right? And that's the best bite, right?

So, you save that for last. So, the point on procrastination is, all of us procrastinate in some areas of our life, right? We procrastinate when we're doing things we don't like to do. We hurry up and do this stuff that we like to do, and we prolong the stuff we don't like to do. And, why we're doing the things we like to do like eating a bologna sandwich, we're thinking of the crust, and we're not enjoying this to full capacity, right?

So, if you eat the crust first, the crust is more palatable because you've got all the good stuff to look forward to.

So, all that means is that the things that you don't like to do, you do first. And while you're doing them, they're more enjoyable because you're looking forward to the things that you do like to do, okay?

Do the things that you don't like to do first. And while you're doing them, they're more enjoyable because you're looking forward to the things that you do like to do.

Does that make sense to you? All of us procrastinate, all of us do, but the thing on procrastination is, do the things you don't like to do first so you can look forward to doing the things you enjoy doing, okay? Now here's the next point.

Failure to Set Good Goals and Plans

Now everybody that you've ever met who is successful has always said you've got to have goals and plans. Well, that's one thing that almost hung me up because I didn't think I had them. I attended seminars, and they call it, *The Art of Setting Goals*. Can you believe that? I'd been to a six-hour seminar, *The Art of Setting Goals*.

Well I thought I couldn't master setting goals, right? They told me to write it down on the three by five card. Put it in your pocket, read it in the morning and as soon as you get up, read it at night before you go to bed. They teach all that stuff, right?

I'm not saying don't do that, I'm saying do that. For me, when I wrote it down, nothing happened. I read it, nothing happened. I don't know how to make plans. I don't know how to follow up. I didn't want to do that.

I was making money. I was moving ahead, but it wasn't with ease, you understand? It wasn't secure movement forward, and then I realized something, and that made a lot of difference to me; and what I realized was I do know how to set goals.

You know why? Well I had some goals in my life. I didn't write them down. All of us in this room know how to set goals. All of us right now know how to make plans to achieve those goals, and right now you don't have to read any books.

You don't have to go to any seminars, you don't have to do anything. You know right now how to do it.

A goal is something that you have got to have - you have to have it. If you have got to have it, and you become aware of it, then you'll figure out the plans. The plans will come to you.

I'm going to tell you a story. When I tell you this story, I bet there's a lot of people in this room that could tell me a story just about like that. There's only a couple of things early on in my life that I knew I wanted. One of them was my own home. I knew at the age of 13, I wanted to own my own home.

And, I was very aware I was going to own my own home. When I was 19, I was doing construction work on a track of homes and they had this one model over there that I really liked. I just kept going back and looking at it, going back and walking through it. It wasn't that it was the best model, but it was the only one that I could identify with possibly being able to get, right? That alone made it the best for me - and I just kept going back and looking at it and finally the developer said, "Why don't you buy it?"

"Oh, you know, I don't have any money or anything and I don't have any credit and all this stuff," I went through the whole thing.

"Listen, why don't you just go buy it?" And he said, "I'll help you. You can do some extra stuff and work off some of the down payment."

"Well, I don't know."

He looked at me squarely, "Do it," and he walked off.

So, the next day on Sunday, I went into the sales office and I wrote out a check for a $250 deposit to hold the house. And, I signed the papers knowing the whole deal was a real deal because if I didn't do it, my money is gone right? So, $250 is a lot of money, especially back then, a lot of money. The house was going to be completed in six months. I had no idea where I was going to get the money for the down payment. The truth of the matter was I had no idea how was going to come in and cover the $250 check! That's true.

But I somehow knew that check was going to get covered before it got into the bank the next day. I knew that somewhere it was going to happen. Somebody was going to buy something I had, you know, my old tennis shoes, something! Somebody was going to give me that $250.

When I signed the papers on the house, I had no idea about how I was going to pay for the payment, had no idea how I was going to qualify, but I forgot all about that once I made the commitment.

I went out there when they started to level off the lot for the foundation. I took pictures, talked to the guys. I went out there when they were doing the foundation. When I did the cement work, I had all my friends over, and we put up some really special cement work. It was just really something. I was really excited about it.

And when they started putting up the walls and everything, I'd bring over all my friends and I would explain to them how the family room was going to be, and how the master bedroom would be, and how we would have the sliding glass door look out over the backyard. It was going to be a step down and I went through that whole deal.

They put the fireplace up, and I went out there and showed them how the fireplace was going to work and everything.

I had no idea how I was going to get the money, but you know the story. Almost to the day and the hour that it came for the final payment for the down payment to get in there. You know what happened? I had the money. Now, I didn't sit down and write it down on a piece of paper. I didn't do that. I didn't read it three times a day, two times a day like they teach it, and I'm not saying that's bad.

I'm saying it was just a total part of my awareness.

Now that story might sound unusual to you, but how many times have you had something like that happen to you?

That's a goal.

You know how to set goals and you know how to make plans.

You know how to do it today.

The difference between $10,000 a year income and $10,000 a month income is the *got to*. That's all. It only has to do with your desire, something that you've got to have. There's never been a goal in your life that you've had that you've not achieved unless you've given up on it.

Have you ever been in a situation where if, *I don't get another $200 the whole world is going to collapse,* and sure enough you got it, right? Because you had to have it.

> **The difference between $200 and $200,000**
> **is not the issue. The amount is not the issue.**
> **The issue is the desire, the amount of**
> **desire that you have.**

I'm telling you the reason that most people don't make $10,000 a month is they don't have the desire to make $10,000 a month - they don't have to do it.

Now, if you've got to have a $10,000 a month income, as bad as you have to have the house, or as bad as you have to have that new suit, or as bad as you have to have that vacation for your lady, or as bad as anything you've ever wanted that you weren't going to give up on... I'm telling you, it's yours. It's a matter of time. It belongs to you. Just a matter of time.

How to Employ Yourself

Now, I'm going to share one other thing with you that will bring this together for you as far as, how do we put all this into practice every single day? How do we go from 8 o'clock this morning to 5 o'clock this afternoon? How are we going to do it?

It's a subject that I call, *employ yourself.*

Why don't you get out a fresh piece of paper for this? Employ yourself. Habits, remember the habits thing? The only way you can get rid of a bad habit is to replace it with a good habit, right? And you've just got to keep switching it. I'm going to talk to about employing yourself, how to employ you.

Everyone says, "It's okay to talk to yourself, but don't answer," right? Don't you buy that story. You want to really get excited. You want to have a good conversation with yourself:

"Yeah, but let me tell you this."

"Yeah, but what about this," right?

And then, just slap yourself around.

You've got to do it sometimes. You've got to get intense just like there was somebody else there. You've got to talk with the inflections, the whole deal. You can't say, "Well, the reason you're not doing well, Larry..." that just doesn't cut it. I had to learn how to employ myself. Sometimes, we need crutches to get us through life. Sometimes, we need mental crutches to get us through life, mental crutches.

You're up here on this stage, and you fall down and break your ankle. You're all by yourself. There's not one other person in this hotel. You fall down right here and break your ankle. You've got to get off the stage, down the aisle, down the corridor, past the coffee shop, out the front door, across the street to the parking lot to get to your car. You've got a broken ankle.

Can you get there? Yeah. Would it be painful? Absolutely. And if you're all by yourself, there's not one person to help you. You could get there, absolutely you can. It'd take a long time, and you could do some irreparable damage to your ankle, right?

You're up here, all by yourself. You fall down and break your ankle, but perhaps you can find something that you can use as a *crutch*. And now, you go down the corridor, across the parking lot, and out to your car.

Can you get there? Can you get there easier? Can you get there with less pain? Probably zero damage to your ankle, right?

So, if you have the ability to have a crutch, then you need to use it.

Sometimes we need mental crutches to make us successful.

Mental crutches. And, that's what I had to develop was a mental crutch. I had to play mental tricks on myself. And to do that, I had to split my personality into two people.

I had to have two personalities, *Larry One*, and *Larry Two*, okay?

Larry One was the boss.

Larry Two was the employee.

Now, I had to split my personality, and I had to talk to myself, and I had to rationalize this whole thing. You want to picture it like this. What if you found out that somebody had a position, or better yet, you just met someone, and you got to like them. They got to like you, and you had no idea what kind of business they were in, but you just liked each other a lot.

And then, after a day or so there, he says, "Hey, listen, I really like you, and I think you're the type of person I'm looking for in my new company, and I've got a position for the right person. It pays $100,000 a year."

And quickly, he's got your attention, right? And you think, *Yeah, I know, it couldn't be me.* Right? And he says, "And I think you're the person for the job." Now, if that happens, someone would have your attention. What happens when you go out to find a job, for example?

You come in contact with somebody, if it's by virtue of an advertisement, personnel agencies, whatever it might be, when it finally gets down to where there is the basic company you would like to work for, and you're the basic person they'd like to have, then you start talking about income. Then you start talking about fringe benefits. Then you start talking about days that you work, hours that you work, etc.

Isn't that how it works?

Well, that's the same thing it is when you go to work for yourself.

The only difference is you don't have this person here that's overseeing you. Remember the bad habits? Remember the guy at the gas station here? We talked about him earlier, why he fell down. Because he kept some prior bad habits that were bad for his business, right?

He showed up when he was working for someone else, but he didn't show up when he was working for himself. Larry One here, and Larry Two.

Larry One says, "Hey, I've talked to you enough for the last two days. I've got something that I think would fit you. It'd pay you $100,000 a year." Larry Two is excited, "Tell me all about it."

Larry One explains his opportunity to him. And Larry Two says, "Okay, what do I have to do exactly?"

"I need you to talk to 10 people a day, okay?

"No problem. I can talk to 20 people a day for $100,000 a year."

"Hey," Larry One says, "only 10."

"All right, when do you want me to start?"

"Right away. How about starting on Monday morning, okay?"

Larry Two is chopping at the bit, "Okay, I'll start Monday morning."

"Okay, we've already decided for this $100,000 that you're going to work six days a week. Is that correct?" Larry One asked.

"Yes."

"We also decided that you're going to work at least eight hours a day during that time period. Is that right?"

Larry Two assured him again, "Yes."

"And you're going to talk to 10 people a day? That's the most important thing that I want," Larry One confirmed.

"I got it."

So, Larry One asks, "Okay, what six days a week do you want to work?"

Larry Two says, "Oh, I don't care," right? (Well, <u>he's got to care</u>, as to his future. You ever see someone go into a restaurant, and they say, "What do you want to order?" and they reply, "Oh, I don't care. Get me anything." Well, you know what you get? Anything. It's what you get. You don't get what you want. You get whatever someone else brings you. You need to care about what happens to you in your life.

So, Larry Two says, "All right, I want to have Sundays off."

"Fine. So, you're going to work eight hours a day?"

"Yes."

"What hours do you want to work, Larry Two?"

Larry Two replies, "Well, I don't care," right?

Larry One digs in, "Well, you choose it."

Larry Two, huffs, "So, okay, I'll start at 9:00. Say 9:00 to 5:00."

Larry One shakes his hand, "You got it!" Okay?

So, everything's all set. Larry Two's excited. He can't wait for Monday morning to come around, start his new job, his new career, making $100,000 a year. All he's got to do is talk to 10 people a day. He's got this in the bag. He can't even believe it. He's not going to believe it until he gets his first check, not ever. He's all excited.

Now, Monday morning rolls around, and Larry Two's ready to go to work. He's trying to get out the door to go do his job. He agreed to start to work at 9 o'clock, and just before he gets out the door, something happens with the kids and with the dog, and he gets a phone call. And as he's heading out the door, it's not 9 o'clock. It's 9:07 when he looks at his watch.

He thinks to himself, *It's 9:07… Oh that's all right. I'll make up for it.* And he goes to get in his car and starts it up, and he looks in his rearview mirror, and who do you think is sitting in the back seat? Larry One.

And Larry One says, "I could be mistaken here, Larry Two, but my watch says 9:07."

Larry Two instantly says, "Oh, you're right. It is 9:07, and I said I was going to start at 9:00, but a lot of things happened," and proceeds to tell Larry One the story.

And Larry One says, "Hold it, right now. You and I agreed that you were going to start at 9 o'clock, and the first day on the job, it's 9:07. Now, if you want to start at 9:07, Larry Two, that's fine with me. But you're going to start at 9:07 every day. It's not going to be 9:08 or 9:17. Whatever time you say you're going to start; you're going to start. Now, do I make myself clear?"

Now, if Larry One didn't care about Larry Two, what would he do?

He'd say, "That's okay. You make up for it a little bit later," right? Isn't that what he'd do? And what does Larry Two develop the first day on his job? *A bad habit.* Larry One cares about Larry Two, so he's not going to allow this bad habit to creep in.

Your habits are what equals your income.

The habits that you have is equal to your income, good, bad or indifferent. And for things to change, what's the formula? You've got to change. You understand? For things to change, you've got to change. So, you've got to change the habits. That's all it is, the habits.

Everything goes along well for a couple weeks when Larry Two is starting to leave, he gets a phone call from one of his best friends that he hasn't seen in six years, and his friend says, "I'm just around the corner. I'm coming over to see you."

And he says, "I'll be here." And he gets there, and they get to talking, and they get all caught up in all those war stories, all the things that's gone on in their lives.

They're going on and on and on, and before you know it, it's 7 or 8 o'clock at night, and he hasn't even gone to work at all. Period. And Larry Two convinces himself, *That's okay. I've got Bob here. Bob is going to be better than any 10 people I could talk to today. This is going to be something. I know he's just going to do great, and he'll start and it's going to be wonderful.*

And they go on and on and on and on some more. They have a nice dinner that night, and it's about 10 o'clock at night. Larry Two's brushing his teeth, getting ready for bed, and who do you think is standing in the shower? Larry One, right?

Larry One says, "Listen, I've been really busy today, and I haven't paid any attention, but I don't remember seeing you at all."

And Larry Two said, "Oh, you didn't, but let me tell you the story." And, he ran through the story, right?

Larry One says, "Hold it, Larry Two. When you were doing construction work for a lousy $10,000 a year, you went to work every day, and you were there on time, and you showed up every single day. And I'm paying you $100,000 a year, and one of your friends comes by, and you don't go to work at all?"

He said, "I need more consideration than that. If you're not going to work like you say you're going to work, then we're going to adjust your pay schedule here, Larry Two. It's going to be adjusted."

Now, Larry Two could look at that two ways. Well, that's being really hard. You bet your life it's being really hard. Larry One cares about Larry Two, and he's not going to let that habit start.

If he lets it start, it's going to happen three weeks from Thursday. He'll be doing it every single day. He'll be starting to slack off because of habits. Lack of discipline starts to creep in.

Everything rocks along fairly well until all of a sudden one day, Larry Two is supposed to talk to 10 people, and he only talks to eight people, and he's heading home, and he said, "Oh, my goodness. Aw, it's just been a terrible day. I tell you though, these eight that I talked to are better than any 20 that I could have talked to. Oh, yeah, these eight are good." He pulls up in the driveway, and who do you think is leaning next to the garage door? You guessed it. Larry One.

Larry One says, "Oh, I've been really busy and everything, and I hadn't talked to you lately, but I only counted eight today."

Larry Two nonchalantly says, "Oh, it was eight, but blah, blah, blah."

"Larry Two, I pay you for 10 a day, not eight a day. If you want to get paid for eight a day, fine. We'll adjust it, but I ain't going pay $100,000 a year for only eight."

Larry Two agrees, "You're right," and he gets in his car, and he pulls out the driveway. The first car he sees that has two people in it, he says, "Pull over," right? He is hungry, and he wants to go home.

See, here's the tendency. The tendency is for Larry Two to say, "Sure, so what it's 9:07, so what? I don't have to be that strict," or "So what if I miss a day and one of my friends comes over?" or, "Alright, I only talked to eight a day. Big deal. I'll make up for it."

The tendency for Larry Two is to lie to himself by saying, "I'm doing okay." Let me tell you this,

You didn't get into direct sales or any other business for yourself to do okay.

Every single one of you in this room was doing okay before you found Herbalife. That's not why you're here. If you got here to do okay, you're doing entirely too much work. There's a better place to spend your Saturday afternoon than here with us if you want to do okay.

Okay, everybody does okay. There's no big deal about doing okay. They don't write you up in the *LA Times* or *People Magazine* for doing okay. *Okay* is not a big deal. There are no commendations for doing okay. Nothing happens. Your family doesn't look up to you for doing okay. Your wife doesn't go out here and get you special dinners for doing okay. That doesn't happen. You get okay responses for okay effort.

You got into your business because you wanted to do excellent. You got into your business because you wanted to do outstanding. That's why you got into your business. You wanted to do exceptional things, not *okay.*

It's too hard to be in your business and just do *okay.* You've got to learn to employ yourself. You understand? Your habits will definitely determine your income.

Your Mental Projector

You are the Projectionist.
Learn to Choose What You Feel!

I'm going to draw you a picture here. And I'm not much of an artist, so I'm going to have to explain it. This is the picture that kind of put it all together for me.

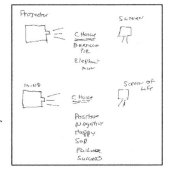

I learned this *employ yourself* concept. I had to learn that stuff. Nobody showed me this. Nobody explained procrastination to me like I explained it to you. I had to learn it. You can find out your own stuff. These are things just to stimulate your thinking here, to get you hopefully going the direction that you want to go.

Now, you know how to build an organization, right?

You know who to look for.

We talked a little bit about *controlling your thinking.*

We talked about bad habits and lying to yourself and procrastination.

We showed you how to employ yourself.

Now I'm going to give you a picture here that would bring the whole thing together.

And this picture, what I'm going to draw for you, for this little box, and you need to put this on your notes, this is a projector. And this projector is much like the projector that we show the film presentations on at night. Now, if you're going to have a movie projector here, a movie projector by itself is nothing. You have to have some elements.

One thing that you need, you need a screen, right? If you're going to see it.

You also need some films, don't you? You've got a list of films to choose from.

This is really important to understand. We have a projector, we have a screen, we have films. In between the projector and the film, we have choice, which means we choose the film. Right? We choose what film we put in the projector. If everything's working right, it shows up on the screen.

Now, you invite me over to your house. And, you've got these new films you want me to see.

You invite me over and say, "Oh, I've got these new films. You're not going to believe it."

I'm excited to see what you've got, "I'm coming, I'll be there." I show up and we do the chit chat, we get all down, we get comfortable and talk and everything. And I say, "Okay, I'm ready."

You ask, "What film would you like to see?"

And I say, "I've got to see *American Pie* again.

"Okay, I'll get the film and the projector, I'll get all set up here, and you get the popcorn." (The natural popcorn, of course.) "It's going to be something. My new sound system is in, it's wonderful."

"Alright, I can't wait!"

Got the popcorn, you've got the film loaded. Okay, we let it rip. We chose to see *American Pie*.

Now, lights go out. Projector goes on. Light comes on the screen. The credits start to roll, and instead of *American Pie* it's *Elephant Man*.

I immediately say, "I thought we were going to see *American Pie*."

You say, "Me too."

"Well, you've got the wrong film in the projector." Right? If *Elephant Man* is showing on this screen, what's in the projector? Projectors aren't known for playing real tricks, you know what I mean? They're pretty conservative, they don't do radical things.

So, do we agree that if *Elephant Man* is showing on the screen that *Elephant Man* is in the projector? No matter what, right? No matter what you think is playing, *Elephant Man* is in the projector, period, over and out. We all buy that story, okay?

Now, we're going to change this just a little bit. We're going to change these films. I'm going to call this film, *Positivity*. We're going to call this film, *Negativity*. We're going to call this one, *Success*. We're going to call this one, *Failure*.

We're going to call this one, *Love*. We're going to call this one, *Hate*.

We're going to call this one, *Happy*. We're going to call this one, *Sad*.

The screen becomes the screen of life. The projector gets changed just a little bit, and we're now going to call this, *The Mind*.

Choice is exactly the same.

Now, a person says, "I have a real positive attitude, but *Negativity* is showing up on the screen." What's in the projector? *Negativity*.

And, another person has *Failure* consistently showing on their screen of life and they say, "It can't be *Failure* because I know I'm thinking successfully?" If *Failure* is showing on their screen, it cannot be coming from *Success*. What's the answer? They've got the *Failure* film in the projector. Remember about lying to yourself? That's what's happening.

The person who has *Success* on the screen, what do they have? *Success* playing in the projector.

Happiness, sadness. If a person's constantly sad, they've got what film is in the projector? *Sad* film. They want to be happy, what do they do? They plug in the *Happy* film.

Now, a person is having a great day with a *Positive* film in the projector, and they have a blowout tire at 4:00 pm on the Harbor Freeway right out here. Now, that's a true test of their attitude. What's going to happen now? Is their film going to change from positive to negative or are they going to keep the same film in the projector regardless of circumstances?

Whatever is showing on your screen is because of what is in your projector.
When there's adversity is when you find out what you really think and really believe.

Anybody can look good when things are going well. Well what about adversity? What do you do then? That's when your true colors come out. Whatever is on the screen is in the projector. And not only do you see what's in there, everybody around you sees what's on your screen of life.

Now, when I realized this I said, "You mean to tell me…" (Remember my thing? Only $25,000 a year. It's all I could think. Remember my deal? Construction work, that's all I could think. I could only see past that one little house that I was going to get, that one deal was all I could do.) I became aware, and I put more things into my projector. And I'll tell you, when I first realized this, I went to work on this one in a positive/negative sense.

Positive. Negative. Positive. Negative. I'd be going along there and every two or three minutes, I'd have to change my film. Every two or three minutes I'd be going along there and say, "Oh my goodness, I've had the *Negative* film in for the last two minutes." And I'd just reach down there and plug in the *Positive* film, right?

You think that's okay. You are set. For about two minutes, then I had to switch them back and forth. I still have to do it today. Today, I'll be going along, and I say, "No wonder things have been going bad, I've had the wrong film in the projector for two days. Two days!"

And then, I put the right film in, and I'm alright for two or three weeks. I still have to do this, just like you're going to have to do it. Find out whatever is on the screen because you've got that film in there. Remember, the key factor here is choice. You get to choose the film.

Problem Solving

Learn to Handle Problems Quickly and Efficiently

Success is a habit, unfortunately so is failure. Vince Lombardi said, "Winning is a habit, but so is losing a habit." Vince Lombardi built the Green Bay Packers dynasty (which nobody thought that he could do.) Following a game, Lombardi and the team reviewed the films the next day. He was more upset if they won and played sloppy, than when they lost but played well. Now why would that be? It wasn't about winning or losing; it was about habits and how they played the game.

Vince Lombardi understands habits. You've got to correct these habits; you've got to work on the habits. One of them is problem solving. We have to talk about problems here. Now to talk about problems, I'm going to have to draw you another picture.

It's a walnut, okay. Why do you crack a walnut? To get inside. Why do you want to get inside? Because the goodies are inside.

All the goodies are inside the walnut, right. So, the walnut right here does you no good, but if you crack the nut, you get inside to the goodies, and you get to eat all the goodies. You're entitled to it because you cracked the nut, right?

Problem solving is a lot like walnuts, it is. You have to learn to solve problems. Here's a formula:

Problem solving equals maturity.

Maturity equals personal growth.

Personal growth equals production.

And, you've got to produce.

So, you've got that problem-solving equals maturity, maturity equals personal growth, personal growth equals production, which is your income.

My point to that is don't shy away from problems.

Don't see how many problems you can get away from, see how many problems you can figure out how to solve.

The bigger the problem, the bigger the paycheck, remember that.

If you solve just everyday problems that everybody can solve, then that's called an average problem solver, average income. The only difference between someone making a living and someone making a fortune is they ask for bigger problems to solve.

Mark Hughes asked for a big problem to solve. How to get fine quality, natural herbal products in the market to control people's weight that would be good for them? And, get it at an economical price? And, to develop up an organization to do it? That was a problem that Mark Hughes had 13 months ago, he solved it. It's solved, yes.

Bigger problems, he could have had the same problem, the same intensity with putting in his lawn in the backyard. The only difference is the paycheck. The bigger the problem, the bigger the paycheck.

Let's talk about babies here for a minute, okay. This is going to be interesting. Babies have problems and when a baby has a problem, how do they let you know about it? They cry. You know when a baby's got a problem because they cry. Let's talk about some of the problems that a baby could have. One of them could be that they're hungry, right, if they're hungry they cry. Then you say, "Oh, I should feed him, right?"

Another problem could be sleepy, could be tired right and want to go to sleep. Another one is, they could be wet, need to be changed. Or, there could be another one where they could be stuck.

Those are the basic problems that a baby has, babies don't have problems other than that. Do you agree they have very few problems?

Adults have problems too, an adult that is immature goes about it the same way a baby does, they cry. They cry about the problem, they don't solve the problem, they cry about their problem. They put their problem on somebody else and that equals immaturity. You have got to learn to crack the nut, okay? So, you get the goodies inside.

Now, sometimes you go to all the trouble of cracking this nut and you don't get what you think. You crack that nut and get inside, and you discover there's no goodies inside at all, there's a worm in there, right, so you don't get paid for that.

Usually when you have to solve problems with worms in them, it involves people. You've got to remember this, the majority of the problems that you're going to have to solve in your life have very little to do with policies and rules and regulations.

The majority of problems you're going to have to solve are going to be personality problems that have to be dealt with.

Sometimes, you'll get inside one of these walnuts, and there will be a worm in there. That's called a self-inflicted problem. A lot of people have self-inflicted problems. They want you to help them crack the walnut. Why? For one thing they need attention.

You've got to find out what are good walnuts and what are bad walnuts. If you examine a walnut real closely, you can generally tell if there's going to be a worm in there. But sometimes they'll fool you. Sometimes you'll crack it and you'll go all the way through it and then you'll find it there. But when you find a walnut with worms in it, and there's no goodies, there's no growth either. There's no growth for them, and you don't grow from it.

There are no rewards from it, but you have to suffer through it. You have to suffer through it because you're a nice person, that's why you have to do it, okay. There are two types of problems you can't solve.

One of them is an emotional involvement. You can't solve a problem that you have an emotional involvement with. You can't solve that kind of a problem. If you do, you'll come up with the wrong decision if you're emotionally involved in it. If you're emotionally involved, you have got to turn it over to somebody else. Anything you're emotionally involved in, you'll come up with the wrong decision.

The second one that you can't solve is when your hammer isn't big enough. You need more experience to be able to handle the situation, so you have to call on your sponsor or mentor; you have to call on somebody else to solve it. You have to call on someone you have confidence in. A third person perhaps, but your hammer is not large enough to solve that problem, Okay now, in solving problems, here's the thing, write this down:

There's no perfect solution to anything.
You strive for 51% accuracy.

Humanity does not have perfection, period. There are no perfect solutions, but here's what you strive for: You strive for 51% accuracy.

If you're 51% accurate or more on the decisions that you make and the problems that you solve, you are going to win. If you're striving for 100%, you're never going to make it. You want to strive for 51% accuracy, and anything above that you're ahead on.

Now, when someone brings me a problem, knowing in advance that most problems are personalities, here's some steps to it, alright, five steps:

Number One: You've got to gather facts. Under gathering the facts, put enough facts. People say you have to get all the facts. You're never going to get *all* the facts. How do you know you've got them all? What happens after you make the decision and one more fact comes in that you didn't realize?

You're never going to get all the facts, but you want to get enough facts to make a good decision. Enough facts means you've got enough information to see that the picture starts to repeat itself. The picture starts repeating itself from both parties, then you've got enough facts to decide.

Now, here's another picture I'm going to draw you. It's a pancake.

Now here's some things about pancakes that we need to talk about. What does a pancake always have? They don't always have syrup, and they don't always have butter. But, there's two sides to every pancake. Both sides are never the same, one side is always a little browner than the other side, right?

Just like a pancake, there are always two sides to a story. Analogies like this help me in decision making.

There's also a thing called *spotlighting*. Know what spotlighting is? Spotlighting is when whoever brings me the problem first, is usually the person at fault in a personality situation, which most problems are. The first one to bring me the problem is usually in the wrong; it's called spotlighting.

They take the spotlight off of them and throw it onto somebody else. That's what they're trying to do, to get the spotlight off them. They are the problem and they want to draw attention to someone else so that you won't see what the real issue is. They don't want you to see their inadequacies at all.

Number Two: Brainstorm for possible solutions. Possible solutions, every possible solution, there's no perfect solutions remember. Any possible solution, find several, not the correct solution, you're not after the correct solution here, you're after possible solutions.

Number Three: You pick two solutions. You pick what is the fairest for everybody involved, and you also ask yourself something like this: *If I choose this solution this time, would it apply every time?* This is very important here. Because if it doesn't, you're now probably getting involved in what? Personalities. If I choose this solution this time, would it work exactly the same way the next time this same circumstance came up? And if it can't, you need to analyze it.

For example, someone says, somebody stole my prospect, right? Possible solution is you could shoot the guy that stole your prospect, or you could shoot the prospect, right? You just have to brainstorm for solutions.

Here's another part to that. You always have to find somebody that you hold in esteem and you've got to say, how would they handle this situation? How would they do it?

Number Four: You choose the best solution. Choose the best solution, choose it quickly knowing that you will make mistakes. But what's your goal? Your goal is 51% accuracy.

When you choose it, here's what you judge – you judge intent. You've got to judge intent when someone has done something inaccurate, you've got to judge their intent. Was there greed involved? Was there malice involved? That has a great deal to do with it, intent.

They might have done it out of intent, which means greed and malice. They might have done it out of ignorance, which means they didn't know. They honestly didn't know. They might have done it out of stupidity, which means they knew, but they did it anyway. Or they could have done it because they had false facts. So, then you've just got to act accordingly.

Number Five: Act on your decision. Once you've made your decision, you act upon it. You act upon it. You decide, you inform the people involved, knowing in advance that everyone will not agree, but you decide, and you act on it and you never look back on a decision, ever. The bigger the problem, the bigger the paycheck.

When someone brings you a personality problem, you set them down and here's the first three things you say.

First, "Folks before we get started, we have got to understand this, what can I do about yesterday?"

And you know what their answer will be, "Nothing." That's part one.

Second is, "If you're here today to be part of the problem, or you're here today to be part of the solution is going to determine my attitude. If you're here to be part of the solution, we'll talk, if you're here to be part of the problem, it's over. Did you come here today to be part of the problem, or did you come here today to be part of the solution?"

And what will they say? "The solution."

Third, I always say, "I want you to know right now, there's no perfect solution to anything. Now, if you agree to those ground rules, we'll proceed." And, we move forward to a solution.

Now, these concepts will help you in solving problems.

The 7 Diseases of Attitude

Know Them, Be Aware of Them, and Work on Them Diligently!

I want to share a couple of things with you here that I feel strong about. It's called *Diseases of Attitude*. I feel very fortunate in my life that I've been exposed to the type of thinking, the type of training that I'm sharing with you now.

Diseases of attitude are a lot like weeds in a garden. To get a good garden we need several things. If you're going to grow a rose garden, you've got to have several things. You need good seeds, good soil, plenty of water, and a really good hoe to have a good garden, don't you? If you're going to have a beautiful rose garden, that's what it takes.

But in the same area of space, to have weeds, what do you have to do? Nothing. To get weeds, you don't have to do anything at all. Weeds will come up all by themselves. You don't need good ground, you don't need good water, you don't need a good hoe, you don't need anything. Weeds will crop up all by themselves.

You don't have to plant weeds. Weeds are automatic.

Rose gardens you have to plant. Rose gardens you have to tend. Weeds just grow.

See, this applies to all areas of our lives. It's almost like man stands at the garden of his wedding, at the door of his marriage. He looks out there and his marriage is in complete shambles and he says, "I didn't intend it to be this way." And of course not, he didn't intend it to be that way. Nobody intends it to be that way. But it is. And I'll tell you how things get in shambles. It's called neglect.

Neglect will do it every single time. One week of neglect can cost a year of repair in your rose garden, can't it? Don't water your rose garden, don't weed it, don't fertilize it for one week in the heat of summer and what's going to happen? It's over for your rose garden.

A person can amble around here for a while and then be lost for a lifetime. You've got to tend your garden. You've got to get out the hoe. And here's some attitudes that we're going to talk about, diseases of attitude.

Number One is INDIFFERENCE.

Indifference is the mild approach to life. Indifference is that shrug of the shoulder. Saying, "Oh, you know I can't get all that worked up about something." That's indifference.

All I can tell you is if you can't get all worked up about something, you need to check your list. If it's not worth getting all worked up over, perhaps it's not worth doing at all, regardless of what it is. Get worked up about what you do.

Swing hot or swing cold, as they say. Even the good Lord said it: I have more respect for the person that does go all the way than the person who's in the half-baked, lukewarm middle here. Strong feelings are what we're after.

Someone's always asking, "What type of people do you like to be around?" My quick answer is always, "Strong-feeling people." I don't care what they feel strongly about. What I want them to do is feel strong about what they feel. It's kind of like back in the real early Christian days. The good Lord needed someone with strong feelings to lead the Christian movement.

Back then it wasn't like it is today. You didn't put 125,000 people in the LA Coliseum to hear Billy Graham on Sunday. Back then, it wasn't good to be a Christian. You didn't go out and publicize the fact and one thing you didn't do was go to the Coliseum, especially on Sundays. The word was stay away from the Coliseum and the good Lord needed someone to lead the charge. He's looking around for someone and His prime thing that He was looking for was someone with strong feelings.

He looks down there and he sees Saul of Tarsus.

You've got to understand Saul of Tarsus. Saul of Tarsus was probably one of the greatest Romans that ever lived. He was also Jewish and one of the greatest Romans. And he was very intellectual, one of the greatest debaters of the time. Saul of Tarsus was really something. You always knew what Saul was into because whatever Saul was into, he went all the way out for it.

Everybody in the community knew what Saul was thinking. Everybody in the community knew what Saul was doing. He was called, All Out Saul, because he went all out for everything that he did.

Saul only had one problem, he hated Christians. He hated them so much that he killed them. Every place he went, he killed Christians and because he was high up in the community, he had letters of authority to go around and kill Christians every place that he went.

He heard about a new group of Christians starting up in Damascus. You know the story. He got new letters of authority, gathered some men around him and he's smoking it to Damascus to get these new Christians. The story goes that he was breathing threats of slaughter. That means he felt strong about it.

The good Lord looks down there and needs someone with strong feelings and said, "My goodness. Look at that Saul. He really feels strongly. That's my man, right there." A bolt of lightning comes out of the sky and knocks Saul off his horse and blinds him temporarily. (It's a recruiting tool that you and I can't use, but if you're the Lord, you know what I mean? Have at it.)

Long story short, Saul gets converted to Christianity and becomes one of the greatest champions of the early Christian movement; one of the greatest men to ever live; Saul of Tarsus, Paul the Apostle. It was really something.

Strong feelings is what you look for. You've got to put everything you've got into everything that you do. Paul later said, "The things that I once loved, I now hate. The things I once hated, I now love." And that's called strong feelings. See, I don't care what direction a person is going in. I want them to feel strongly about what they feel about.

Put everything you've got into everything you do. That's the formula for real success. That goes from making a fortune to kissing your lady in the morning. *I will promise you that adventure awaits you in both cases.*

Number Two is INDECISION.

Indecision. It's called mental paralysis. Indecision will bring you to your knees. Indecision is when a person is on the fence. They can't quite decide which way to go. Indecision is when a person knows they're crippled with this disease.

The person says, "I know I'm on the fence, but I just don't know what to do." Sometimes you have got to make the decision knowing the 51% accuracy factor and knowing that you have got to get off the fence. It makes no difference what side it's on. It doesn't make any difference if you get off on the wrong side.

What makes a difference is that
you practice the habit of making decisions.

See, a life full of adventure, a life full of success, is a life full of many decisions. Indecision is the greatest thief of opportunity. Indecision is the greatest thief of time, greatest thief of happiness.

You got to learn to decide quicker, you got to learn to decide faster, you got to learn to decide better. Not reckless, not careless, but you've got to decide and move on. Indecision will bring you to your knees.

Number Three is DOUBT.

Doubt is like a plague. The worst doubt that a person can have in their life is self-doubt. It's the worst, to doubt yourself.

A person doubts, "Well, I don't know if I can do all that well." Why would a person entertain that thinking at all? A person doubts if he can make that much money. Remember the projector? If you're going to think about something, why not think about positive things? A person doubts if it'll last that long. Pretty soon people get good at doubting. Pretty soon the person can be a practiced doubter. They get really good at it. And I'll tell you what happens, they end up with an empty cup. An empty cup is what's in it for the doubter.

Turn the coin over, become a believer. Remember that trust is better than doubt. Always. I'm not telling you that you're going to win with that formula every time, but I am going to tell you you're going to win with trust a lot more than you can win with doubt.

Trust is a better deal than doubt.

Number Four is WORRY.

Worry can cause you so many problems:

Worry can cause you health problems.

Worry can cause you social problems.

Worry can cause you personal problems, economic problems, family problems, all sorts ...

Worry can drop you to your knees and reduce you to a beggar overnight.

Worry is a bad habit to get into. You can't be a worrier.

You can't be like the little old lady in Cleveland. She used to say, "My goodness. You know I can't believe this nuclear bomb, the nuclear things going on all over the world. I just can't believe it." She's always worried about a nuclear bomb coming. She said, "If one of those things were to go off here, I'd go all to pieces."

Of course, she would, right? But why go to pieces before the bomb falls? Why do that? To reduce yourself to a beggar overnight?

I used to be a super worrier. I did. Not a super warrior. Super worrier. My family wished I'd have been a super warrior. But I wasn't. Worry. You've got to give it up as a bad deal, worry. You got to treat worry like it's excess baggage.

Substitute worry with positive action. I want you to remember this, the heavy chains of worry, are always forged in idle hours. The heavy chains of worry are always forged in idle hours. Get in action. Take positive action.

Number Five is OVER CAUTION.

Some people are always just cautious. This is called the timid approach to life. Timid approach. Some people always test the water before they take the plunge. They test the water out with their toes before they take the plunge.

Some people wait for better days to come. Better days are never going to be here. You have to take the days as they are and make them into what you want them to be. Better days aren't coming. When has there been a better day? There hasn't been a better day. There are 24-hour segments that we have at our disposal for success/failure, happiness/sadness, positive/negative. There are 24-hour segments every single day; that is what we have.

There's no such thing as better days.
There are days. Period.

Take the days how you find them and make them into what you want them to be. I'll tell you one of my biggest cautions always was risk. Risk. I'd say, "Well, what if this happens? What if that happens? And then what if this happens? And then what about that? What if that happens? What about that one, huh?" It used to be my attitude.

There is always risk. Always risk.

People who chronically fail, always look at the risk in the opportunity. People who always succeed, look at the opportunity in the risk. You can't get away without risk.

Nobody's entitled to go through this deal called life without risk. You think you can have success and happiness without risk? It's an impossibility. Nobody gets off without having risk. It's part of our life. Let me tell you. Life is risky. I'll tell you how risky it is, we ain't getting out alive. Try that deal out.

I had someone tell me, "You guys are always talking about opportunity, opportunity, opportunity, here in Herbalife. And what happens if I get going and all of a sudden I start building up a little bit of inventory here, start conducting my business, I'm walking across the street and I get run over by a car, break my arm here, break my leg, and I end up in a hospital, can't work, who's going to take care of my family? Who's going to pay my bills? Herbalife?"

The answer to that question is, "Of course, not."

I'll tell you what I told him, I said, "Listen here, when you're walking across the street, instead of it being a car that hits you, let's have it be a truck. And not only does it break your leg this time, but it breaks your arm, breaks your back, breaks your neck, crushes your skull, you end up in a hospital, complete vegetable for the rest of your life. How about that one?"

He said, "Don't make fun of me."

I said, "I'm not making fun of you. My wreck's better than yours."

You can't design a nice one-legged wreck. Can you? You can't do that. So, if you can't do that, why design any wreck at all? Why look at that side of it? Someone's always looking for safety and security.

Let's say I need safety and security. Well, if you want safety and security, we'll put you in the corner. We'll get you a sheet, we'll get you a blanket, we'll bring you food and water every single day, you'll probably live to be 100 years old, safe and secure in a corner. You say, "Yeah, but what a way to live." That's right. What a way to live. Safe and secure.

Number Six is PESSIMISM.

The pessimist always looks on the dark side. The pessimist always looks at the reason why it can't work, why it won't work. We know the story.

To the pessimist the glass is half empty.

To the optimist the glass is half full.

We know that story. We just got a new place out on the beach. Boy it's nice. You walk outside and you put your feet in the sand, it's just unbelievable. I can't even tell you how good I feel there, and I know I look good, too. That's probably the best part about it. I had a friend over and he said, "My goodness, the taxes must be high here." You step out and put your toes in the sand and he says, "The taxes must be high." Can you believe that?

Got a view that is so beautiful. And, he can't even believe the view, yet he says, "The taxes must be high," and he doesn't even live there. He can't enjoy the sand between his toes and the smell of the ocean because he's concerned about the taxes.

A negative accountant I once worked with kept saying, "What if we go broke? What if we go broke?"

And I kept saying, "What if we get rich?"

See, the pessimist doesn't look for virtue, he looks for faults and once they find the faults, they start to enjoy the faults. The pessimist looks out the window and doesn't see the sunset, he sees the specks. He doesn't see the beautiful painting on the wall, he sees the cracks, how ugly it is. It's ugly. We don't need to be that way. It's not becoming to anybody. I don't care who you are. It's ugly. Get rid of it.

It doesn't take long for pessimism to break your life down to where it's not worth much more than a warm pitcher of spit. Just wanted to get the point across. Didn't want you to forget.

Number Seven is COMPLAINING.

Complaining, crying, griping…spend five minutes complaining and you've wasted five minutes. You can't complain. Who are you to complain to anybody about anything? Where do you get off complaining to somebody about something? Who are you to do that?

Imperfection can't judge imperfection, period. Crying, complaining, griping, it won't work. I'll tell you a story, a story of Old Testament fame, about the children of Israel. It's a good example here.

Through a series of miracles, God got the children of Israel, got them free as slaves and they're heading towards the Promised Land. You know how it goes.

They're going to the Promised Land, got them freed as slaves and they're heading to the Promised Land. They're free now and heading to the Promised Land, not slaves anymore, free, going to the Promised Land.

You know what happened? They started crying, condemning, complaining from day one. They complained about the food, they complained about the weather, they complained about the leadership. They complained about each other.

They complained and they kept complaining and crying and condemning so long until God got it up to here, I guess. And He said, "Trip canceled." They never made it. They died in the wilderness.

Going to the Promised Land and crying and condemning and complaining, they never made it to the Promised Land. That's how serious that one is.

Those are the seven diseases.

You've got to know about them.

You've got to work on them.

You've got to become aware of them.

Five Major Ingredients
to Turn Your Life Around

Apply them at the Same Time
for Predictable Results

All of us are here today. We came here today to turn our lives in a new direction. We're not here for anything else. You remember that deal about lying to yourself? Tell yourself while you're here today, there are a lot of other places you could be besides spending four hours at the Bonaventure Hotel with us. You could be at any place you wanted to be.

You're here today because you want your life to be turned in a new direction. There are some ingredients that have to take place. There's five major ingredients (I'm going to share them with you here) that go into the day that turns your life around.

These ingredients have to be in a 24-hour period, 24-days per month, 24-months, but there are some ingredients, five major ingredients that goes into turning your life around.

The First Ingredient is DISGUST.

You know what a disgust means? Disgust means you don't like it like it is. Disgust means that you had it up to here. You're not putting up with it anymore. No more will you live with it like this. See, a person could have it with embarrassment of not being able to pay their bills on time. They say, "I have had it, no more."

A person could say I've had it with giving a dollar when they always want me to give more. A person could have had it with a sick feeling, when a man knows that his wife is down at the store shopping and she's looking at beans, two cans of beans, one marked 37 cents, one marked 39 cents and he's sick inside knowing his wife is going to choose the 37 cent can of beans and she doesn't even like the brand. You know why? To save two cents. And the man says, "I'm not living like this anymore. I have had it. No more are you going to see me on my knees in the dust looking for pennies. I'm going to do something about it."

When you see a man could have it with mediocrity. He could have it with not being some kind of winner. He could have it with not having challenge. He could have a lack of excitement, love and caring, but when a person says, "I've had it," I'm telling you, look out. That could be the day.

The Second Ingredient is DECISION.

You have to know what you want. Almost everybody in my life that I've met can tell me what they don't want; but almost no one in my life I've met can tell me what they do want. Most people spend more time planning their three-week vacation every year, than they do planning their future. You've got to find out what you do want, and I'll tell you this about decision. It's not easy. Decision is not easy.

Winston Churchill called it, *The Agony of Decision*. You don't want that agony of decision, that sick nausea feeling. You get that cold sweat pops out on your forehead. You're lying in bed late at night. It's a midnight hour, but you've got to decide. I'll tell you what I've found out in my life, that generally making a decision is the hardest part. That's the hardest part of almost anything I've ever done is the decision. If a person could just wade through the heavy waters of decision, they could climb the mountain almost every single time.

The Third Ingredient is DESIRE.

You have to *want to*. This whole book has been about these five ingredients. You have got to *want to*. You've got to develop your *want to*. I wish someone had desire for sale. I do. I wish that we could package it in little bottles, because if we could package desire and you could take a couple of tablets and they would increase your desire every day – watch the wheels come off!

Here's what I would do. I would tell you to go home and liquidate all your assets and come back and buy every bottle of desire your money will purchase. Buy every bottle of desire because that's where it starts. I'll tell you this about desire – it comes from deep within you. You can't clip out a coupon in the magazine and send for it. It doesn't work that way. It cannot be bestowed upon you by some benevolent magistrate someplace. You have got to develop it.

Your desire can be cultivated. It can be cultivated by a meeting like this today. It can be cultivated by getting involved with a group of people. It can be prayed for. A lot of it comes from books that I've read, people I've met, my family. The only thing I'm sharing with you here is every single day, add more weight to *your want* and ask for it. Search for it.

Fourth Ingredient is ACTION.

Decision can turn you in a new direction; it's action that takes you in that new direction. I'm going to give you a word to go with action – *massive*. It's called, *massive action*. Take all-out, massive action. Don't be like the distributor who says, "Okay, I'll pass out a few brochures." He'll always be broke. Don't be like the one who said, "Okay, I'll make a few contacts." Listen, you can guess their bank account. Or, like the girl who says, "All right, I'll try a sales party and see what happens." Listen, that's not the success, that's not how you keep from starving to death.

If you're going to take action, take enough action, massive action so the community won't have pity upon your family. You know, do something that's all-out and massive. Real, sustainable success comes from all-out, massive action.

Fifth Ingredient is RESOLVE.

Resolve simply means, *I'll do it*. Resolve means, *I'll be there*. Resolve means, *You can count on me*. Resolve means this: You pick out your mountain in life, wherever that mountain is, whatever mountain that is, and you say, "I'm going up to the top." And, you do that.

And there's going to be people to tell you, "You can't climb mountains, you don't have any experience."

You say, "I'm going to the top."

Someone else will say, "Come on, choose another mountain, that's too rocky."

You say, "I'm going to the top."

Someone else will say, "Come on, not that one... That's too slippery."

And, you say, "I'm going to the top."

See, there's something about when someone makes that kind of commitment to themselves, there's something about it that does it. You see, I remember the things in my life that I took a wishy-washy way of attitude. I remember when my daughter used to come to me and say, "Listen, Dad. Can we go on a picnic this weekend?"

And my answer would be, "Sure," but nothing would happen. I couldn't understand when she went away, she wasn't happy. Kids are smart, they know. They know the slightest little thing. She knew that if the wind blew that weekend, we weren't going. If someone got a headache, we weren't going.

Now she would come and ask again, and the answer would be either, *yes* or *no*. And she was just as happy with a *no* as she was with a *yes*. Just as happy. Why? Because either way, the result was going to be the same. We were not going to go on a picnic. I had no resolve to do that.

So, you got to practice a little resolve every day. Whatever it is, you're climbing that mountain. You got to have the "do or die" attitude. That is what you've got to have. Someone tells you, "You can't go up it's too rocky, too steep, too slippery,"

You say, "Listen, here, I'm going up. You're either going to see me waving from the top or dead on the side. I'm not coming back."

Now that's called heavy resolve. There's something about the *do or die* attitude. It's almost like if someone has to do it or they'll die. It's almost like time, faith, and circumstance come together, have a hasty conference, and they say, "Listen, John says he's going to do it or die, we might as well let him have it." Resolve moves providence.

You've got to be willing to practice the little resolves, or the big ones will find you hiding in the closet every single time.

You are Enough
Demand the Best of You

What we've been talking about here today, is getting favorable results in our lives. Those favorable results come from right inside here (points to self). That's where they come from. You don't have to have any special talents, any special energy, any special anything. You have got enough of everything you need right now. I want us all to know something. We've been selected for this Herbalife team, we have.

There are always success stories, before and after. And there's going to be a time in the next two, three, five, seven, 10 years (I don't know how long it's going to take), when Herbalife is the finest company of its kind. And we'll be written up in the magazines, and over here is going to be the "before and the after" pictures.

Someone's going to be reading and say, "What a wonderful success story. Look at that. A schoolteacher did that. Look at that. A construction worker did that. A homemaker did that. Look at that, a doctor. Listen, look at them now. Isn't that something? How come I never found out about these opportunities?"

And they might be walking by that hallway right now, this minute, and never find out about Herbalife. Things don't just happen. Things happen just - and you're here today for a reason, and you need to pay attention to that reason. And we've all been selected for it.

I want you to know right now that you've got enough ability right in your entire being to make this thing work for you right this second. You've got enough to make it work. The difference is going to be in the little things that you do. See, I'm a big sports fan. I really like football, too. Let's talk about spring training.

The rookies always check in to camp before the veterans; they have to work there first. You know the difference between the first-year rookie and the 10-year veteran? They both have the fundamentals of the game the same and that's what I'm trying to share with you. You got enough fundamentals right now to make it work.

The difference between the veteran and the rookie is that the veteran becomes the veteran because they do a little bit more, they become a little better every single day, every day. It's done in inches; it's not done in yards. It's done in inches.

That's that little bit of extra excitement that you're going to have to muster up, that little bit of extra attitude control that you're going to have to have, that little bit of extra sincerity, a little bit of extra faith, that little bit of extra fun.

You have to live up to your best.

You have got to demand the best out of you!

If you can't demand the best out of you, then you need to take a real strong look at everything that you're doing. No matter what it is. Joseph Kennedy had a sign on his desk, and when I heard about this, it really helped me out because I was always real tough on myself. Do you know what that signs said? It said, "Once you've done your best, the hell with it." And that's all I'm saying to you today.

I want you to learn to be strong in your life,
all areas of your life. I want you to learn
to be strong,
but I also want you to learn to
develop your strength without being rude.
Become strong, but don't become rude.

I want you to learn how to win in life,
win in everything,
win the conversation game, win everything,
but learn to win without pressure.

I want you to learn how to be bold,
learn how to be bold without becoming a bully.

I'd like to see you learn how to develop your
pride in everything that you do. Have pride in it -
but develop pride without arrogance. Pride without
arrogance.

I'd like for you to learn how to be thoughtful
about all things and everybody, and about yourself.
Learn to become thoughtful without becoming lazy.

I'd also like for you to learn to develop your
humility. Become humble, minus timidity.
Become humble, but don't become timid.

I'd like for you to learn to become kind. Kind to
everything and everybody, especially to yourself.
But develop kindness, without weakness. Become
kind, without becoming weak.

I'd like for you to learn how to become gentle but become gentle without becoming soft.

I'd like for you to learn how to make new commitments every single day to your faith, your family, to your friends, and to your future. I'd like to see you learn how to be willing to sacrifice the small things in life, the things that are truly important.

Helen Keller said something once, and it really stuck with me. I'm going to close today with it because I think it kind of says what it means to me. What she said was, "Sometimes the most beautiful things in the world cannot be seen or heard. They can only be felt in the heart."

And that's how I feel about this afternoon and I wish you all good luck. Thank you very much.

Photos

My mentor, Bobby DePew (center) with Mark Parkhurst and, me at 24 years old. Mark was #53 in El Paso, Texas. A remarkable example of the reality of what The Mental Projector, S.I.N.L.O.A. and The Thompson Rule 80-15-5 can do for anyone in network marketing.

Me with my daughters, Leah and Lari, in front of our new Cadillac Eldorado.

The old ford I drove into the car dealership (rock and everything.)

And, my brand spanking new, gold Cadillac Eldorado.

Top of the stairs at the legendary Paris Communique Training.

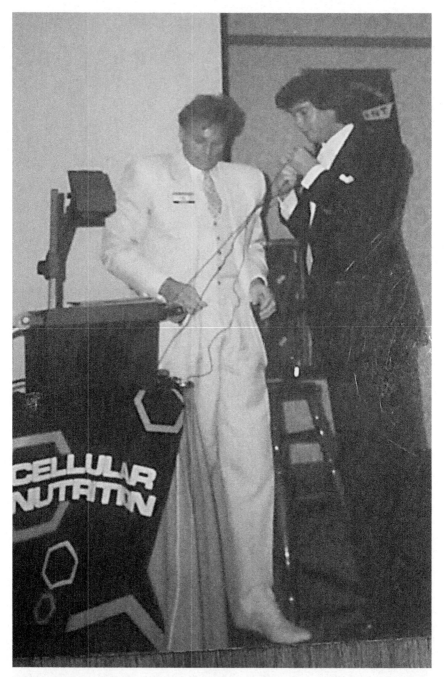

With Mark Hughes at one of our first distributor meetings, note the overhead projector.

Mark Hughes and me working the room. We had incredible energy that was magnified when we were together. It was really something.

My mentor, Jim Rohn and me with distributors.

Mark Hughes, me and Jim Rohn. A monumental moment in the upswing of Herbalife International after the FTC allegations.

Mark Hughes, me and Jim Rohn at 1987 Universal Theatre President Summit.

Me with Mark Hughes at Corporate School, Monterey, California, 1984.

At a Supervisor School. So many incredible opportunities to meet and work with distributors which is what I loved most.

"We got this." That look and feeling are indescribable to me.

Riding up in a car in Australia. Look at that suit!

Jeff Roberti and me. Right, at the 50th Anniversary NAMP Awards Ceremony. Years and years of friendship.

Above, Dan Waldron and me at an Herbalife Extravaganza and still connected all these years later.

Jack Silva and me.

Then and now.

Karla Ingolio at Herbalife International and later at our Gig Summit.

At the wedding of Rick and Michelle Teague where I walked Michelle down the aisle.

Carolyn Tarr, me and my "adopted" daughter, Vicki Tarr Sorg

Guido Buch, Carolyn Tarr with Taylor and me.

Rolf Sorg, Owner and Founder of PM International

Rolf Sorg and me in Cuba on my 70th birthday.

Joachim Heberlein, Taylor, me, Rolf and Vicki Sorg at the 2017 World Congress in Frankfurt, Germany

Training with Sammy ElGhoul at Spain University.

Asia Pacific Extravaganza.

Asia Grand Tour

Presenting at a distributor workshop in Italy.

Rolf Sorg and me at PM International Christmas party.

Rolf Sorg in Switzerland pointing to Larry Thompson's Blue Ink training.

Taylor and me at the Asia Launch.

One of my all-time favorite students is Carsten Ledulé. He was the #1 Distributor at PM International for 25 years.

Carsten studied my Wealth Building System over and over. What a privilege to go to his home and to enjoy spending time with him.

Here it is! One of the first audio training sets of its kind. Carsten is what *The Millionaire Training* and the LT WealthBuilding Academy are all about...giving distributors the fundamentals and concepts that are necessary for growing a successful network marketing business.

2018 Direct Selling News Top 100 Awards Ceremony, PM International was #36 in the world.

2019 Direct Selling News Top 100 Awards Ceremony PM International was #24 and this year they hit $1 Billion in sales and was #13.

Being recognized as Rolf Sorg's mentor at PM International 25th Anniversary.

Taylor and me receiving special recognition for our contribution to the success of PM International.

Taylor and me in Mexico City.

Taylor and me broadcasting for Wisdom Wednesdays and the LT WealthBuilding Academy

Taylor and me training at the first Gig Summit in Dallas, Texas.

Jeff Weisberg, me and Jeff Roberti.

Kyle Wilson, Founder and Partner of Jim Rohn International,

John Maxwell and me at a leadership conference.

Jeff Roberti, Steve Jamieson, me, Taylor, Cheryle Cortes, Kyle Wilson, Jay Bennett and Jeff Weisberg at a Dallas Cowboys game together. Friends for life.

Dan Stammen, Jeff Weisberg, Jonathon Roberti, Jeff Roberti, Harris Williams, and me at Siesta Keys breakfast.

Jeff Weisberg, me and Jeff Roberti

With Jay Bennett at The Gig Summit in Dallas, Texas

Ron Henley, Jeff Weisberg, me, Jeff Roberti, Jonathan Roberti

Ron Henley, me and Jeff Weisberg showing a flyer of a World Tour that Jim Rohn and I did in December 1992.

Frank Mulcahy, Jay Bennett, me, Jeff Roberti, Dan Stammen, Rick Teague and Jeff Weisberg at The Gig Summit, Dallas, Texas.

30 Year Millionaire Training Reunion. Dan McCormick, Jay Bennett, me, Tish Rochin, John Solleder, and Ted Charchuk.

Me and my amazing sister, Tish Rochin – the lady truck driver. She was the first Herbalife distributor in the state of Texas.

I'm grateful for so much. My daughters, Leah and Lari, for starters.

30 Year Millionaire Training Reunion. Jay Bennett, Dan McCormick, me, Tish Rochin, Taylor and John Solleder.

John Solleder speaking at the 30-Year Reunion of The Millionaire Training.

Being recognized at the Association of Network Marketing Professionals for 50 years in the network marketing industry. Brian McMullen, John Solleder, Dan Waldron, Jeff Roberti, Taylor, me, Karla Ingolio, Jeff Weisberg and Garrett McGrath.

Dan Stammen and me at the 50 Year AMNP recognition ceremony.

Jeff Roberti, Lisa Grossmann and me.

Before Rank Makers, Ray Higdon as the #1 Earner of the company we were working with at the time, along with me, Taylor and Jessica as the top female earner (before she was a Higdon.)

A gift from Ray and Jessica Higdon thanking me for 50 years in the network marketing profession

Special memories celebrating by 50 years in network marketing with my family.   Back Kandyce, Taylor, me, Kyla, son-in-law, Bryan. Front: My daughter, Lari, granddaughters Makenzie and Ryan, and Kassy.

Kandyce, Taylor, me, Kassy, Kyla and son-in-law Cole.

My daughters Lari and Natalie Tasha.

My daughter, Natalie Tasha, and me.

Success
Stories

Jeff Roberti
#1 Distributor, Juice Plus+

Growing up in Sarasota, Florida, my family was not wealthy. We didn't have any of the higher education or fancy backgrounds that others had. What I always did have was a great work ethic. I was always a hard worker. Whatever I did, I was constantly the best at it, be it mowing lawns, waiting tables, cleaning pools, working construction, or stocking shelves at the grocery store. Starting in junior high, I had a burning desire to put in my best effort and a willingness to learn. I frequently found myself frustrated when I would come across some sort of limit working for someone else.

While waiting tables at a beach and tennis resort (along with two other jobs), my longtime friend, Danny (Dan Stammen, Co-owner WorldVentures Holdings), and I were always figuring out what we were going to do with our lives. I thought I was going to be a real estate tycoon by becoming a broker with all sorts of agents under me. I had gotten my insurance and real estate license and was looking forward to having a career that would bring me abundance and financial independence.

One night, fate stepped in; Danny told me that a company called Herbalife was going to be hosting a meeting at a local performance hall. I remember thinking, *Herbalife? What's Herbalife?* I thought the name was kind of funny sounding.

Danny told me, "Oh yeah, these people are selling this weight loss product, and all these average people are making above-average incomes."

That night I got sent home early from the restaurant because we were slow. I believe everything happens for a reason, and it was God's divine intervention. I took it as my sign and headed to the presentation. I was so skeptical at first. I was sitting in the back row with my arms crossed thinking I had all the answers even though I had no money. Then, out comes Larry Thompson and he starts talking about being your own boss and earning what you're worth. Larry began sharing stories of everyday people earning extraordinary incomes.

I got excited. I remember thinking, Wow, you've got to be kidding me. These people are making $10,000, $20,000, $30,000, $50,000 a month? I thought, *If they can do it, I can do it. They are no better than me.*

I decided to get started immediately with a Supervisor Pack. I didn't have the money, so I borrowed money by taking a lien against my car. When my pack arrived, I remember putting on the LOSE WEIGHT NOW, ASK ME HOW! button that came with the kit and I started looking through the flipbook. I was in my early twenties, and I didn't know a lot of people who were as hungry for success as I was. Most of my friends were wasting time partying at the beach and didn't have anywhere near the same work ethic I had.

The first step was to run ads in the newspaper, kind of like today's social media. Concepts are constant, and the basics and fundamentals will never change. It was a technique I used to help attract a critical mass. I needed to get people in front of me so I could share the story, the company, the product, and the opportunity. I didn't have money for an office space or a hotel conference room to do the presentations, but I still figured out a way to do three presentations a day with a group briefing. I got very creative and innovative with my newspaper ads, and I figured out how to run these ads and get the phone to ring.

During this time, I got my hands on Larry's *The Millionaire Training* and wore those cassette tapes out. Those tapes became my original training as far as understanding the concepts, basics, and fundamentals of how to build a business. I would listen over and over again and take notes which kept me in the game. I would run the ads and do the briefings, month after month, person after person. It wasn't easy, though. Nobody was signing up to join. I was often crying at night with no idea what to do. I had all this product, and no signups, but I just kept doing it. I stayed in the game and did it over and over and over again. I believed what Larry was telling me. A few simple disciplines done consistently over and over would eventually equal multiple rewards.

This stagnation would continue for three or four months. I didn't have enough money to book an actual conference room, so I would meet with people who responded to my newspaper ads in hotel lobbies or restaurants. I would do a presentation at 11:00 a.m., 1:00 p.m., and 3:00 p.m. with some Tuesday and Thursday night meetings thrown in. This was not an easy time in my life; I often got kicked out of hotels for trespassing. I became friends with some of the service workers, and they wouldn't mind too much as long as I tipped the waitresses refilling my iced teas and didn't disrupt guests.

Things were looking pretty dark, and at my lower points, I would question and doubt what I was doing. One day, a man whose name I'll never forget, Grover Flowers, came to one of my meetings and liked what I had to say. He said, "I'll take one of those Slim and Trim Kits, and I want to buy an extra one because my friend needs to lose some weight." Grover gave this kit to his friend Ed Powers, who was a former salesman for the Fuller Brush Company. Ed was in very poor health, and he ended up getting great results from the product.

Grover signed up to become a distributor, then Ed signed up under Grover, and I enrolled them both under my dad who was still living at that time. That sale was what got my business rolling.

Ed went out and became a bonus winner in his first month. His sales were so high, he qualified for all of us to fly out to Los Angeles, California for corporate training. I had never been on an airplane. I had never been out of the state of Florida! I was a waiter used to making only one or two grand a month and all of a sudden, I had gotten lucky. But it wasn't luck; this all happened because I didn't quit, and I kept at it long enough.

When I flew out to Los Angeles and sat in the training room with my long hair, my one suit and a skinny little tie getting to meet all these incredible people for the first time, I felt like I had died and gone to heaven. I could feel the excitement. When Larry started speaking, I had chills go through my body. Larry began discussing some of the ideas in *The Millionaire Training* and here I was getting to hear it from him live and with intensity. (Larry gets so fired up when he's speaking. It's almost like a rant with lots of go, go, go!) I responded to that on a deep level. At that training, everything clicked. By the time I boarded the airplane to go home, I was a totally different person.

Everything changed, from my presentations to the way I walked and talked. I had absolute confidence and certainty in my position. I was bulletproof, and people could feel that. During my time at corporate school with Mark Hughes and Larry Thompson, I found myself surrounded by schoolteachers, grocery store checkers, mattress salespeople, carpet cleaners, and truck drivers, who were all making $50,000 to $100,000 a month. I now was on fire and unstoppable. I worked day and night (18-20 hours a day) fully engaged and immersed in what I was doing. I just kept working and working. I did well for myself even though I was not a big earner at that time.

I tell people I got my Ph.D. in direct sales and network marketing during the two-and-a-half years I was at Herbalife. Larry impacted and affected me giving me the belief that I could do it. I gained the perspective that, if they can do it, I can do it, too. Larry would often pose the question, "Would you rather have the briefcase with $1 million in it or the briefcase with the skills of a person of someone who can earn a million dollars?" I picked the briefcase with the skills.

Unfortunately, in 1985, Herbalife faced a massive FDA lawsuit, and sales dropped significantly. Everybody's checks were falling, including mine. I stayed as long as I could. It's one thing to be broke and not have money, but it's even worse to get a little taste of success, and then be broke again. Everything I made was put back into the business. I was loyal and committed and didn't want to leave Herbalife, but I was renting a room for $180 a month with only a mattress on the floor. I was at my lowest point financially. Even though I was broke, I had a sense of strength and confidence. I knew going back to waiting tables wasn't an option for me. Fortunately, in January of 1987 a friend of mine from Jacksonville, Florida introduced me to the company, Juice Plus+.

At this time, I was 24 years old and thanks to Larry, I had my Ph.D. in direct sales and I was ready to get to it. I figured out a way to borrow some money again so I could sign with Juice Plus+. Somebody believed in me and gave me a loan so I could buy a little bit of product. Within the first three to four years, I've sold $2 billion worth of product. I was working endless hours like there's no tomorrow because part of me didn't believe it was going to last. So many of these types of companies are here today, gone tomorrow, but God blessed me and gave me something that was solid, stable, and lasting. I'm still with Juice Plus+ to this day.

I often go back and think, *What if I hadn't been sent home early from waiting tables? What if I hadn't met Larry Thompson?* Who knows where my life would have been? I thank God that Larry changed my life. I give him the credit and the credit is due. He took a broke waiter who was hungry and put me in a learning environment that got me exposed to *The Millionaire Training.* I listened so many times I wore those tapes out. You can't forget training like that; it becomes part of your DNA. Still, 40 years later, I listen to those tapes before I'm getting ready to go up on stage or traveling internationally. I've lived and worked in over two dozen countries, sold billions of dollars' worth of product, and built a massive organization and residual income. I stay in the game today because I love what I do. I have success and fulfillment.

I am fortunate to have a business that's full of relationships, love, connection, and growth. Aren't you the happiest when you're growing, and there's progress? I have an opportunity to contribute and pay it forward. It gives me rewards both emotionally and spiritually when I get to do something bigger than myself – something that matters, that's mission-driven, and cause-oriented, which allows us to touch and change people's lives.

I tell people to look at their check as a measuring stick. The bigger your check is, the more significant impact you've had with your product, service, or opportunity. It's a gauge of the lives you've affected and touched, directly or indirectly, through what you're doing. Success without fulfillment is the ultimate failure in life. I decided many years ago to retire *into* my business, not *from* my business, because if you love what you do, you get to add value to people's lives. There's emotional and spiritual revenue that comes from the work you do. You get to become rich in relationships and long-term relationships equals long-term success. Your focus becomes meeting other people's needs, not your needs, which adds value to their lives, creating raving-fan relationships with priceless rewards.

I was at my company's big convention today, and I'm always up in the front row, taking notes (which I learned from Larry). He always says, "The million-dollar seats are in the front row, Baby." As I'm sitting there, I'm hearing all these stories coming across the stage, and it moves me emotionally. I'm crying, seeing these average people share what's happened to them. It's not about the money or position. It's about who they've become. It's getting to hear about the adversities and challenges and how their lives have changed. When you've played a role in that, even a small one, it feels priceless. You can't put a value on it. I thank Larry today from the bottom of my heart. He's impacted me, and I in turn, have been able to change countless numbers of people lives around the world because of his teachings and *The Millionaire Training* which we now get to read and share. From Larry's training, I learned the fundamentals, and it's given me real clarity, and clarity is power because it allows you to cast a vision.

When it comes to Larry's *The Millionaire Training,* it's not a "one and done" deal. You don't just listen once and set it aside. You've got to read it over and over and over. I've said before, "It's not when you remember, it's when you can't forget." It becomes part of your DNA. I know those principles inside and out. You have to make a point to metabolize and implement what Larry is teaching you, like understanding the importance of employing yourself. There are so many great chapters, and you have to break it down and not only apply and integrate it in yourself but then teach it and share it with others.

Larry's trainings are like the Bible of network marketing. They are timeless and foundational to anyone's success in this industry. The principles in his teachings will never change. You want to build your business on rock, not sand. You need solid basics to build from, and to do that, you have to start with *The Millionaire Training.* It's non-negotiable. Read this over and over and internalize it. Do it until you can't possibly forget it. It will give you the strength to go out there and do what I did, even when everybody was telling me no. Because of the confidence *The Millionaire Training* gave me, I was able to keep moving forward even when times were hard and I was crying into my pillow nightly.

So many people in my position would have given up, but I believed in myself and had the wherewithal to keep taking that next step because Larry's training was so embedded in me. I know it sounds sacrilegious equating it to the Bible, but Larry's teachings are like reading scripture in the sense that you read scripture one day, and you get one thing from it, and then you reread it the next week and get something completely different from the same passage. It's the concept of meeting you where you are in your growth with what the words are saying.

Another critical aspect of the business I've learned from Larry is to keep things fun, simple, easy, magical, and duplicatable. There's so much stuff people try to teach others to make them believe they have to go through all this training and personal development, but the kick is, you have enough in you right now!

You are good enough right now to go out and share something you believe in.

The longest journey in life is from the head to the heart. I've always told my people to have emotional sincerity. It has to come from the heart and truly be there to serve and share that gift of health or whatever your product or service is. You have to put other people's needs ahead of your own. You have to avoid making it too complicated. Keep it simple. You want people to be able to say, "What I just did with you, could you do that for someone else?" If I can do it, you can do it, and plugging into *The Millionaire Training* gives you the belief, vision, clarity, and strength to be successful.

Tish Rochin
Chairman's Club,
Herbalife International

 As I sit here thinking about this journey God has had me on for the last 40 years, I am in awe at what has happened in my life and how God used Larry to start me on this amazing journey.

In the 1970's I was a single mom with two kids to support. I had to figure out how to do it on my own and I thought, well, men support kids. That's when I realized I needed to get a job that a man could do but that I could do physically. First, I found a job as a clerk typist for the California Department of Transportation (CalTrans), and the funny thing is I couldn't even type! After about a year of doing that, CalTrans opened up the maintenance division to women.

I applied for the job and I got it. I worked on the highway driving trucks and equipment and maintaining the freeway for 5 ½ years and I loved it. In the early part of 1980 as I was looking into the future, I couldn't see me as a little old lady working on the freeway. Around the same time, my brother Larry called and asked if I would be interested in coming to Texas to help him with a project he was working on. I was the happiest I had ever been so couldn't imagine leaving, but he told me to think about it and he would call back in a month. This was a big decision for me because I was in a good relationship and I had the best job I ever had. I was making about $1,200 a month, had sick leave, vacation time, and health insurance. Yet, for some reason, I decided I was going to do it. I was going to Texas. So, in June of 1980 I jumped in my Toyota with my daughter Leslee, my significant other Vern, and my best friend, Brenda, and we headed to Texas.

Along the way, we stopped at my parent's house to stay the night. I was taken aback when my parents told me they had been going to church and got baptized. I was surprised about this because we didn't grow up in the church. The next stop on our trip was in Arizona to visit Brenda's parents. Her mom started talking about God. I couldn't figure out what was going on. After a pit stop by Larry's in Plano, Texas, we went on to New Orleans to visit Vern's dad and stepmom. For three days his stepmom went on and on about her religion. Looking back, now I know this was God working in my life and preparing me for what was about to come.

We made our way back to Plano and then Leslee, Vern and Brenda all flew back to California leaving me with Larry to move forward on his project. Then, after a couple of days – I remember it was a Tuesday night – I'm watching television and Larry comes out fixed up a bit. So, I asked, "Where are you going?"

He said he had just started going to a Bible Church. My response was, "You go to a Bible Church?"

He said, "Yes, do you want to go?"

I asked if they dressed up and he said that it was casual. All I had were my work Levi's and my dress Levi's, so I put on my dress Levi's and off to church we went.

The preacher was teaching some interesting stuff, but since I didn't know anything about the Bible, I didn't really understand it. Then, afterward, this lady invited us to her house for a get together. We went and the first thing they did was to crank up the music and bring out some wine. Not too long later, there was a knock on the door, and I couldn't believe my eyes, it was the preacher! I couldn't believe it because I thought you couldn't do things like that and go to church.

So now I am thinking that Larry is in a cult. We argued all the way home, but he said the guy is teaching the truth, I've never heard him contradict himself once. After that, the only reason I went back was to see how they had him brainwashed... was it a word or a phrase? I didn't know but I needed to find out. Come Sunday night, Larry and I headed off to church again. At the end of the Bible class, in the closing prayer, the preacher said, "You can have just a thread of faith in Jesus Christ and have eternal life or you could burn in hell."

I'm sitting there thinking, well, I could muster up a thread of faith. So, I did. I believed in Jesus Christ as my Savior. Now, as a Believer, the Bible messages started really opening up to me.

I was helping Larry with his new project, which ultimately did not work out. In the meantime, this guy, Mark Hughes, kept calling for Larry and leaving all these messages. Then, one day, Larry comes in to talk with me and tells me he is going to California to meet with Mark. While in California, they discussed what was going on with Mark's new business, Herbalife. Mark was really excited and wanted Larry to come work with him. They ended up drawing up the marketing plan on a restaurant napkin, and Larry agreed to go back to help Mark build Herbalife. Once Larry got back to Texas and informed me of his decision, I was devastated. I was only in Texas for three months and now he was going to leave me here. I didn't know what I was going to do, but I'd been going to

Bible study for long enough to know that this is where God wanted me to be.

Larry had been gone for a few weeks when all of I sudden I get this box in the mail. Larry had sent me an Herbalife distributor kit with some weight loss products in it. He told me to get on this stuff and start talking to people. I thought he was crazy. Why he thought I could do this was beyond me. He knew that I knew how to work hard and was teachable, but I didn't really have much weight to lose.

I did what he said though and lost a little weight and gained some energy. Then, I was introduced to a guy named John and he had a lot of weight to lose. He ended up losing 75 pounds in 90 days. Now, we had a story to share. Let me tell you, we had to have good results because those Herbalife protein shakes were nothing like they are today. You wouldn't just sip this stuff; you'd have to gulp it down real quick because they were potent, gritty, and really gross. But, boy did they work!

I still couldn't believe Larry wanted me to sell this stuff. I was no salesman, but Larry kept telling me, "You can do this!" He said all I needed to do was to wear this button that said LOSE WEIGHT NOW, ASK ME HOW! (which by the way, I felt was as big as a satellite on my shoulder), and talk to people.

He gave me this script to follow that read, "Are you seriously interested in losing weight?"

If they answered yes, I would ask what kind of weight-loss products they had tried before. They'd name off a few things they had tried, and I would say, "But you haven't tried Herbalife."

In order to get more business, I started placing ads in the local shopper's guide that said, LOSE WEIGHT NOW, ASK

ME HOW! My phone started ringing off the hook. I read my script, asked them how they wanted to pay for the product, and scheduled a delivery time. Back then, we didn't have UPS, FedEx or any type of delivery service, so every order had to be hand-delivered. Boy, I was running myself ragged going all over Dallas to deliver my products, and it didn't take long to figure out that I needed to come up with a better plan.

I decided to deliver products to Garland on one day, Dallas on another day, and Plano on another and so on. This worked much better. Because I was out making product deliveries, I couldn't answer the phone, which meant I was missing out on business. Back then, there was no such thing as answering machines, much less voice mail. Again, I had to come up with a solution. So, I ended up hiring an answering service to take messages while I was gone. I would return calls when I got home and schedule more deliveries.

Initially, I was living off the retail profit I made because that was the only money coming in while I was building my business. So, I'm out there selling all these products just to keep a roof over our head and some food on the table. Some of my customers became my best distributors. I'd tell them if they needed to make some extra money, I could show them how. I'd say, "Once you begin losing weight, people will ask you what you're doing. I can sign you up as a distributor, and you can make the extra $500 - $1,000 a month, or I can make that profit, the choice is yours." That is how I built my team.

Larry and Mark said, "Use – Wear – Talk," so that's what I did and that's what I taught my team. It was that simple and that duplicatable. Together, my team and I, were able to retail and wholesale our way up to the President's Team, which was the top level of Herbalife at the time.

It wasn't easy being the first distributor outside of California, but Larry and Mark were encouraging and guiding me from afar. I needed to make this business work. Unfortunately for me, I wasn't a businessperson; I was a truck driver. But, that wasn't the worst of it… I looked like a truck driver, acted like a truck driver, and talked like a truck driver. If a word had more than four letters, I couldn't pronounce it. Needless to say, they had to clean me up a bit. On the other hand, one thing I had going for me was that I was willing to do the work. Larry and Mark told me that to build my business, I needed to talk to 10 people a day about the product and 10 people a day about the business.

They also told me if I did that every single day, I could earn $30,000 - $60,000 my first year. I didn't know any different, so I did exactly what they told me to do and I didn't deviate. If it was 9:00 on a Sunday night and I had only talked to nine people about the product, then I'd run out to 7-11 and find someone to talk to.

Since I wasn't a businessperson, I was more comfortable retailing the products than I was building the business. That is until I had the opportunity to be at a training Larry and Mark were holding in California. From this training came Larry's infamous "Millionaire Training." This training blew us all away. It was outstanding and propelled Herbalife forward like no one could imagine. The event was recorded, and *The Millionaire Training* was put on cassettes. Distributors would listen to those tapes over and over again until the tape wore out. It was so funny because every time I would get into a distributor's car, they would have *The Millionaire Training* playing. Little did we know back then what an incredible influence and impact this training would have on the entire industry.

The Millionaire Training reinforced what Larry had already being teaching me; the training made it real and put it all together. I finally realized why I had to talk to 10 people a day about the product and 10 people a day about the opportunity – it was Safety in Numbers and Law of Averages (S.I.N.L.O.A.) I learned about the Goldmine Principle that I couldn't build my business alone that I needed a team of people working toward the same goal. We left The Millionaire Training with enthusiasm and the momentum we needed to take our business to the next level.

We started teaching our team the principles and concepts of The Millionaire Training. We put the 90-day plan that Larry gave us into effect. Every day we had to use the product, wear the button and talk to 10 people about the product and 10 people about the business. We worked with our team using the "Tell, Show, Try, Do" principle, and not accept any excuses by applying "I don't know about that, all I know is..." We put the work in consistently and persistently, day in and day out for 90-days. Then, we would do it all over again for another 90-days, and then another, and another to keep our momentum rolling!

Larry was the key to my success as my business grew. It's a process to build, grow, change, and become better. Larry was always there with training, advice, and a listening ear when I needed it. He had the most influence when it came to setting the tone for all the distributors. He wasn't soft, he would tell you like it is. He told–people what they needed to hear not necessarily what they wanted to hear. Everyone respected Larry and his teaching. Part of his magic is his ability to get people to believe they can do it when they don't have enough belief in themselves. Larry has a special gift to recognize the potential in someone. He would zero in on someone in my downline who I may have never noticed, see their potential, build them up, and sharpen their skills – skills many times they didn't even know they had. Time and again he was able to pick out people who were willing to put in the work to be successful. And, that is exactly what he did with me. He saw the potential in me that I never knew I had. He never doubted me and sure enough my first year I made $59,000.

Looking back on my life, God obviously had a much bigger plan for me then I could have imagined when Larry brought me to Texas. God used Herbalife to orchestrate His Plan. I learned early on in my Herbalife career that if I was going to be successful, I needed to keep my priorities straight. I had to put my spiritual life first, then my family life, and then Herbalife. It wasn't always easy. There were hard times, both personally and professionally, and there were times when Herbalife came under attack, but we stuck it out and came back stronger than before. One reason we were able to have this "sticktuitism," as we called it, was because we trusted God. I would have never imagined God was working in my life back in 1980, but yes, looking back He definitely has a perfect plan.

So, here we are nearly 40 years later, and *The Millionaire Training* is just as relevant and useful today for building a business as it was back then. The tools and concepts Larry taught us are exactly the same, they never change. Those concepts still apply today for whatever endeavor you embark upon, or just for life.

It is so true what we used to say, we can take the Herbalife distributor kit with Larry's *The Millionaire Training* drop it on an island somewhere and the person who finds it can build a successful business. When we attended *The Millionaire Training*, no one ever could have imagined how that training would change the course of network marketing history, much less, be the network marketing playbook 40 years later and still making a difference.

I am grateful Larry believed in me and encouraged me to spread my wings and move to Texas. Because he did, I found God. Together, they helped me, a lady truck driver, build a successful international business that has flourished beyond my wildest dreams.

Trey Herron, Chairman's Club, Herbalife International

When I was 10 years old, my parents were struggling financially. Of course, I was totally unaware. They were doing the very best they could to take care of me. Everything changed when my parents joined Herbalife. I remember my dad's health significantly improved, our vacations got better, and Christmas had a lot more presents. Everything was on a positive upswing. Seeing this transformation left a lasting impression on me that shaped my future.

Many kids grow up hearing about superheroes from their parents; in our home, those superheroes were people like the legendary Jim Rohn and, of course, Larry Thompson. Every time we were in the car together, my dad, Bill Heron, would play *The Millionaire Training* tapes. Dad was always telling me stories about Larry.

When I was really into cars, dad showed me all sorts of pictures of Larry's cars. Back in 1983, there were two popular Mercedes models, an SEL and an SEC. Larry liked the front of one car and the back of another, so he bought one of each, cut them in half, and made a limo! Who does that? Growing up hearing stories like that, I felt like I already knew Larry and I certainly was influenced by him, even before joining the network marketing industry.

In 1984, trouble started brewing between Herbalife and the FTC. My dad chose to leave Herbalife at that time. He then bounced around to six or seven different companies before landing with Body Wise, where he became their #1 distributor for 36 months. Then out of the blue, while I happened to be home from college, he gets a call from Larry and Mark Hughes telling him it's time to come back to Herbalife. I remember this phone call because Larry and Mark had invited Dad to go to Los Angeles to meet with them and my mom didn't want him to go saying, "Don't you go, don't you go. You know they'll get you, if you do!"

Long story short, they got to him! And he was officially back with Herbalife in 1992. At this time, lots of changes were taking place at Herbalife, When I was 19 and back home visiting from college, my dad happened to have an Opportunity conference call on speaker. I decided to sit down in his office and listen to the call with him. During that call, a 25-year-old man was discussing how he had made $1,500 the previous month. (Believe it or not, that was the story that sold me on network marketing and not the fact that my parents had made millions of dollars over the years.)

I just didn't think that kind of success was possible for me at my age, but I was hoping I could make an extra $1,000 a month working around my class schedule. After the call, I looked at my dad and said, "I think I can do that." and he turned and looked me straight in the eyes and replied, "I know you can, but will you?"

I told him, "I'd like to give it a try." Before I knew it, Mom was sitting down with me on the living room floor going over the products.

At that time, Herbalife had a program called *The High Five Club*, and you started with a Success Builder order, which had 1,000 volume points worth of the products inside. If you sold all this product within 10 days and got your receipts turned in, you received a plaque with a picture of Larry and Mark in their suits and their cars on it. I remember that plaque perfectly because I wanted it. I had grown up hearing Larry's stories, and I wanted to be like him.

The first day back at school after receiving my Success Builder order, I headed to one of the college sorority houses. I ended up selling the entire thing and ran out of products. I called my dad and said, "Look, I'm out of product, I need more." Instead of excitement, there was this long pause on the line before he finally responded, "Well who stole it?" Can you believe it? He asked me, "Who stole it?" As a result of that first day of sales, I ended up making the High Five Club and earning that plaque, which I proudly displayed in my college dorm room.

My business started from there, but I hadn't gone to a training yet, and my dad kept telling me I needed to go to one. I finally got around to it and booked a trip out to Los Angeles where I attended a two-day training with Mark, Larry, and Jim Rohn. These sessions blew me away. At the time, I was a sophomore in college, and I remember taking so many notes; notes that I still have today. After being introduced to Larry, I told him that I took more notes these past two days than I did during my entire freshman year of college. It's funny looking back on this because the notes I took there, have made me a lot more money than my college education did.

I related so much to Larry's trainings, both at Herbalife and *The Millionaire Training*. They have left a dramatic impact on me. I've learned from watching and listening to Larry, and I've taken his strengths and messages and implemented them into the trainings I do on stage today. Storytelling is such an essential part of Larry's method, and I incorporate that same message when I'm speaking to a group. For example, it's easy to get up in front of a group of people and tell them they need to recruit from their "center of influence," but how do you get people to want to do that? By storytelling. You're giving people a compelling vision of how to accomplish that.

In *The Millionaire Training*, Larry talks about communicating with feelings. I was recently with my mom, discussing the impact Larry has had on my career, and she mentioned that there's always something from Larry's training fused into every training I do. His stories have stuck with me for years and have molded me as a trainer. When I teach people in my organization, I use Larry's approach.

In this day and age, it's easy to get distracted by all the shiny objects and new things surrounding us, especially those who are just getting started with network marketing. However, even with new developments like social media, when you get down to it, the basics are always the same. The lessons in *The Millionaire Training* are timeless.

My story is different than many of those who join network marketing in that I've never had any other job. I started in this industry at the age of 19 and built it into a career. One of the key takeaways I got from Larry was to employ myself. I know this wasn't as big of a challenge for me as it is for some coming from other industries. I've never known anything different. Often people want to be their own boss, but they are terrible at it. And, if you start with Larry's methods as the foundation of your business, you'll have the right mindset to build up from.

At first, things moved very quickly when I joined Herbalife. I made it into the Millionaire's Club within the first eight months, but like many, I got into my comfort zone and spent 13 years in the President's Team. Even though I've now been in this business for over 27 years, it's been only in the last year that I've made it to the Chairman's Club. Now, I intend to make it into the Founder's Club in the next few years.

I've seen crazy, explosive growth over the past two-and-a-half years, but this has been 25 years of buildup to get to this point.

We hear stories all the time of people join the network marketing industry for the first time and move up fast. I believe it's important to share my story because there are many network marketing veterans who have been around a long time who think their time has passed for that kind of exponential growth. I hope they are inspired when they see that my most significant accomplishments happened after 25 years in business *in the same company.* I have heard Larry say many times, "For things to change, you've got to change." I would quote this to my team endlessly; but honestly, I was saying this for them rather than for me. I thought I was good where I was at, but I came to realize I needed to say these words to myself. I had to change for things to get better. The pin level I was at with the company was exactly equal to my leadership level, and I knew then I had to change. I had to kill off the person I was and grow into someone better.

It was time to stop chasing levels and pins within the company and instead pursue more with a purpose. That was three or four years ago after reading a book about an accountant who worked for his family business and realized it wasn't for him; he went on to become a Navy SEAL. It was ultimately a story of finding your purpose, and it made me think, *Had I been in network marketing for the past 20 years just because my family was involved with this industry?*

I began to ask myself what my passions are and what excites me. What I realized from this time of reflection was that I love being on stage training others. I believe a lot of that comes from watching Larry and all the things I learned from him. I still want to be like him. I remember the last time my dad and I were in a car together, and we were talking about things we had never talked about before. We talked about the network marketing industry and why he had joined this business. He mentioned that the first time he went to an Herbalife meeting and saw Larry on stage, he had wanted to be that guy with the microphone.

Dad was passionate about teaching others just as I am, and it's really what I love most – training, building up leaders and mentoring. When I realized that my purpose was to help others with their success, rather than reaching a certain level or getting a particular pin, I changed. And, then my life changed.

Inspiring, motivating, training, and teaching others is what I love to do, and I've come to understand that network marketing is exactly where I am meant to be.

At Herbalife, the leaders are always telling us, "Build locally, think globally." I developed my business the other way around. After being the first in my family to graduate college, I joined Herbalife full time. At this point, the company was opening Thailand and my Dad encouraged me to move there to diversify my business. During my six months living there, I met a man from Singapore. At that time, Singapore did not allow network marketing, but I kept this person's contact information, just in case the market someday opened up.

About seven years later, the market did end up opening in Singapore, and I reached out to my contact there are started building. Because things were growing there, my wife and I sold our house and cars, put everything into storage, and lived in Singapore for three years. Our business ended up growing into Vietnam, Malaysia, and parts of Southeast Asia. We found out we were going to have a son. We planned to stay in Asia and let our son get a dual passport, but my dad passed away, and our families encouraged us to move home and have the baby in the United States.

We moved back to Mississippi, but still had the mindset to build the business outside of America so we traveled back and forth to Asia. When our son reached school age, we knew we weren't going to be leaving. It was only then that we committed to expanding our business locally. Unfortunately, Mississippi is the most impoverished state in the country with a lack of access to proper nutrition in many areas. We realized people right here at home needed Herbalife, so we chose to stay and grow our business here. It's been a long process of continuous growth over the past decade. In the past, I would have simply said, "Forget this," and found a new country opening up to work in. But now, with Herbalife in over 90 countries, we're simply running out of new places to go. That's a good thing.

Some people in the industry say that our method is old school and outdated, but no matter what others may say, for us that mentality still works. Over the last few years, the most considerable portion of growth within our company has been social media based. We tried to do that with our teams to attract a larger audience, but it just didn't fit us. We've found that social media works as a better platform for training our organization. The key for us has been focusing on those core set of skills we learned from people like Larry and staying faithful to those teachings.

Network marketing has truly become a multi-generational industry for our family. Our son, who is now 13, has previously never shown much interest in the business. However, this past summer, we took a trip to Asia. We were traveling from country to country, going to lots of meetings and hearing the personal stories and income testimonials from distributors in Herbalife. Several weeks later after getting home, we were sitting down to dinner, and I asked my son what he wanted to do when he grows up. For the first time he replied, "I want to be an Herbalife distributor." Once he turns 14, he's going to sign up as a distributor and get going with that.

Our whole family is extremely grateful to Larry, not only the training he's provided but for his friendship over all these years. When Dad passed away, I was living in Singapore at the time, and immediately had to hop on a plane and travel 36 hours to get back to home. I'll never forget being at my father's graveside and looking up and seeing Larry. That meant everything to me and showed me who he is as a person. He's been a massive part of my success in the business and will always have a special place in my family's heart.

Rolf Sorg
Founder, PM International

Over the last 25 years, Larry's business methods have had an enormous impact on my success in network marketing which has culminated in PM International hitting over $1 Billion a year in sales. This didn't happen by accident, and I am extremely grateful I met Larry in the early stages of starting my company.

Five years before meeting Larry, I began working part-time for a direct-sales cosmetic company. I had recently finished a car mechanic's apprenticeship and was studying economics and engineering at university. I was in debt and living off my parent's support. A mechanic I knew was driving my dream car, and when I asked him about it, he said direct sales was the only reason he was able to afford it. I didn't know anything about direct sales, but I thought, if he can do it, then maybe I can do it, too. Three years later, I was the company's #1 distributor with over a million a month in sales.

Unfortunately, that business went under, and I found myself having to start over again at age 30. Thankfully, I was conservative with the money I earned and had savings to fall back on. In August of 1993, I took a risk and reinvested all the money I had made, took out a loan for $500,000, and started what would become PM International.

Within a year, I faced my first business crisis – a competitor copied my products and opened a subsidiary within 15 miles of me. This person also gained access to my database and contacted my leaders and distributors with promises of them making more money and extra bonuses.

Fate stepped in when I received a phone call from a woman in America named Carolyn Tarr, who was working for Larry Thompson. (Having grown up in Germany, I didn't have a frame of reference for who Larry Thompson was. My only thought was I had nothing to lose, so I made an appointment with her.) The first thing she did when she came into my office was play a recording of Larry speaking before a group of 10,000 people. It was at that moment, I realized that Larry was an absolute giant in the network marketing industry and my company was the baby. I quickly understood I was going to get to learn from the best.

Carolyn invited my leaders and me to attend Larry's Wealth Training seminar just three days later. This event couldn't have come at a more opportune time. Our sales were down 50%, and I was going to attend with an open mind and a willingness to learn. I gathered up the 20 most influential leaders in my group to attend with me.

What Larry shared that day, blew me away. I believed every word that came out of his mouth, and I knew instinctively I needed to implement this training with my team. I knew that Larry was looking for a company to train, one that would become as legendary as Herbalife. I wanted PM International to be that company.

My anxiety was at an all-time high waiting for that meeting, but what happened at midnight talking with Larry changed my life. He challenged me. He asked me how deep my passion for success was and what kind of effort I was willing to put into this endeavor. I was going to prove to him just how serious I was about pursuing this and how much of a burning desire I had to work. This kind of partnership doesn't come around every day. I knew right then I was going to put all my efforts into mastering his modules and learning whatever lessons Larry Thompson had to teach me.

If I wanted my business to succeed, I was going to have to outperform all my previous results. At the time, we were a very tiny company that only did $2.5 million in sales during our first full year of business. I knew this would not be an easy endeavor, and I also knew that with Larry's training and guidance, it would be possible. Larry agreed to partner with me.

Larry made sure his assistant called me every day to check that my team and I were doing the training modules. It was during these trainings that I learned some of my most valuable skills, like how to set the pace of your team by being a role model and demonstrating that to them. He made sure I was doing the best I could and working hard to show my team what was possible. Through the training modules, I also learned an effective Daily Method of Operation. It can be painful to face your numbers every day, but when you see your day-to-day activity, it puts a pulse on what is and what isn't working, and that's what ultimately builds success.

I could quickly see the effect Larry's training was having on my business. My team and I picked up the pace and worked like hell. In August, we were selling $250,000 a month. In September, we were up to $277,000. By October things had really kicked in and we were selling $400,000 per month. Because we were such a small company to begin with, the impact we were seeing from implementing Larry's training was fast.

Come November, we doubled our sales to $800,000 and in December we had over $1.7 million in sales. That was 1994. This number would have been even higher except for the fact we were not prepared for this kind of rapid expansion, and we ended up running out of product towards the end of December and early January. But it didn't even matter that we started a little lower in the new year because we had built momentum. PM International was now on solid ground.

Over the next two years, I continued to work very closely with Larry, and it was an invaluable experience. From him, I learned that you could have the best product in the world; however, if you don't tell the story in a way that gets them to see and feel what you see and feel about the product, you will experience fewer positive results. You have to promote the product and paint a picture that gets people excited about what you are offering them. When people see your excitement, it becomes contagious and gets them excited as well. It becomes a shared experience and that can only happen with real stories. Fake stories don't work.

Besides Larry being an incredible role model to me, he also demonstrated how important it is to never give up and that there are methods that build consistency which trigger long-lasting success. PM International is a perfect example of that. Taking over 27 years to reach $1 Billion a year in sales is not the fastest story in the history of network marketing, but it is one of the most consistent stories.

With this younger generation of network marketers coming up in the digital age, I think back on my younger self and remember that stage of my life and the unlimited potential I felt. I see that same passion and desire to go hard after something in many of the younger people in my company today.

Regardless of social media and the internet, you still have to have a burning desire to succeed and a teachable attitude if you want to accomplish your goals. Larry's teachings are as relevant and practical today as they were when I started in this industry over 30 years ago, perhaps even more so.

Most people are looking to stay in their comfort zone. They think that technology can replace hard work, but that isn't the case. If you are willing to step up and do the job and implement Larry's techniques and strategies, you will see success. And, like an athlete training for the Olympics, you have to work your butt off. Success isn't handed to you, only you can put in the effort.

In today's world of network marketing, social media can be an excellent tool for communication. It's a platform that allows you to concentrate on your contacts and gives you significant reach, but it's no replacement for the basic fundamentals that build loyalty and deep relationships. That sense of meeting with someone and knowing them creates team spirit that you can't imitate the same way in the online community.

Nothing in the social media realm can replace the strategies and tactics you get from Larry's training. You have to stay focused and based around that model. You need to be setting the pace for your team and be in constant contact with your people. They need to know that you are excited about what you're doing with your business. Larry lays everything out for you super clear and simple in his training.

Another formative aspect of Larry's training is the ripple effect of success it has had on my life both in and out of the network marketing space. My wife, Vicki, and I believe strongly in giving help to others by creating a margin in our company to give back to charity. We decided to partner with World Vision and have had the opportunity to sponsor over 2,300 children to help provide them with education and resources for their future. Again, because of Larry's emphasis on consistency, we've been able to keep this partnership with World Vision going for over 20 years with no plans of stopping.

Through the years, Larry has been a great advisor and a constant inspiration. He helped give me the confidence I needed to build myself up and make my business what it is today. His ability to see the big picture and evaluate things from the outside helped open me up to new possibilities and the chance to see growth I didn't dream possible. He truly is the best promoter I have ever met in my life and a true master at sales strategies. When I signed my contract with him back in 2011, he told me we were going to hit a billion in sales by 2018. He always was a little faster than me (it took until 2019), but he wasn't far off. And now, he's telling me we're going to hit $3 billion in the next two years. I believe him.

Karla Ingolio
President's Team,
Herbalife International

 My background is waitressing and for a while, I was working at a doctor's office in San Francisco, California. That's where I heard about Herbalife. My doctor was looking for a weight loss program that was going to be healthy and nutritional to put into his practice, and his doctor friend recommended Herbalife.

Now, I had done a lot of things to try to lose weight and get healthy. There were so many crazy things I tried. One thing I personally had done is a seven-day fruit juice fast. I lost 10 pounds in seven days and gained it back in one day of normal eating and I was so frustrated.

Anyway, I was an overweight waitress, going to college and did my two part-time jobs. As a waitress I was only making about $800 a month, and with all the time of commuting over the Bay Bridge, paying for tolls and gas to work at the doctor's office, I only profited an extra $250 a month.

My doctor had me invite all his patients into the office to hear about the Herbalife program where they could lose weight and be healthy. This lady, Pam, drove all the way from Aptos (80 miles one way) to give that meeting.

I thought, *Okay, this sounds really healthy and I'm going to try this because it's something that's natural and herbal. And, if this doesn't work, I just need to accept myself as being fat and overweight.* (I was splitting my size 16 pants so I never imagined I would go into a size 8.)

I started on the product. I was just a customer and had no interest in doing any business. What happened was my energy tripled that very first day and everybody at work noticed my energy shift. Soon, they started seeing me getting smaller and smaller.

They started asking me, "Karla. What are you doing?"

I told them, "Oh, I'm on this Herbalife stuff. It's amazing."

They said, "Karla, go get me some!" I thought, *Shoot instead of referring everyone back to my doctor, maybe I can just get, you know, get a discount and pay for my own product that I'm using.*

That was my first goal was just to have it where I could use the products for free. Before I knew it, this amazing thing happened where that person got results and then their person got results. Everybody was getting results. The first month, I was only working five hours a week with Herbalife because I was going to school, working at the doctor's office and waitressing so I had very little time. But, I made $800 that first month which matched what I was making as a waitress, and I wasn't even really trying!

I became like a billboard. Everyone could see what was happening! I had never done any type of business and I never saw myself in any type of business.

I was 21 when I started Herbalife and Herbalife was growing so fast then that even though I registered, I didn't get my distributor kit for two and a half weeks because they were putting them together by hand.

When I received my registration pack, it had my own product to use, but it also had a list of things I could buy. One of those things was a set of *The Millionaire Training* cassette tapes. My sponsor insisted that I needed to get these. He told me, "They are done by the vice-president of the company. It'll really help you."

When they arrived, I played them in my car and everything he was telling me was simple. But, it was also so profound. It was something that I could apply. I was basically on my own and in a place where I didn't have a support system, and *The Millionaire Training* tapes became my support system. I would listen to them over and over and over again. Some of the concepts that were on there and what I learned and what I applied made a huge difference.

So, as an example, when Larry talked about when he went to buy his Cadillac Eldorado, and when he wanted to buy his first house and up until the final day that he only had the down payment. Larry and *The Millionaire Training* taught me that you put your intention out there, you work hard, you have a great attitude and you just keep going forward with it. It was a persistence and consistency that I could see. I thought, *You know, I might not have the skill, but I do have persistence going for me!*

Larry said, "What you lack in skill, make up in numbers." So, I believed that if I just kept going, I could do like this guy did. And, he was so down to earth. That's what I loved the most about listening to Larry.

When I started building my business, something happened in my life that I didn't expect. You know, life can take certain turns. I thought my life's purpose was to be a chiropractor, so that is why I started working at the chiropractor's office to begin with. But, when the office manager embezzled $92,000 (which almost put the doctor under), I was the first to go. My chiropractor who got me on the product said, "You know, Karla. Because of this, and given that you're the newest employee, we're going to have to let you go."

I started crying and I said, "But this is what I want to do! The other people who work here don't want to be a chiropractor like I do."

He sat me down and said, "Karla. Don't worry, you can get rich with Herbalife." I looked at him and I started crying more. Brand new person, right?

Well, I started my business in the worst part of Oakland, which I found out later had the highest crime rate in the whole Bay Area. Even though it was a rough area, my business started picking up. The second month I made $1,200. And then the next month, I made even more.

I did what Larry and Mark told me to do. They said, "Use the product, wear the button, and talk to people." I didn't know anything about ads. I didn't know anything about flyers. I thought the only way a person could talk to people was if you were asked about your LOSE WEIGHT NOW, ASK ME HOW! button. That's how backwards my thinking was.

I would just put the button on and go about my day. Sometimes, I forgot that I even had it on. I'd be in line at the grocery store and somebody would say, "How?" I'd be caught off guard, but I'd start talking. It worked, because I was too shy otherwise to go up to talk to people.

In 90 days, I started experiencing some financial freedom. I was making extra money. I was going to school and getting people at school on the product. Then, the doctor's office called me back and asked if I wanted to come back. I said, "Um, can you let me think about it over the weekend?"

Over the weekend, I realized that I could help more people with what I was doing. I felt confident because I had *The Millionaire Training* tapes and was being taught what to do, and how to do it. I learned about The Gold Mine Attitude which kept in my mind that even though it feels like you're digging and digging and digging and digging, you could be an inch or two away from really striking it. Every time I would talk to people, I would think, *Okay, maybe this is it. This is it. This is it.* That attitude kept me going. And what's so amazing is Larry and Mark said, "If you just use the product, wear the button, and talk to people on a part-time basis, you can make $30,000 to $60,000 a year.

My very first year, part-time, I made $30,000. They told me, if you put in more time, more energy and build an organization, you can make $30,000 to $60,000 a month.

At that time, the most I could think about was doubling my income because that is what Larry and Mark taught me. When I started making $2,500 a month, I thought, *Oh my gosh, what if I could make $5,000 a month?*

My sponsor was no longer doing the business and it was Pam, my upline, who would call me every so often. It seemed like she only called just to say, "Karla, you were the number one producer this month."

I thought, *Really? In an organization this big, I'm the #1 for volume in retailing the product?*

I was encouraged by that. I had to learn how to employ myself, which is in *The Millionaire Training* and putting the 10 pennies in one pocket and then crossing it over to the other pocket. They said, "If you just talk to 10 people a day about the products and 10 people a day about the opportunity, that's all you need to do."

Well, at the beginning, I never got to 10 people a day, but I knew that if I was persistent and consistent and didn't let go of my dream, my ambition, my goals that it was going to happen.

I became a Supervisor, which was $2,000 in business volume two months in a row, or $4,000 in business volume in one month. I did the $2,000 two months in a row. That qualified me for Supervisor School, which was in Sacramento, two hours away. It was my birthday and my fiancé at the time said to me, "You're going to go to another meeting?"

"Yeah, I am," and I drove my army green VW Bug with primer on it. It really wasn't the prettiest thing in the world, but it got me everywhere. So, I drove all the way. This was the first time I got to meet Larry and Mark in person. I was so blown away. I just sat there after hearing Larry and Mark that I sat in that room after everybody had left. I was looking at my notes and gathering up my things when Larry, who was still in front of the room looked up saw me. He looked at me then came down off the stage and walked up to me.

"Hi, I'm Larry Thompson."

"I know. Oh my gosh, it's so great to meet you," I said. "It's actually my 22nd birthday today. And, I felt like there was nothing more I could do better than to be here today for my birthday for my future. And being here learning from you is my present."

"Oh my goodness. Happy birthday," and he gave me a hug. I thought to myself, *Oh my gosh, to meet the vice president and being so new, and this is the guy I've been listening to on The Millionaire Training cassettes. It was so surreal.*

I listened to *The Millionaire Training* on the way there and on the way back. I memorized those tapes. I listened to them so much, I knew what was going to be said next.

The Millionaire Training talks about how easy it is to have a great attitude when everything's going great for you. But what happens to you if you have a flat tire? Your real true attitude comes out during adversity.

My fiancé and I broke up. I was devastated. My mother passed away from cancer. My dog died. All of it was within 90 days' time. Everything that was closest to me was gone.

I had to move from the Bay Area down to San Diego with my brother and my sister. I'll never forget this. The day I was moving my brother and I loaded up a truck and my little VW Bug. It was 12 o'clock noon, and I said, "I'll go get us some some snacks and stuff for the road." He was continuing to pack the truck.

I was only gone 15 minutes and when I came back there was a cop car there, which wasn't unusual in that area. And I said, "What's going on?"

"Well, your two suitcases and nightstand were just stolen out of the truck."

My brother, Blake, loves joking with me because I'm very gullible. I said, "No. Come on. Why are they really here?"

"No, Karla. I went in, just to use the bathroom for less than two minutes. And when I came back out there were two huge guys running down the street with your suitcases and the nightstand."

All the clothes I owned were in those suitcases.

As we started down the road, I cried for the first four hours driving to San Diego because of my heart break of leaving my relationship. I cried so much that my head was hurting, but I was listening to those training tapes.

Moving to San Diego, I gave away my entire business that I had built. Back then, we didn't have places where we could ship like we do today, and we had to buy in case lots. It also cost a lot to make long distance phone calls then. All my business in the Bay Area I gave to one of the distributors in my 1st line, Francesca.

We're driving through LA in my VW Bug. I'm noticing my lights are getting dimmer and dimmer and dimmer. By now, it's nighttime. I tried to honk the horn to let my brother know that there was something wrong and my horn wouldn't work. So, I finally flashed the little bit of lights that I had left at my brother.

My car died in one of the worst places of LA. I gave away my business and all my clothes were stolen. I'm leaving the guy I thought I was going to be with for the rest of my life. And, I'm moving to a place where I only know my brother and my sister.

Blake and I had to stay at a hotel. I didn't sleep that night because given we were in a bad area of LA and all my stuff was in the truck, I was worried more stuff was going to get stolen. I kept looking out the window throughout the night.

The next day we took my VW Bug to the shop. Now, the funny thing is that in a VW Bug, the battery is in the backseat. I had put my plants in the backseat and the water I added to the plants ahead of time leaked onto the battery. Luckily, all I needed was to have my battery jumped.

I made it down to San Diego. Now here I am with no customers and no distributors. No clothes. Hardly any money. And that was the only time I ever thought, *Maybe this isn't for me. Maybe I need to do something different.* I remember thinking I would have to stay on these products because I feel so great. And, if I stay on them, I'm going to have to talk about it. So, I was only ever out of the business for 10 seconds.

Besides, I remembered Larry saying, "The skills that you build can go anywhere with you. If we were to take a parachute and throw you out in any city and you had to start from scratch, and you had a briefcase of skills or briefcase of a million dollars, which would you want? You want the skills."

I got back up and rebuilt my business, and it was nice being in Southern California because then I could go and see Larry and Mark in person because I was down there and it was my dream.

On *The Millionaire Training* tapes, Larry talked about what you put in your mental projector. I would put in my mental projector my intentions of what I wanted, and I made a dream board. I just worked towards that.

One of my dreams was to become friends with the president and the vice president of the company (Mark and Larry), which seemed like way too big for me at the time, but I did that. I also wanted to be friends with the top two distributors who were women; Geri, the grocery checker, and Larry's sister, Tish, the lady truckdriver, because I looked up to them and they were the first two women millionaires in the company. Mm hmm. I thought, *If they can do it. I can do it.*

I became close friends with both of them.

I went back to waitressing because I thought I needed a center of influence. I thought, *I'm going to pick where I want to work.* I picked this beautiful place called the Boat House. The boats would come up to the dock and they would come into the restaurant. It was beautiful right on Harbor Island in San Diego.

The lady who interviewed me ended up being one of my top distributors. (She also married my brother.) I started getting royalties and my business was growing. I constantly listened to *The Millionaire Training.* Anyone I registered who was serious about the business had to have *The Millionaire Training* tapes, too.

That was a staple because it taught me how to get through adversity. It taught me how to Employ Yourself. It taught me The Goldmine Attitude. It taught me so many principles that I could take and apply in my business and my life. It would help me get through the rough times.

Through the major controversy in 1985, we went from almost 500,000 distributors down to 20,000 distributors in less than six months.

It was a massive Exodus.

I knew then that this company was going to make it because Mark and Larry were leading it. I just knew it was. I never even had a doubt. You need to keep that projector clear in your intent because "Whatever the mind of man can conceive and believe, he can achieve."

I truly believed in Larry, and Mark got me to believe that anything that you want, anything that you desire will come true – unless you give up on yourself.

I thought, *I'm not going to give up on myself. I chose consistency and persistence, no matter what, and I'm NOT drawing a line in the sand.* (Drawing a line in the sand is saying, "I'm only going to do it "until," unless this happens. For example, I'm only going to do this for 90 days unless this happens. I'm only going to do this for the next year, unless this happens. So, NOT drawing a line in the sand means that you do it until you do it.)

All the people that I have ever exposed to *The Millionaire Training* tapes were very fortunate to be able to listen to them. Now, to be able to read it and have it at your fingertips, highlight it and have as a business guide, What a gift.

Herbalife has given me an amazing lifestyle for decades and I was in semi-retirement for 17 years raising my two girls and being a very present mom. I had an assistant to help me with my business, a cleaning lady, gardener, a cook at times, so I could be the one with my girls.

I was the team soccer mom and the one-day-a-week volunteer in their classroom. (I loved being the treasure box lady.) I had the most amazing sleep overs for them and their friends. I took them to swimming lessons, softball, soccer, volleyball, even one of them to acting lessons. I have always been their biggest cheerleader! I gave them EXTRAVAGANZA birthday parties that would last six- to eight-hours and kids would cry when the parents wanted to take them home because they were having such a blast!

I helped them do their annual 4th of July Lemonade and Brownie sales at the local parade where they would earn $85 to $110 for 1 ½ hours' worth of work starting at age four. I started them young to become entrepreneurs! Now both girls are Herbalife distributors and my oldest, at age 25, just upgraded to her 2nd home with over 3,000 sq. ft. on six acres in Missouri.

Jeff Weisberg
Top Earner and Entrepreneur

 I believe network marketing is the greatest industry out there. I started in this business when I was only 19 years old and I've been here for 3+ decades. I love that it allows an average person to make an above-average income and an above-average person a chance to get rich. I originally joined Herbalife in October of 1983 when I was 23 years old. Living in Los Angeles, I was seeing bumper stickers and people everywhere wearing the button, "Lose weight now, ask me how." I had to know more. My partner and I drove over to the Herbalife headquarters in Culver City in hopes of meeting the owners, Mark Hughes and Larry Thompson, but they weren't in. We met a young sharp gentleman in a suit & tie driving a Mercedes convertible and talked with him. We gave him our number to call us and never received a call. A big mistake & why it is so true that 'the fortune is in the follow-up'.

We soon learned there was an Herbalife meeting in Santa Monica and there we met John and Lori Tartol. We hit it off with them and ended up joining their down line and the rest is history. I had a pretty fast start and won a production bonus in November during my first full month. I was in the Top 25 for personal production in the company, so in December I was invited to Mark's house for a private training with the other production bonus winners.

I'll never forget the beautiful, intimate setting where I got to meet Mark and Larry for the first time. Mark had a huge house (which was Kenny Rogers' former home in Bel Air). All of the winners were gathered together talking when Mark and Larry suddenly made their appearance. They came down the staircase, Larry wearing a double-breasted suit, complete with shoulder pads, and Mark with his long, flowing hair looking almost too perfect. They began mingling with all the guests. I'm thinking, *What an incredible experience I'm getting to have.*

In January of 1984, I qualified for Corporate School. Several of the people I met at that training, I am still friends with 36 years later. Seeing Mark and Larry on stage speaking before a group was amazing. The message was simple – Use the products, Wear the button and Talk to people. Those are the only things they talked about. It was all nuts and bolts, simple and focused. It didn't involve hours and hours of you've got to do this, and you've got to go there. They never talked about what to say, where to go, or what to do. It's very different from what everybody does today. It was as simple as could be.

Obviously, we didn't have a lot of the technology like we do today. I think when you add in technology, it clogs up everything going on. Back then, the only way you could meet people was a face-to-face or a three-way call. You couldn't do a conference call with 30 people or have a Zoom meeting like you can now. We wore a button and put stickers on our cars. That was the majority of our advertising (with the occasional flyers on cars and ads in the newspaper).

Back then, we had to learn how to have direct interaction. If you couldn't talk, then you couldn't do the business. Today, most people hide behind the internet. They hide behind, "Let's learn all these systems for Facebook. Let's learn all these algorithms for Instagram. What time do you post? How do you post? How's your lighting? What's your tagline?" All the minutiae that we didn't have. In many ways, it was more manageable because we weren't distracted by all those small aspects.

The model was simple. Use the products every day. Become a product of the product and get your results. The better your story, the better your business is going to be. Back then 70% of the country was overweight and today 70% of the country is overweight; everybody always wants to lose weight. Plus, there wasn't as much noise as there is today with so many companies vying for the same marketplace. Between the button, the bumper stickers, and just talking about what happened to us on the product, we learned the basics early. You talk with people about what happened to you on the product and talk about what happened to others on the product. Talk about what happened to you in the business and talk about what happened to other people in their business.

Larry taught us to always dress sharp. "You always want to look good. You might only have one suit; make sure it's clean and get a couple of ties. Make sure you're presenting yourself properly."

I quickly learned, the more we did it, the more it worked, and the more confidence we gained. I didn't doubt it because it was simple. I'm not going to say it was brainwashing, but we had such a strong belief in the business, the product, and in Mark and Larry, that we probably would have done anything they told us. But, they didn't have to tell us to do crazy stuff because it was just that simple.

We would go to Corporate Schools with hundreds of people in attendance; some were making a minimum of $4,000 a month to people like Jim Fobair earning over $100,000 a month and every month, the concepts were the same. It was not the newest, latest, and greatest training each month. Larry always taught us the same ideas from the beginning. "Concepts stay constant, techniques change," he would say.

Today, we are in a technique business rather than focusing on the concepts. There's a big difference.

There were concepts I learned back then that I still use all the time. Larry always told us, "For things to change, you've got to change. For things to get better, you've got to get better." He frequently used stories to illustrate his points. He would talk about fried bologna sandwiches and how he didn't like the crust on the bread, so he would eat the crust first because he hated it. Then he would get to the inside because he liked it the best. That story was a metaphor on the concept of procrastination. Get done what you don't like (the crust), and then work on things you do (the inside).

He also gave the example of having a "goldmine" attitude. What if you went out exploring and came across a goldmine? Floor to ceiling, wall to wall, gold coins. What would you do? Would you run an ad in the newspaper, would you put flyers on cars? No, you'd pick up the phone and call your best friend. Those are just a couple of the concepts he taught.

There were all these different concepts in *The Millionaire Training* that weren't Herbalife concepts. They were life concepts. Yes, they worked in Herbalife, but they also worked in real life. I was in Herbalife until the end of 1985, and I've listened to *The Millionaire Training cassette* tapes far more times since then because it has nothing to do with the product, the opportunity, or the company. It's all about these concepts Larry teaches that are still true today.

I don't think anybody in network marketing has had a training program listened to more than *The Millionaire Training*. Not just by more people but listened to *more times* by more people. Every time I listen, I always come across something I've forgotten. Some of us in the industry call it the Bible. You've just got to give somebody in network marketing this book or a digital version of *The Millionaire Training* and tell them to keep absorbing it; that's all you need. I don't care what company you're in, what product you've got, what compensation plan you have, or what country you're in.

Think about how often you watch a movie more than once. You know the movie's going to be the same. It hasn't changed, but for some reason, when you watch it again, you see something you haven't seen before. Or you watch a part you totally forgot about. *The Millionaire Training* is the exact same way. Reading it or listening to it once is great, but when you read it or listen to it a few times, you pick something else up. When you're listening to something, you don't absorb it all. The first time you might focus on Larry talking about The Goldmine Attitude. The next time, your attention might be on The Fried Bologna Sandwich concept which is a great metaphor for procrastination.

After leaving Herbalife, I took these concepts with me to start my own business. All those skills and concepts apply to life. Remember, it's not Herbalife training, it's not networking marketing training. It's life training.

I've never had a real job. All my experience has been in the network marketing industry and as an Entrepreneur. I'm 60 now and started when I was 19 and if it weren't for network marketing, I wouldn't have been able to raise my 2 sons as a single parent and be a stay-at-home dad who works out of his house. I learned a lot at Herbalife and did well financially while I was there, but that wasn't the big takeaway. My big takeaway was my training with Mark and Larry. I learned how to be disciplined and avoid procrastination, which is essential when you don't have a boss looking over your shoulder and keeping you focused.

To illustrate that point, I want to share the ultimate Larry Thompson story. You are going to love this. It's 1984, and I'm a 24-year-old kid making over $20,000 a month (which today is probably $60,000 to $70,000 a month). I bought an airplane and learned how to fly. I did several crazy things like that. However, my business was just kind of flat. So, I called Larry one day, and I said, "Can I talk to you?"

He replied, "Sure, what's up?"

I told him how my business was kind of flat, and he asked me what my check was for that month. When I told him he started laughing, telling me, "Do you know how much money that is?"

"Yeah, that is a lot of money, but I just can't seem to get to the next level. All in all, things are going great, and I'm loving Herbalife, but things aren't moving."

He then proceeds to say, "Do me a favor, go get your calendar." (Back then, we had old school paper calendars.) I go and get my calendar, not knowing I'd walked right into Larry's plan without realizing it. He told me to open it up and then asked me about the previous Monday.

"How many people did you talk to on Monday?" How many people did you talk to about the product or the opportunity?"

I can't remember what I told him exactly, but I had some excuse. He tells me, "Okay, no problem. Tuesday, how many people did you talk to?"

"I think I was with my mom. I was doing something with her, and a couple of other people."

He says again, "Okay, no problem. Wednesday. How many people?"

"Well, I had a friend in town that day, so we were hanging out."

Now, I can't use the exact vernacular or diction he used, but it was laden with truck driver, long-haired hippy construction worker language. I'll give you a cleaned-up version.

He said, "Do me a favor, don't effing call me again until that calendar is full." Then he slammed the phone down, and back then, you didn't hit a button to end a call. He physically had to slam the phone down on the receiver.

All I could think was, *Did that "you-know-what" just hang up on me?*

I sat there thinking about what he had said and done, but it didn't hit me correctly at that moment; however, it sure did a couple of days later when I was listening to *The Millionaire Training*. I was listening to his concept of what our job description is in this industry. Asking ourselves, what do we get paid for? We don't get paid for yes's, and we don't get paid for no's. We get paid for talking to people. Say hello, talk to a few people, and make a few dollars. Talk to a lot of people, and you can get rich. Our job description is talking to people about the product, talking to people about the opportunity. Nothing else we do matters. Everything else is an afterthought.

The fact that I had gone three days in a row without meeting and talking with people showed Larry precisely where my head was. I was in the top 50 income earners in the company at this point and working the business full-time; the fact that I didn't talk to people hit me hard. The next time I saw Larry, I walked up and thanked him. That was 36 years ago, and to this day, I still remember the ringing in my ear when he slammed the phone down.

That was a defining moment because he didn't just flat out say, "Remember the concepts I taught you about being your own boss and being disciplined." He didn't get on the phone and feel sorry for me and tell me, "Oh, I'm so sorry to hear that." and pat me on the shoulder, telling me, "Go get them, Jeff." He just hammered me.

He let me figure it out for myself.

It boils down to self-responsibility. Keep things simple. Use the products, wear the button, and talk to people. What's our job description? What do we get paid for?

We get paid for talking to people. Remember that.

It made me realize again, *Wow, he's right about this, he's right about that.* He was right; I was wrong. I had a big team, and I was doing well and making money. Sometimes you plateau, and that's okay, but to get to the next level, what are you going to do? The basics.

Take sports, for instance. The fundamentals are the fundamentals, Neither Larry nor Mark ever diverted from the fundamentals. When I would attend corporate school (which I did many times), it became almost boring. I already knew what Larry was going to say. And, if I would ask a question at corporate school, I had better get ready for an answer I didn't like. The delivery was not, "Oh, okay, Jeff. Yeah, that was a great question. Thank you for sharing that with us."

No, they embedded it in our DNA of how simple it was, and human nature is what makes it difficult. During the training, I would often be thinking, *Mark and Larry, it can't be that easy. It can't be that we're just here to talk. It can't be what we get paid to do. It can't be 10 Pennies. It can't be The Goldmine Attitude.*

You can use all the concepts in *The Millionaire Training* to become a better mom or dad. You can use them to become a better spouse. You can use them in life. You can use them in sports. You can use them in anything. Yes, Herbalife was a weight-loss company, but we didn't spend time in our corporate school talking about products and going over the compensation plan.

A problem today is there are so many different versions of what to do. As great as the internet is for network marketing, it's also a negative. Today, I can sit here at my house, you can sit here at your house, we can have somebody sitting in Japan, and we never have to leave. So, your skillset, those muscles that you're building, get weaker. Mark and Larry hammered the fundamentals into us over and over again, and they worked. Why wouldn't you do what somebody is teaching you if it's working?

When I left Herbalife and went into regular business and then got back into network marketing, it already was so ingrained in my mind that I didn't have to even think. I can sit here 36 years later and tell you the Fried Bologna Sandwich story word for word. I can regurgitate it without having to listen again. Today, people are trying to learn too much without integrating any of it. It becomes more useless information.

Instead, focus on the basics that you get in *The Millionaire Training*. At the end of the day, it's not what you say, it's how you *feel* about what you say. You have to remember that whoever talks to the most people wins.

Thanks to network marketing, I was able to be at home with my boys all the way through high school. I coached 26 sports teams. I was one of the few dads able to volunteer in the classroom and go out on field trips because I was in network marketing. Because of Larry's concepts, I learned to employ myself. When my sons were four and six, I suddenly became a single dad. I was like a juvenile delinquent growing up, such a terrible kid. My sisters and my parents were like, "We've got to get these kids in therapy because they've got a whack job as their dad."

However, sometimes when things get dumped into your lap, you have to turn a *should* into a *must*, and you get better. I'm not saying that if I was still married to their mother that I wouldn't be a good dad. But obviously, I'm a better dad than I would have been because I had to be the dad and the mom. Adversity causes your capacities to grow. As Larry's saying goes, "For things to change, you've got to change. For things to get better, you've got to get better." Again, that's not Herbalife, that's life.

I'll share an example of implementing Larry's concepts during that time of my life. Since I was raising my boys on my own, I had to get disciplined. In the beginning, I didn't have as much time to work on my business. However, as soon as they entered school, I hit it hard. I'm following Larry's 10 Pennies and moving quickly. When they're out of school, I was with them, but after I put them to bed, I'm on the phone again. Boom, those 10 pennies are moving quickly. Again, it's because of Larry's emphasis on being the best version of you, and what that requires. Now my younger son is a senior in college and the older one recently graduated college. I've learned a lot. We've traveled internationally together, and they've been to events with me. I told them to go to college. I dropped out of college to do network marketing, but I told them they needed to be in college because of the connections, and what you can learn.

My boys have gotten to spend time with Larry, his wife, Taylor, and their lovely girls. They've met friends of mine from all over the world. They understand the network marketing arena. It's interesting because a lot of their friend's moms and dads are successful, but they aren't able to cope. They aren't able to travel all over the place, because they're too busy working or building a business, or they've got a high-powered job they can't leave. Thankfully, my boys were able to see that money's important, but time and freedom are more important.

Yes, you've got to have money to do things, but you have to have the time to enjoy it. I didn't want my sons to see me putting off enjoying life until I was 70 or 80. You want to start enjoying life sooner than that. Now that my sons are adults, I see them implementing the things I've passed on to them from Larry's concepts. They're very outgoing, they're movers and shakers, they're leaders. It's because I passed on what I learned over the years, and it's made a huge impact on their lives.

If you haven't already, find a company you believe in and put your head down and get to work. You need a product and an opportunity, but it's not about the product, the opportunity, or the company; it's the leadership and the people involved. At the end of the day, compensation plans are compensation plans and products are products. The focus has to be on the leadership of the company from the top down.

Mark and Larry had one of the only companies I've seen in my career, where the company trained you. They knew what to teach from their personal experience before Herbalife. It wasn't about starting a company and then teaching their people what to do. No, they already had experience and were already successful, so they drove it from the top down.

Most companies don't do that today. You have an owner who might be a CEO or corporate guy, or maybe a formulator, a doctor, or an inventor or something. They're not marketing people. They might be businesspeople, but they're not marketing people. This industry is called network marketing, not network business. If you keep it simple, *The Millionaire Training* is remarkably as relevant today as when it came out in 1981. Whether you sell skincare, weight loss, hair care, services, remote controls, whatever your company is, it doesn't matter. It doesn't matter what your compensation plan is. Follow *The Millionaire Training*, because it's proven it works for over 40 years. These concepts are not something Larry just came up with yesterday. You've got somebody with over 50 years of experience in the network marketing industry.

No matter what company you're with, stay focused on *The Millionaire Training*. I'm not saying don't get involved with your company, don't go to your corporate events and all that. But ultimately, I believe you've gotta keep it simple. Right now I can go on Facebook or Instagram, and there's dozens of people offering training. The funny part is though, all of them put together don't have the experience Larry has. Larry has been doing network marketing longer than these people are old. It's easy to get hooked by the latest, greatest shiny object, or the fanciest, newest trainer, or the guy that got lucky one time in a deal but never can do it again. Larry's concepts are constant. These are things that are not going to change another 50 years from now. We'll all be gone, but they'll still be going. If you follow the simple basics, no matter what your company is, you're going to be successful. If you keep jumping from trainer to trainer, idea to idea, or technique to technique, you'll be continually going in circles. It's better to stay with the basics and master the half a dozen concepts.

I'm not being negative at all, but I know many top people in this industry. They're not Rhodes scholars. They're not PhD's. They're not professionals, yet they're still uber-successful because they learned a handful of skills, and did them repeatedly, instead of learning 50 different skills and doing them once or twice. I have a story to exemplify that point. Back in 1991, I'm in Europe with Jeff Roberti opening up a company. We're going to meetings and doing some traveling. I went to pick up Jeff from his hotel, and he wasn't ready yet, so I went up to his room to meet him. I get up to his room, and on his little cassette player, he's listening to *The Millionaire Training*. The important thing to know is this is ten years after these tapes were released, and five or six years after Jeff had left Herbalife. Here is a man who in 1991 has already put away $10 Million and he is still listening to *The Millionaire Training*, carrying it around with him in his bag.

You have to remember, you can always try to get the latest and greatest, but the question is, how much experience and how much adversity has this trainer gone through? With *The Millionaire Training*, it's nearly 40 years' worth of experience. And as far as adversity goes, no company has been pounded harder than Herbalife by the Federal Trade Commission.

If you look at the guys who are still around since the early 1980s, they learned from Larry personally and listened to *The Millionaire Training* religiously; they are still making seven-figure incomes to this day.

In July 2004, I was at a Jim Rohn Leadership Event. I was at a table eating lunch with Jeff Roberti, BK Boreyko, Jim Rohn, Dennis Waitley, Brian Tracy and Ali Brown. I was sitting next to Jim Rohn talking about my background and that I had been involved in Herbalife in the early days. A discussion of Larry came up and I'll never forget what Jim Rohn said, "Larry Thompson is the best trainer I have ever seen." It brought happy tears to my eyes then, and it brings happy tears to my eyes now.

Rick and Michelle Teague
Top 10 Distributor, Modere

Michelle: I started in the network marketing industry back in 1984 when I was only 19 years old and working at a restaurant in Houston, Texas. Late one night a few Herbalife distributors walked in and were seated in my section. At the time, I was miserable. I was working two jobs and going to school to become a dental assistant. I remember thinking to myself a lot, *What am I doing with my life, because right now I'm not enjoying any of it.*

I grew up in a super small, southeast Texas town. It was a great little town to grow up in, but the day after I graduated, I moved because I had a feeling there was something more for me out there in the world. I just wasn't sure what.

Even though it was super late when they came into the restaurant, there was something extra bright about this group. They were different from the usual late-night dining crowd. They were fired up having just come from doing an Herbalife opportunity meeting. For some unknown reason I was being drawn to their table. Because I wasn't super busy, I'd find things to talk to them about. Finally, one of them turned to me and said, "Have you ever thought about owning your own business?"

I don't know why, but immediately I responded, "No, but that sounds great." Two nights later, I went to an Herbalife opportunity meeting and signed up, my life hasn't been the same since.

Long story short, I ended up moving to Dallas, where I worked with Larry's niece, Leslie, and sister, Tish Rochin. It made all the difference being around people like Tish, who mentored me in every part of my life. After attending a couple of hours' worth of Larry's teachings, I learned so much. I didn't even know people could do what he was talking about doing, but I thought to myself, *Oh, my gosh, anybody can do this!*

Even though I was only 19, I had worked in three restaurants and was going to school. This was not living. Every day was the same. Every day, I had people telling me what to do and where to go and when to take my lunch break. Even school felt like prison.

When Larry and Herbalife came along, I realized I didn't have to stay in a box. It was time to start finding out who I was and what I wanted.

Larry is so good at making sure other people understand that anybody in the world can have the same kind of success as he has had in this industry. For me to realize this at such a young age was such a big deal. I didn't have a lot of money or skills and I didn't even know what the sales profession was or the concepts it involved, but it was all eye-opening and exciting, thrilling and crazy, and even a little scary sometimes.

I remember thinking, *Who is this guy? How did he learn this?* and *How does he know how to go straight in and get right to the point?*

First, Larry is an excellent storyteller. He would always use a story to hook you in. I could tell you so many of his stories verbatim today, just because I listened to them over and over again. Repetition was something Larry frequently mentioned. At his presentations he often explained how repetition made such a difference.

The funny part was, people weren't showing up saying, "Oh my gosh, we've heard this all before." People were going to hear it repeatedly because they knew hearing it again and again means it's going to work better for them, and they will understand it better. Repetition moves it from our heads into our hearts, and then from our hearts into action where what we actively do makes a difference. If something is just in your head, you don't have it. If you're a believer, your actions are going to show it. You have to lift your weights and be responsible for *your* business.

I think we miss that point today when we go from podcast to podcast looking for something new, when we really want to ingrain in ourselves what we already know to work. That's why it's important to read *The Millionaire Training* over and over.

At this time in my career, Larry's *The Millionaire Training* was included in the Herbalife distributor packs on audio cassettes, and I was always listening to those cassettes. I would often make the three-hour drive back home, listening continuously to the training. Or, I would listen to *The Millionaire Training* right before I was about to present at an opportunity meeting. I listened to that training more than anything else during that time of my life. That training always helped put me in the right mindset and kept me able to talk about what I was doing with others. Soon, I started making as much money part-time as I made working fulltime anywhere else. What I was accomplishing by the age of 20 made me feel like this business was the right fit for me.

It was no longer all about the money, but more about the mindset. I was focused and knew this is what I wanted to do for the rest of my life. I loved the freedom and lifestyle this industry gave me. I could live the life I wanted to live and answer to my own rules.

I knew it was important to me that when I got married and started a family, that I wouldn't fall into this robotic, no-life way of living. I wanted to see my kids all the time and be around my husband as much as possible.

When I met my future husband, Rick Teague, who was an attorney, I remember thinking, *Oh crap, I don't want to marry an attorney.* A lot of my family and friends were thrilled I was marrying a lawyer, but I was not super excited about that fact. I knew he was going to have to go into work every day, work crazy long hours and I never would get to see him, and he would never get to spend much time with our future family.

Rick: I was just tipping my toe into Herbalife when I met Michelle at an opportunity meeting in Dallas. We both had driven 200 miles to attend. Unfortunately, from opposite directions. She was still living in Houston at the time, and I was living in Stillwater, Oklahoma. I had my law practice in Tulsa. I would come to Dallas on occasion to pick up Herbalife products because it was the main distribution center for our part of the country.

In what I call my former life, I spent nine years in college and had not one, but two, law degrees. I started practicing law as an oil and gas attorney in the early 1980's when the oil and gas industry was doing well. Business was excellent. I thought that was because I was smarter than most and worked harder than most. I had the degrees and the big ego to match.

In the mid-1980s, all that changed. The oil and gas industry took a nosedive, and many of the smaller, newer companies that I worked for started going out of business. You can guess what that did to my income. My dad was a college professor at Oklahoma State, and he had gotten into Herbalife through a whole different set of circumstances. He tried to get me to join Herbalife for the better part of a year and finally succeeded when my income and satisfaction with my legal practice kept declining to a point where I could no longer say "no." In short, because the oil and gas business was drying up, I was being forced to take a lot of legal business that I had no desire to do, mainly things like bankruptcies, divorces, traffic tickets and criminal matters.

When I joined Herbalife, I didn't plan on making a career change. I met Michelle and occasionally started building my part-time Herbalife business around Dallas and eventually ended up getting a desk at Tish's co-op in Richardson. After that, Michelle and I started talking more, and eventually, I was mysteriously invited over to Tish's house.

Now, since Michelle and Tish had to make sure I was a Christian before I was officially "approved" as a suitor for Michelle, they both tricked me by asking me to come over to Tish's house to take a look at her video cassette recorder (VCR) because it "was broken." Within a few seconds after arriving and checking out the VCR, I immediately determined that there was absolutely nothing wrong with it. Further, I also instantly learned that this was a total set up when Tish, who was obviously and completely unconcerned with her VCR, turned to me and asked, "Rick, if you died right now, where would you go, to heaven or hell?"

In response I told her the truth, which was that I would go to heaven because I believed Jesus Christ died for my sins and I was consequently saved. To sum it up, I had inadvertently passed Michelle and Tish's thinly veiled litmus test and was officially stamped with their seal of approval.

Michelle: I was first led to Christ by one of the Herbalife distributors that came into the restaurant that night in Houston. After joining Herbalife, this person shared the Gospel with me, and I started attending church with them as much as I could so I could learn about God. It was at that point that I knew I wasn't going to date anybody unless they loved Jesus as much as I did.

Rick: After passing "the test," Michelle and I started dating, and I began to take more notice of the work she was doing. When I joined Herbalife, I was not familiar with the network marketing business at all. I was hanging around other Herbalife colleagues and was learning some tips and seeing their success. What blew my mind was seeing that there was one month where our upline leader and friend, Tish, made $93,000. I knew Tish worked hard, but I also knew she didn't have a high school diploma; it got me thinking. Here I was, a big shot, white-collar attorney with a large ego and nine years of college and two degrees and my law practice falling apart, and Tish without her high school diploma is the one making $93,000 in one month!

I had no idea people could even make that much. It opened my eyes, and my mantra then became, "if she can do it, then I can do it," and for 35 years since then I've been trying to catch up with her, but still haven't as far as total lifetime industry earnings.

Michelle: Rick and I have been working in this industry together since we met over 35 years ago. I was living with Tish and in addition to building my Herbalife business I was also Tish's assistant, so I was frequently around the family working on things here and there. I began hanging out with Tish, Larry, and his daughters as much as I could. The whole family is super generous and grateful, and they lived a life very different than the atmosphere I grew up in. Everybody was positive and doing their best to help others be their best. I took notice of that.

When Rick proposed, I began to think about our wedding day and what I wanted it to be like. For various reasons I had become estranged to my stepfather over the years, and although I did have a biological father in California, I didn't have a strong relationship with him either and that bothered me. To make matters even worse neither of them were Christians either, so when it came down to it Larry was literally the only believer I could think of that had the qualities of someone I wanted to walk me down the aisle. However, I was also very nervous to ask him mainly because I wanted to make sure his daughters were okay with it because none of them were married yet. I remember him talking to his daughters and then agreeing to do it. I was so thrilled because I couldn't think of a better person who had changed my life in so many ways. Larry and Tish both had a significant influence on my Christian life. Even Larry's teachings in person and *The Millionaire Training* on audio tapes interlaced with the Gospel and Biblical doctrine. Having him walk me down the aisle was such a special moment and a real act of kindness. It's a great memory to look back and reflect on to think I had such a good man with a positive, loving influence on my life, walking me down the aisle.

Rick: After joining Herbalife in November 1984, we ran into lousy timing when CNN ran a negative story about the company in January 1985. I didn't understand the importance of timing back then. Even though the company's situation at the time was much less than ideal, my first full month's check was $3,400, which at the time seemed pretty good to me. I ended up chasing that initial high check for three years but never could recreate or increase my initial results. At that time in the company, things weren't going that great for anybody.

Michelle and I then got married in December 1987. Two weeks before our wedding, I ended up leaving Herbalife and joining NSA after talking with some colleagues who had joined the company the year prior. After joining this new organization, I was finally able to put all the training I learned at Herbalife to work for the first time ever in a really good timing situation. I simply started applying the wisdom I had been taught in my "boot camp" years, and things really started working like they were supposed to.

Next thing you know, in just a few short months we had 800 people on our team and when I got my first $6,500 check, I knew it was time to quit my law practice for good and go full time into network marketing with NSA. My time at Herbalife showed me people like Larry and Tish who were successful, and it showed me the possibilities of what financial freedom offered. It was because of their example I was able to make the 90-degree turn from being an attorney to staking my flag and becoming a full-time network marketing professional who has now been in this business for over 35 years.

Michelle: We may have switched to another company that happened to be better for us timing-wise, but we applied every single principle we had learned from Larry. We didn't add to it or take away from it; we simply did what Larry taught us, and then suddenly, we had success. Fortunately, or unfortunately, depending on how you look at things, we've had to change companies several times, but each time we made a switch, we did the same things. We would take Larry's principles and teachings and do it again in another company with different products.

It didn't matter because it worked every time. Rick and I have been working together for thirty-something years, and that's because we got educated by the best and applied what he told us to do. Nothing has been perfect along the way, but we've never doubted a single second how we should go about doing things. You see that it works, and you just do it over and over and over again. That's the bottom line.

Rick: Having a background as a tax attorney has given me a bent towards complexity. There's hardly anything more complicated on this planet than the Internal Revenue Code and the law that goes with it. That's why it was mind-boggling to me when I started learning from Larry and seeing how practical and straightforward his approach to business is. I am a very analytical and detailed person, but complexity does not duplicate well. Learning from Larry was my complexity antidote.

I listen to Larry's *The Millionaire Training* over and over again to keep me on the straight and narrow in regard to simplicity. Even to this day I have to continually remind myself to focus on what can be *duplicated* instead of what I *personally have the ability to* do. For it to truly duplicate it has to be *achievable* by someone who's 10 levels below me in the company, who's halfway across the country, and who's never even done this type of business before.

During my three and a half years at Herbalife, I learned from Larry and Jim Rohn the fundamental principles of duplication. My time there became my network marketing training ground, and it's what has enabled Michelle and me to make an ultra-successful career out of network marketing.

Over the past 35 years, our greatest claim to fame is *not* the money we've earned, even though it's a lot. This is because we know plenty of people who have earned *more* than we have. However, very few if any of those people, especially outside of network marketing, have been able to spend more time with their spouse or their kids while they were growing up than we have. In a nutshell, beyond the money it's the flexibility, time freedom and lifestyle that comes with the money that really matters. In the end, it means being able to earn dream income while keeping your priorities straight... kind of like having your cake and eating it too.

Even to this day, we are continually learning and revisiting Larry's teachings. We're members of the LT WealthBuilding Academy just to be able to watch *The Millionaire Training* and use many of their other resources.

The LT WealthBuilding Academy, Gig Summit, and the Facebook group give us a constant and much needed refresher course in "anti-complexity." In the legal world, you have continuing legal education. In the medical world, you have continuing medical education. In network marketing you need continuing education as well, and Larry's resources are the perfect curriculum.

Michelle: Because of our training, we can get down to the bones of what's going on. We may be using the internet more rather than nailing signs on poles or leaving notes on peoples' cars like we used to do, but at the end of the day, it's about talking to people. Larry ingrained this in us so deeply. You need to be talking to lots of people.

Make up in numbers what you lack in skill.

That is something I tell everybody on my team. You might have to speak to a few more people than someone else does, but eventually you can potentially get the same results. While you're learning this business, you may need to talk with more people than someone who has been doing this two or three years, because you haven't reached the same skill level yet. However, you can make that up by increasing the number of contacts you reach out to while you're building your skills.

Larry is big on just getting out there and doing the work, and while you're out there, the skills will grow. You have to have the confidence that if I do these things, if I contact 10 people per day, it *is* going to happen. When I met Rick, I was making more money than he was in Herbalife, yet I didn't have nearly the same level of education that he had.

You can always tell who the "smart" people are at a presentation. Some of them are humble, and some of them are not. They don't like being told a simple way of doing things; they want it to be complicated. Some actually thrive on that complication in school and life. Larry would take that rug right out from under them. He would shake up their thinking and tell them to humble themselves.

We constantly strive to bring those same ideas to our team. We still use Larry's same principles and concepts from when we started nearly 35 years ago. They remain effective because they are all just simple fundamental principles that work no matter what you're doing. They even can be applied to your normal, day-to-day life for greater success.

Rick: I would add that one of the most significant takeaways from Larry and *The Millionaire Training* is his three-legged stool of success: have a burning desire, a willingness to work, and being teachable. These principles are the cornerstone of everything else you will do.

Michelle: I don't know anyone in the network marketing industry who knowingly or unknowingly hasn't been positively affected by Larry Thompson in one way or another. Larry has created a ripple effect that goes well beyond the network marketing industry. His influence in our lives has been a blessing to our family that I never would have imagined possible when I was just a young girl leaving my small town for the big city in my Toyota Corolla. I had no idea what was coming, and to be part of Larry's legacy is an honor. Rick and I have had the privilege to talk with thousands of people, and so much of what we share comes from Larry's influence. We give him credit for that. Almost every word that comes out of our mouth when it comes to training, encouraging, or giving a little pep talk to our team has got its roots in something that came from Larry. Larry has done more than he ever set out to do. I would say God ordained him for this, and he hasn't missed his calling; that's for sure.

Rick: When I think about the massive impact Larry has had in the network marketing world, it astounds me. He often talks about 100% certainty and 100% uncertainty, and you know there had to be a time when he felt that 100% uncertainty and wanted to quit. Thankfully, he didn't, and here he is with over 50 years in the network marketing industry. His influence reaches far beyond the money he's helped people make to the concepts of lifestyle, free enterprise, and a good dose of the Gospel mixed in.

Perhaps the most mind boggling thing is that the influence Larry has had over the *last* 50 years is just the tip of the iceberg compared to the exponential future impact he will have throughout the *next* 50 years and beyond, especially when you consider the reach of all the top earners, company owners, management teams, and industry insiders who have all been impacted by Larry and his mentorship. All I end with is, "Wow, we are forever grateful."

Jay Bennett
Top Field Executive, Isagenix

 When I look back on my life, it's plain to see my first passion was football. I remember seeing a guy with a letterman's jacket and thinking, *I want one of those*. My parents didn't want me to play, but I desperately did. After bugging my parents for two or three years, they finally agree to send me to football camp to see if I'd even like it. So, I got to attend Roman Gabriel's football camp, and it changed my life.

During this time, the Los Angeles Rams were a big deal (early 1970's). The best players who were teaching me were All Pro's and Hall of Famer's – people like Roman Gabriel, Merlin Olsen, Jack Snow, Rosie Grier, and Deacon Jones. I learned so much that week, and I fell in love with the game. That camp was a prime example of how having a mentor (someone who can hold you accountable) can teach you to go to the next level.

After that camp, I started playing Pop Warner football. I was 11 years old and didn't even know how to put on my pads or helmet, but I got out there on the field and enjoyed it. From there, I went on to play football for 10 years through high school and college. It was kind of incredible that I got into college at all. My grades were so bad, I flunked two classes. Somehow, I found a way. Football was everything to me, and once it was over, like many retired athletes, I struggled with what to do with my life.

I ended up taking a job working for a food company. It was very boring and mundane; I found no enjoyment or passion for it. Most of the people working there could care less if you were part of the company, and I knew I had to find a different opportunity. I was more than dissatisfied with my current situation. I started looking through the job ads in *The L.A. Times* and came across an ad that read, "**Get in $hape**." I liked health and getting in shape, so this sounded like a cool opportunity for me. I thought this was an actual job interview, so I called and set an appointment.

I was surprised to find that at the job interview, there were 14 other people and myself. We were sitting in a cramped office listening to guy with a little presentation book sharing an opportunity about Herbalife. He starts flipping the pages and talking about the company.

Here are the products…

Here is the compensation plan…

And, here are the options for joining…

Then he asks, "Who wants to get started?" Man, it was like a fire drill!

Fourteen people got up and ran out the door as fast as they could; everyone except me left. I liked what this guy presented because I could grasp the concept of geometric progression and residual income. Plus, I loved health, so everything converged. From what I could tell, I could do what this guy was doing, and I already knew I was going to go for it!

He showed me other people's checks and the incomes they were making, and I thought, *If they can do it, I can do it*. I didn't wait and let the grass grow under my feet. I told him straight up, "Let's do this deal."

He responded, "Come back tomorrow, and we'll submit your first order." He showed me this sliding scale of Product Volumes with which to choose your first order.

I choose the top of the scale, which was a $4,000 Retail Order, this got me a 50% discount on products forever, and it was all the money that I had!

This product I was buying was my one shot if I wanted to pay rent, put gas in my car, and eat that month. I believe one of the best things you can do is put yourself in a "do or die" situation. Not an attitude of, *I'll get around to it after I watch some TV shows*, or *Maybe I'll make some phone calls.* I had a sense of urgency spurring me on.

That was May of 1983, and my first full month was in June. That first month I had 38,000 Volume – I scored a $6,800 bonus check! When you combined that with my wholesale and retail sales, my total was over $10,000 in earnings for my first full month in business with Herbalife. In 1983, $10,000 was a massive amount of money. And, you know what? At Herbalife, they wouldn't even consider that to be a big deal. It was what people expected you to do. I was just another one of the distributors going after their goals like they were.

Making $10,000 my first full month in business became my story. Now, I was able to present to my friends, family members, neighbors, old football buddies, and coworkers and put my team together.

It got me launched. Getting a fast start, set the foundation that catapulted my business. It's a much better story to say I made $10,000 in my first full 30 days then it is to say I've been doing this for three years and now I'm making $500 a month. I don't find that particularly inspiring.

Another beautiful thing is I met my wife through Herbalife. In 1985, I was attending a company meeting. After being introduced to her, I knew instantly she was the one. I don't know if it was immediate for her, but it definitely was for me. We've been married since 1987 and been in network marketing together the entire time. There have been "Exhilarating" highs and "Knock You Out" lows in this business for the 33 years we've been together, but we're in this together.

I love that we met through network marketing because she can relate to me and the industry. Many times, within the network marketing space, I've seen spouses not support each other. It becomes very difficult to build the business when one person is giving their all to make the business work and the other just has negative comments all the time, which creates a negative environment in their marriage. This makes the business even more difficult and it produces a disconnect within their marriage.

My wife has always supported my endeavors even when my failures truly outnumbered my successes. After all these years, She has become my manager and coach, and she's able to see things from different angles. We complement each other well, and I'm grateful for that.

Around 1985, things went south at Herbalife. The FDA and FTC came after our company and we went from $100 Million Volume a month to only $3 Million Volume in a month. Over 100,000 people quit the business within a short time. It was like a nuclear bomb had gone off.

Not once did Larry Thompson and Mark Hughes give up the fight. For seven years, they fought their way back to the top to become what is now a $5 Billion a year company. It was not without great sacrifice. Mark and Larry sold their houses, cars, and countless possessions to keep the business afloat. It was a difficult, stressful time.

In a lot of ways, it was that initial devastation of Herbalife that built the network marking industry to where it is today. Many of the Herbalife distributors who left, went on to different companies and now they are now the top executives and distributors within the industry.

If you think about it, it's similar to the persecution of Christians leading to the spread of the Gospel 2,000 years ago. What happened at Herbalife is what eventually took network marketing to another level!

It was my experience at Herbalife that got me addicted to network marketing. It's a good addiction to have, not a bad one like drugs or food. It becomes an addiction because once you've tasted that level of financial freedom and gained control of so many areas of your life, you want more from life, you don't want less.

After leaving Herbalife, I had so many failures with different companies because it's challenging to find a legitimate company like Herbalife that's consistent, has the right products, the right compensation plan, tools, systems, and company culture. Bringing all that together is very difficult.

You would think it would be somewhat straightforward, just have the right product and marketing, right? But there are a lot of pieces to the puzzle, and all those pieces have to come together.

In the span of 20 years, I was with 20 different companies. I would get involved with one, stay for a year or two, it would fail, and then I'd move on to the next one. These failures happened time and time again.

After things had gone bust with my 18th company, I found out Larry had started his own business. I thought, *All right, let's rock and roll!* I didn't know what the company was or what the products were. I just knew I wanted to be a part of it because of the belief I had in Larry. For two years, I got a front-row seat with Larry on every decision he made with his company. During that time, I learned so many things that took me to another level. Larry is always innovative and on the cutting edge. In 1995 he bought a website for his company and at that time, this was cutting edge. We were amazed you could get on the world wide web and see this information on a computer.

We utilized technology and had a futuristic take on network marketing. There was one time where we had this event called, Midnight Madness. The goal was to get someone to upgrade to the $1,000 distributor package, and by doing so they would move up to the next rank in the compensation plan and be in the "Golden Circle."

I remember that night making so many phone calls during this Midnight Madness Promotion! Calling people in our downline, people outside our downline, people who weren't even enrolled yet, just trying to get someone to sign up for the package upgrade.

Then it gets to be 11:59 pm Pacific time, right before the cutoff time, and I call this guy in Florida (so we are talking 2:59 am Eastern time) who was definitely asleep when his phone rang. I pitch the promotion to this guy and share with him he needs to buy this package so he can advance to this next rank and get to the top of our company's compensation plan. I tell him with urgency, it's the last minute of the promotion, and it has to be done right now!!!

I don't know if he gave me his credit card in his sleep or if he actually did know what he was doing, but either way, he gave me his credit card number, and I got his order in.

I always try to communicate to people that anybody can do this, no matter what level they want to be involved. You want to make sure everybody feels comfortable with the level they are performing, that's the key. Larry has a concept that 80% of people in network marketing want to be in this business part-time, just to make some extra money. I never want to make anyone on my team feel uncomfortable for working the business at that level. But if I'm always talking to someone who would like to be in the top 5%, I would tell you that there's no better plan than choosing to block out the world and not let anything get in your way. You have to be willing to stop the planet from rotating on its axis for you to make this top level of success happen.

At my company now, I'm in that top 5%. But, that's after 19 other failures. Herbalife was one of them, as was Larry's company. My current company is Opportunity #20. I always knew at some point I was going to be successful. It just turned out that #20 was the right company. People see my success and think, *Yeah, well it's easy for Jay, he's been involved with 20 different businesses,* but do you also realize what a liability that was for me?

I was now part of the NFL (that's No Friends Left). So many people ran the other way. When I would call, people wouldn't listen to anything I had to say about anything. I had to dig deep in the mud and dirt. I was digging because it was painful. None of my family members would get involved or even buy the product. I was only able to build up my business by asking for referrals and getting into cold market lists, to get the ball rolling and gain some traction.

So many of the skills I have developed have come from Larry's teachings. Larry always says, "Peter was a disciple of Jesus. If you want to become a Christian, you can do it by being like Peter." In a similar sense, Larry was a disciple of Jim Rohn. Larry really embraced his training and philosophy of success, but definitely found his own style to communicate it to the field.

I kind of relate it to Jim Rohn being the schoolteacher and Larry being the football coach. The same concepts, but one guy is in the classroom on a blackboard, and the other guy is out on the field telling the team what they're going to do. Jim was always the teacher and Larry was the field general.

One of the critical things that stuck with me from Larry's principles is a mantra passed on to him from Jim Rohn. You read about it in *The Millionaire Training* – for things to change, you have to change. There's a natural tendency to point fingers outside of yourself, but if you accept the fact that you're the one in charge, you're embracing the philosophy that everything you could ever want can come your way. As I've gotten older, I often look back and think, *Gosh, I wish I would have done this, or I wish I could have done that. I should have done this, or I should have done that.*

I think that way even about football games in college that we lost 40 years ago. The only regret you should have is when you know you didn't do your best. When you know that you gave less than your best effort, then there's genuine regret. Thinking back on my career, for the most part, I can say I gave it 100%, but I certainly have isolated cases where I was going at half speed, and I regret those moments. For the most part, though, whether good or bad, I did it at a 100% level. I might not have known what I was doing, but at least I gave it my best.

The most important principles Larry taught me over the years come right back to the same basics I learned at Herbalife. I've taken those same concepts with me to every company where I have been a distributor. At Herbalife, we were told to (1) use the products, (2) wear our LOSE WEIGHT NOW, ASK ME HOW! button, and just get out there and (3) talk to people.

I think it's so brilliant: Talk to people and share the products. Simple, right? Those are still the fundamentals I use today. I also think it's important to keep in mind the characteristics to be successful that Larry speaks about. You need to have a burning desire, a willingness to work, and be coachable. If you don't possess those qualities, the simplicity of the basics are not going to work well for you.

It's the same thing with Christianity. Some people say being a Christian is so difficult, but if you think about it, it's about the basics. Reading the Word, being in prayer, and having fellowship with other believers. Those are the fundamentals. If you combine those fundamentals with a burning desire, a willingness to work (learn), and being coachable, you can be shaped into an incredible Christian.

I've gleaned so much wisdom from Larry over the years, but one of my favorite things he always says is, "You're good enough, you're tall enough, you're short enough, you're big enough, you're smart enough, you're dumb enough. You're enough. No matter who you are or what you bring, it doesn't matter."

I love that way of looking at things because so often we compare ourselves to others. We have to remember to embrace who we are. You have the ability and wherewithal to meet your goals. It doesn't take anything special to be successful with the network marketing model, which is what makes it so great. Regardless of the product or compensation plan, the Basics are all the same. It's about what you are willing to bring to the table.

As a disciple of Larry's since 1983, I've been listening to his audio training for over 37 years. I remember I had this big old CD player that I kept with me in my jacket or sweats, and I would listen to *The Millionaire Training* as I walked around my neighborhood. This routine went on for years, so it's no mystery why Larry's teachings are embedded in my brain and heart; it's become part of my DNA. I'm beyond thankful to Larry for his mentorship over the years. Even with all his success, Larry remains humble and grateful, and it's an honor to be a part of his legacy.

Jack and Julie Silva
President's Team
Herbalife International

 Julie and I met Larry Thompson in 1987 through a conference call. At the time he was vice president of Herbalife and we had just joined the company as distributors. Larry was talking about how you could take these nutritional products to the marketplace and change people's lives. Well, at that time in our lives, I was working about 12 hours a day selling Cadillacs and Julie was my inventory control manager at the dealership.

I wasn't earning what I felt I was worth, and Julie was open for opportunity. I never will forget that first conference call with Larry because we got so excited when he said, "You've got to fly to Chicago, and we'll meet you there at a distributor workshop" I couldn't believe we were going to Chicago to this business meeting.

The only other time I ever had been on an airplane, I was five or six years old. I couldn't remember much about it and now, I'm 25 years old getting on an airplane, going to Chicago to be trained by the Larry Thompson. We were excited because we were now business owners and we believed we could make this business work.

Going to that meeting in Chicago changed our life. I was an athlete growing up and Larry just came across to me like

Vince Lombardi the great football coach. He spoke my language and I felt honored to be in the same room with this man. There were many other successful distributors at this business workshop. It was very exciting for us to be there.

That's when I got my hands on *The Millionaire Training* tapes, and they became a staple in my daily routine for growing our distributorship.

I took *The Millionaire Training* seriously. It gave me the courage and the confidence that I could do this, and it gave me the fundamentals, the foundation, and a new way of thinking that I never thought before.

For example, I didn't realize procrastination is one of the biggest business problems people have. I procrastinated in a lot of things and I had my weaknesses that I knew I had to fix. I had to change some old habits and replace them with new habits like doing the things you don't want to do first, just get them out of the way, don't put them off until later which opens the door for procrastination.

I can honestly say, I don't think I would have made it if I didn't become a serious student of The *Millionaire Training* every single day in those early days.

As a kid, I was always setting goals and making plans. So, when Julie and I worked every day, we had our goals and plans. We would compete with each other to push each other.

I didn't have a problem with that one, but here's what I didn't understand about goals and plans. I was taught you had to write them down and check them off. I had a problem writing them down and checking them off. I struggled with that until Larry said, "Listen, a goal is something you have to have. And, if you have to have it, no matter what, it's yours. It's just a matter of time until it happens," He said. "You don't have to write it down and look at it every day."

A goal is something you have to have and Julie and I had to be successful. We had to make it happen. So, that really made a huge difference for us. But the reality is a goal is just something you have to have and if you have to have it, it's yours. It's just a matter of time.

In *The Millionaire Training* I also learned about communicating with feelings and not words. See, I didn't do well in school; I didn't have good English. I was concerned when I thought it was the words that were important when talking with people. When I learned it's how you feel about what you say that is more important than the words you use, that was huge for me to understand.

The Millionaire Training also helped me tremendously with not just putting a plan together but also following through on my plan. It taught me about holding myself accountable. If you talk to enough people every day and stay consistent, then you're going to be successful.

The Millionaire Training laid down that framework for us. Julie and I had to stay inside of that framework to be successful. We had to stay very consistent at talking to lots of people every day. If we had operated outside of that framework, we would not have made it.

Our first year we became one of the top achievers in our company. Our fifth year, we achieved the top 1% and still today, 30 plus years later, Julie and I are among the top 1% who are most successful in our industry. We thank God every day for the opportunity and for meeting the great people that we have met along the way.

I only can imagine where we would be without *The Millionaire Training.* It's made our life greater than we could have ever dreamt being able to provide stability for our family all these years. Julie, and I have been married for over 30 years since our beginning in Herbalife together. We have a great life truly living the dream as they say.

I can tell you the most important thing we have done is to recruit lots of people into our business. You've got to bring in new people, front lines every month and you have to develop a good retail customer plan.

Of course, you feel bad if someone doesn't make it in your business, but I never got wrapped up in feeling really bad if a person didn't make it as a business owner. It's not our responsibility for others' success because we are all independent distributors. Our responsibility is to bring in new customers and recruit new distributors who do the same as we do. We lead by example and that's how we've always done it. We have been there when our people needed us. Be there when they call you, be there for them when they reach out to you.

We never brought our problems to our people. We would listen to others talk about their problems and always say with compassion, "Okay, now let's talk about your business plan this week. What's going on?"

Today I will do video room meetings with distributors and I'll do one-on-one calls with distributors. I'll even go out into the streets with them and teach them by example. We'll go out and talk to people and I'll show them how to talk to people about the products. There are only a handful of things you need to say about your products. We show them what to do until they can do it. If they don't do it, I just go find someone else who will do it and will talk to people.

I don't spend too much time trying to convince people to do what I do. I spend most of my time finding people who believe in what I am sharing with them and that is my best advice for you, too.

Thank you, Larry and Taylor. It is a privilege for Julie and me to be a part of this amazing story.

.

Lisa Grossmann
Top Rank Distributor, Pruvit

 Although it would be many years later until I had the privilege to meet Larry Thompson in person, through *The Millionaire Training*, he had been my coach, my mentor and I felt my friend since almost the beginning of my career. Through his stories and teachings, I was able to shift my thinking and understand the principles of our profession and learn the strategies to build it successfully by duplicating it with others. The impact that it had on me has created a ripple effect in my business and sphere of influence that reverberates to this day.

When I started in this profession there was no internet; self-help was a shelf in a bookstore. There was little to no generic training available and what was there, was limited to *what* to do, but did little to address the mindset you needed to do it effectively and consistently. Moreover, even that was dependent on the company in which you happened to find yourself.

Network marketing came into my life when I was in my mid-twenties and in some circles, I would have been considered a success financially, but I was in fact very unhappy. As I learned and often share with others and when I speak, "Even if you win the rat race, you are still a rat." However, the freedom I caught a glimmer of spoke to my soul and I leaped in and very quickly realized that I did not know what I was doing. And, I didn't understand it enough to figure it out. What I did understand from what I was hearing, was that getting to events was important, so I committed to go to the next event in Toronto. I was told that if I hit a certain rank, I could attend a special school where the top earner in the company would be the trainer. Somehow, I got to that rank – I had to do it. I had to learn the secrets that were eluding me.

I didn't realize it at the time but qualifying to go to that school was the first big lesson that I learned. I was already different by the time I got there so I listened with different ears. My first big wakeup call was how impressed I was with the top earner simply because his background prior to network marketing was so unimpressive. He was my age, had been a waiter and yet he was earning in a month what most people at the time would have been happy with as an annual income. What stood out for me was rather than finding what he said to be complicated, it was his gift of simplification that seemed to be the secret of his success.

Over the course of three days he kept referring to his mentor, Larry Thompson, and how much he had learned from him. He spoke about Larry's *The Millionaire Training* and how he still listened to that coaching via cassette tape consistently. I knew that I had to have that program. Of course, it was not available in a generic format at the time as it had been designed for Herbalife, the extraordinary company that Larry founded. That didn't matter to me. With some searching and digging, I managed to get a set and it became my Bible in the first decade of my career.

I listened to it over and over again. I filled notebook after notebook with what I learned and rose through the ranks and the incomes in my endeavors.

I took a hiatus from network marketing for several years and when I decided to come back to it, I could not find the tapes. And I wanted them. One of the earliest things I learned from Larry is what you feed your mind is paramount to achievement and that was the best mental food I had ever come across. So, in the early days of the internet explosion my search on eBay led me to another set and I started listening again. I am not sure why the seller wanted to let these tapes go, but I'm so grateful he did because I attribute them to part of my success today.

What was amazing to me is once again, as I was in a different place when I listened to the tapes, I understood things in ways I didn't the first time. I realized that it all comes down to the story we tell ourselves, the narrative that becomes our truth. This stage of my growth was more internal than the first go round had been. And *The Millionaire Training* is so timeless, that while much had changed in the way of technology and opportunity, human nature really never changes and the information was every bit as relevant 10 years later and still remains so today, nearly 20 years after that.

Though I had listened to Larry almost every day for 10 years, it was only then that I realized it was more about what we think, our mindset and the story we tell ourselves that is the real gamechanger. One thing Larry always emphasizes is that we're worried about what we feed our bodies, but do we spend enough time worrying about what we feed our minds?

Once that hit home for me, it changed everything. I started to realize that the narrative we tell ourselves is the loudest of all, and it's very easy to go out and feed your mind with things that will reinforce a story that doesn't serve you. That mindset will keep you from contributing at a high level and not allow you to realize that you see things from a narrow confine of where you are rather than where you could be.

Consistency and repetition will hone your skill but what you think and how you see the world will directly influence if you will actually stick it out and not quit. Larry taught me to "Keep the main thing the main thing". People often think the main thing is a paycheck or how much they're earning. Money is a part of this business, but if the leadership and team expansion don't happen, you're not going to keep the money or maintain what you did to get it because you can't achieve success independently.

You can make somebody who isn't very highly evolved in their thinking work hard and be a record salesperson, but that doesn't guarantee they are going to be able to lead others well. It's only by building depth that you create a legacy and provide a means of change for the people around you.

Constant personal mental growth and listening to/reading powerful truths over and over is what makes that happen. You can hear something and say to yourself, *That makes sense*, then you listen to it again and think, *Now, I see something I didn't see before*, but eventually, if it resonates with you and you're immersing yourself in it over and over again, you can articulate it to others because it's no longer what you hear, it's what you think. It becomes embedded in you. We're not talking about duplicating system strategies that have worked, but duplicating leadership.

Take Michael Jordan, for instance. Yes, he has natural talent and ability, but he became the Michael Jordan we know because he practiced more than anyone. He shot more free throws than anybody, to the point that he could pick up a basketball and do it in his sleep. He was in a zone. If you see excellence in any space, you're going to find that same level of dedication.

The fact that anybody can join the network marketing profession is both its greatest strength and its biggest weakness. You can have people on your team with the highest level of commitment or no commitment at all. Larry taught me to be selective in who I recruit because you agree to go to work for them. If I meet someone and they whine for an hour, the last thing I'm going to want to do is to be in business together.

When I finally had the privilege of meeting Larry and heard him echo what I thought were my thoughts (only because I had heard them so many, many times), I remember thinking, *Oh, my gosh, we think the same*! And, then I realized that he is the person that planted those thoughts in me. Those thoughts were no longer repetition or imitation of Larry; they had become embedded in me with a whole different complexity and depth.

It's kind of like learning to ride a bicycle. At first, you're uncomfortable and aware of every movement you're making, but with practice and repetition, it becomes second nature. It's no longer a struggle, and you're going off muscle memory. It's the same thing with putting Larry's teaching into practice. One day, you are thinking the same as they are thinking without even trying. That's when you know everything has changed. You're succeeding, achieving ranks, and accomplishing the things you set out to do. It's working because you're following the mentors you've chosen to follow.

One of Larry's most underrated qualities and greatest contributions is his ability to choose the right words matched with the proper delivery. He understands that language matters. One little nuance in the delivery of the message greatly can change how it's received; it's more than just the words themselves. Larry had his own mentor, Bobby DePew, whom he studied and learned from and Larry would listen to his speeches over and over again on reel-to-reel tape. Larry would master his voice inflections, timing, and the language he used.

Often people don't realize that even though it's sometimes useful to simplify a message, you can't always simplify the message to the point of what I call "fortune cookie wisdom," where the message loses all meaning. The great minds cannot articulate everything they need to say into 140 characters on Twitter. When I started listening to Larry and realized language matters. I wanted to be able to communicate with people and paint a picture for them. I wanted to be able to get people to see things that could change their life, and if people don't see it, they're not going to aspire to do it themselves. What Larry taught me was the importance of telling a story.

I've been in this business for over 30 years, and I finally got to meet Larry in person when we spoke at the same event. I was freaking out because here was this icon I've looked up to for a quarter of a century. I base so much of what I do on his principles. I think every successful person has been guided by mentors if they want long-term success and getting to meet one of mine was a massive moment for me.

As I think back on Larry's teaching and influence on my career, one of the critical points that sticks out to me is the phrase, "Marry the process and divorce the results." You have to understand that our job is not to convince anybody, and whatever they decide at that time doesn't mean it's the final answer because, as Larry says, "The fortune is in the follow-up." To understand that we are not here to convince anyone to do anything and that if someone says, "No," that it is not a personal rejection. Whatever people decide today is just for that day. And that *No* does not mean never. Don't respond in a way that robs yourself of the ability to have a follow-up conversation the next day or the following week or in a couple months. It's all about the process, and you can't get emotionally attached because everyone has a right to their choice just as you do.

Your goal is to have a wealth of people to follow up with at all times and to operate in a way that people wanted that seventh exposure from you because you didn't make them angry the first six times you called.

I've been revisiting the *The Millionaire Training* for years, and I'm always gaining something new from it every time I listen. Something I continually take away from Larry's teaching is not to prejudge and get so caught up in my stuff that I forget that it's about somebody else. I need to continually touch base with people because new timing can create massively different results. Even though *The Millionaire Training* was recorded in 1981, the knowledge is timeless. Wisdom doesn't change. It's timeless because we're dealing with human nature, and that doesn't follow trends. Delivery mechanisms and techniques vary, but concepts and principles don't. They are the DNA of this business and the hallmark of longevity and a legacy of success.

The legacy I am building now includes my daughter, Hillary. I am beginning to see a lot of second-generation people coming into this business. The millennials coming into this profession are more likely to think for themselves. They are not motivated by the same things that motivated my generation. They tend to be more minimalistic and less interested in the big fancy car. They are about the company that makes the car being socially responsible. Nowadays, with the internet and gig economy, if people don't want to have a boss, they have many options. When I was young if you didn't have an education or the right pedigree, there weren't many options to be an entrepreneur outside of network marketing.

Today, more people are choosing this profession because it gives them the ability to leave a legacy. You have the opportunity to teach somebody everything you know and hope that they do it better than you, and if they're successful, you're compensated accordingly. Where else do you see that happen where you can teach somebody all your secrets and make money because they do it better than you? That gives me great hope, and I do see a bright future for our profession, one where my daughter can excel. Network marketing had become a much more inviting atmosphere than it was when I started. When I began, you had to be pretty tough and have thick skin. Now I have hopes that my great-great-granddaughter will be working from home, presenting to someone, somewhere across the globe, with a hologram but utilizing the same principles and guiding wisdom that's been around for generations.

I'm very proud of what Hillary is accomplishing in this field. Being in the second generation of this business, people often attribute your success to your parents, so you have to work that much harder to get out of your parent's shadow and prove yourself to others. I had her listen to all the people I respected, because like I said before, wisdom is wisdom no matter the time or the place. When Hillary went to one of Larry's conferences, she came back and asked me, "Have you heard of this guy?" and all I could do was laugh.

"Have I heard of him? I was raised on him!" Hillary was raised on the same principles and values as all of us because long-term success leaves clues.

Larry's concepts have stood the test of time because they teach you *how* to think rather than *what* to think. There are no shortcuts to success, but there is the leverage you can gain when you're educated by people who have accomplished what you want to achieve and headed where you want to go because they're invested. Spend time with people who want to open people's minds.

I'm thankful that Larry Thompson has spent his career doing just those things. He has a legacy he's built and has never let any obstacles stop him. I love the fact that he's never retired. He's still out there, giving all his energy to sharing information with another generation. I respect and admire the fact that Larry has continued when it's no longer about money but out of a desire to help others and pass along this timeless wisdom so that the pebbles he has dropped in the pond of this wonderful profession will continue to ripple around the world without end.

Frank Mulcahy
Top Earner, LegalShield

 I first had the opportunity to meet Larry Thompson when I began my direct selling career with Herbalife in 1982. During those early years, I quickly related to Larry's teachings and looked at him as a person who cared about others. I immediately looked at him as a mentor from afar. Many of his lessons and core philosophies helped me to go onto achieve unimaginable abundance over the next 38 years. The most significant thing that changed my life was a simple two-cassette tape set Larry had released called *The Millionaire Training*. I listened to those tapes so many times that I wore them out. One of those lessons, which I held within me but had never tested for 30 years, changed my life when I was at my lowest point.

The Millionaire Training was critical in helping me attain the massive success that I have today. I would like to share with you how Larry demonstrated the necessity of taking a sabbatical, even if it's only one day, as in investment in your future accomplishments.

When I began at Herbalife, it was Larry's simple duplicatable, repeatable process that allowed Lynne and I to earn over $18,000 a month. We used Larry's guidance to build an incredible business that had distributors in Canada, Australia, England, and the USA. Still being new to the direct sales industry, I made a point to study *The Millionaire Training* by listening to the training over and over. It was at that point I was able to build an unshakeable core belief system, which later gave me the ability to weather the many storms that life would throw my way.

After three years of tremendous success, things changed drastically within 60 days. In early 1985, Herbalife and several other direct sales companies faced false accusations from the U.S. Food and Drug Administration and the resulting Senate hearings. These hearings caused significant damage to the Herbalife brand and the incredible work thousands of distributors were doing to bring health and income to our customers. A short time later, I decided it was time to leave the business when my monthly residual check had dropped off to only $800 per month.

Thankfully, I was able to use the life skills I learned from Larry to build several businesses over the next 15 years. Fate would have it that I would have the opportunity to work on several projects with Larry and his mentor, Bobby DePew. Later on, I also would have the good fortune to be introduced to legendary entrepreneur and motivational speaker, Jim Rohn. From these three men, I developed the set of skills that would become the tapestry of beliefs that form my philosophy in life. I wouldn't fully realize the value of these lessons and how they would put me back on the track to "true residual wealth" until a critical time in my life 26 years later.

My lifelong goal had been to retire by age 50. In June 2001, I was able to make that dream a reality and retired on my 50th birthday. Lynne and I sold our business and moved back to New Hampshire to be with our children and grandchildren. We were able to purchase our 6,500 square-foot dream home on 26 wooded acres with a 7-acre private pond; it was simply beautiful.

It wasn't long before I became bored with retirement, and I started buying investment properties. I planned to collect rent, change light bulbs, go fishing, and let the real estate create passive income and appreciate in value, allowing us to set up a legacy for our children. I was up to 57 rental units when the economy crashed along with the housing bubble in 2007. I lost almost $5.5 Million in assets, along with my pride, my dream home, and my inspiration. Thankfully, the incredible lessons I learned from *The Millionaire Training* tapes allowed me to create that Unshakeable Belief System. I am convinced that all the lessons I learned from Larry became my philosophy on life and business. I knew deep in my heart that I could succeed in any field as long as I didn't quit. As Larry said to me once, "You have never not achieved your goal, unless you quit pursuing it."

I never had any doubt that I would succeed again, especially in this great land we live in called the United States of America. As Larry always said, "They're not building boats to go to Cuba." I still believe that this is the most magnificent place to start your business and to achieve your goals.

It was then that I began searching for something special I could do, something that I could be proud of that would provide genuine value to the consumer. That's when the Lord brought me to the company I work with now, LegalShield. Today, people see my success, and they probably think I had it easy. They may believe I had lots of connections, associations, and a vast database. I didn't have that. What I had was a deep belief system that, in America, we can achieve whatever we set out to do.

It wasn't easy to start over at age 57, broke and out of resources. Lynne and I had to give up our dream home and move back to Texas. I quickly realized that the job market for people over the age of 40 is challenging. We all know people who are looking for something to grab on to, something to believe in, something that can change the rest of their lives. I was hopeful this opportunity in employee benefits, identity theft training, and seminars would be the answer. My starting over was rough because of my debt at the time, and I was not 100% committed.

In my first 90 days, I made less than $1,900, so I thought about quitting until Lynne, my incredible wife, partner and best friend since 1980, said, "Frank, I have never known you to quit anything; so why quit now?" Wow, how lucky I was to have her support and unwavering love.

I was feeling lost and unsure of what to do next. It was during this darkest time in my life that I went back to the early journals that I kept from listening to *The Millionaire Training* tapes. In my notes, I found the simple strategy that involved taking a sabbatical and asking myself four powerful questions that needed answering with brutal honesty. I remember Larry's words echoing, "Lie to your spouse, lie to your sponsor, but have the ability to tell yourself the truth." Then I membered he also said in your darkest hours you need to get away and take a sabbatical if you want to develop a plan to succeed.

I set aside time for my day-long Sabbatical. I took a couple of yellow legal pads, found privacy, and had a real hard, serious talk with myself. I had to look at things the way they honestly were, and not how I wanted them to be. I did not want to put my head in the ground like an ostrich. I had to ask myself tough questions.

I focused on four questions Larry called, *The Four Ifs*.

Amazingly, I had that lesson within me for almost 26 years, but I had never needed to put it to the test before like I desperately needed to do that day. The Sabbatical is *The One Thing That Changed Everything* when my back was against the wall. I was able to create the blueprint I needed to succeed one more time.

Because I followed Larry's methodology, in less than nine months, I was able to create a stable six-figure income. That income has now turned into a multiple six-figure *residual* income. It has also allowed me to create an income that I can pass on to my children and grandchildren.

I want to share this same process with you in the hope that it will benefit you or someone you know.

Question 1: What if I learn? What if I take the time to stop and learn about the opportunity I have in front of me?

I asked myself, *What would happen if I developed a daily, weekly, monthly Method of Operation*? What if I studied the leadership, products, compensation, mission statement, purpose, longevity, support system, and other competing brands? I evaluated everything in my life. What is and isn't working? Who is helping me succeed, and who is holding me back? After a rigorous and careful study, I had the vision, and I knew with unwavering confidence that I had found the right company. The founder has outstanding character; the opportunity and compensation plan was incredible and simple like Herbalife's plan. It had leadership with integrity, just like Larry Thompson and Mark Hughes had in my early years. They had a product of the highest quality, no competition, and not replicable. There was a high demand for the service, no inventory, no capital investment, the possibility of residual income, and to top it off, my initial investment was less than $200.

Question 2: What if I try? What if I put all my effort into the program? I'm not talking about a half-baked, lukewarm attempt. What if I implemented a daily, weekly, and monthly *Method of Operation*? If I applied it, how far could I stretch? How far could I take my talent? How far could I go if I shared this process with others?

I remember Jim Rohn said he was talking to some second graders one day. As he set up a two-foot bar, he asked them if they thought they could jump over it. Some said yes, others said no, and others didn't know. Jim asked them, "Well, how do you know unless you try? If you knock it over, try a second run, and another, and another."

Jim put a word with the word "try." Try *until*. That one word has stuck with me since the first time I heard him say it. We don't stop a baby from trying when they fall while learning how to walk. We just laugh and say, "Nice try. Try it again, and again." Go out there. Talk to your associates, talk to your customers, and speak to your upline, but you keep trying, and you keep trying *until*.

Another critical lesson I learned from Larry, "The heavy chains of worry are always forged in idle hours." In other words, if we get busy, become productive with our time and stick with it, the problems of life disappear. He also taught me the invaluable lesson of learning *How to Employ Yourself.* Larry taught us, "If you want to get rid of a bad habit, replace it with a good habit."

Question 3: What if I stay? What if I stay committed for 1,000 days?

Now, 1,000 days may sound like a big commitment, but when you're talking about your life, your career, your retirement, 1,000 days is a small fraction of time. You accomplish this by breaking it into segments. You utilize the first 90 days to establish momentum, the next 90 days to advance momentum, and the 90 days following that to maintain your momentum. Repeat it again and again until you get the results you desire.

Question 4: What if I care?

Larry said, "If you care a little, you can get some results. If you care enough, you can get incredible results." That's the posture my wife and I take to the marketplace. We care more about the results the customers get from our products than the money we make selling them. We care more about the success of the associates we bring into this business than the money we make from those associates. I will share with you that if you develop that same philosophy, that same pride, where you can go out there and care, you can have incredible success as well.

These four questions gave me a crystal-clear path to follow, but these four questions were just the beginning.

After being in LegalShield for nine months, the founder, Harold Stonecipher, called me and said, "You and Lynne have an incredible story people need to hear." I immediately asked him why he felt that way?

He said, "When you lost everything, you were down for the count, yet you stood tall, you looked life in the eye, you took charge, and changed your life without complaining. You just simply went to work and did it. That is an incredible lesson for others."

Mr. Stonecipher then asked me if I could do him a small favor. I said, "Of course, what would you like me to do?"

He said, "I would like you to speak for 30 minutes and share your story with 17,000 people at our annual convention." At that time, I had never spoken to more than 100 at any event, now 17,000 people? They brought in all the big money earners, the board of directors, 200 attorneys, and put them in the first 30 rows. It was a scary assignment for me because I was never on the big stage before.

I didn't realize you cannot look up at the spotlights in the rafters. They will temporarily blind you, and your notes become a blank sheet of paper. I started speaking, never once looking at my notes. It was difficult telling the world that I lost millions, I lost my home, I went bankrupt. But then I shared how it was just a little setback. The magic was that I had built this Unshakeable Belief

System off of Larry's teachings. I had the chance to share some the most valuable lessons I ever learned from Larry.

First, I spoke about *The Five Major Ingredients* that go into the day that turns your life around. Second, I shared *The Seven Deadly Diseases of Attitude* and how they will reduce you to a beggar overnight. That belief system allowed me to address 17,000 with a message from my heart, it was my philosophy.

Larry always taught that if it is in your heart, you will be able to deliver the message. That experience was the foundation of my becoming the international speaker I am today and I now have spoken in 29 countries to over a million people.

It was the most incredible and humbling experience I have ever had because so many of those folks were able to relate to my journey. After I spoke that day, I had 650 to 700 people approach me and ask to either take a photo, sign their book, or just talk to them for a moment. They all took away different nuggets from my 30-minute talk. But they were not my nuggets. They were the invaluable lessons I learned from that original set of *The Millionaire Training* tapes. I was able to share with them that no matter how bleak things look, it will work itself out if you have faith in your skills, company, products, and marketplace.

The most incredible part was that even though I touched their hearts, the audience did more for me in return. They reaffirmed 650 to 700 times that my belief system was right on track; that helping and serving others will always benefit us in the end.

I want to let others know that the journey I took is duplicatable. It's a repeatable, proven process that can put anybody onto a fast track of success no matter what they do in life, whether they are interested in my opportunity or something else.

A quote from Helen Keller says it best, "Sometimes, the most beautiful things in the world cannot be seen or heard but can only be felt in the heart." That's what Larry and Taylor Thompson mean to Lynne and me. That's what our business means to my wife and me.

I wish you the best, find your dream, take a Sabbatical, and ask yourself, *The Four Ifs*.

Larry, thank you again for pouring so much into so many, I am honored and blessed to call you a friend. I will be forever grateful.

.

John Solleder
Senior Platinum, Immunotec

 I was about to graduate from Seton Hall University in Northern New Jersey. It was 1983. At the time, I was working part-time selling health club memberships in a Nautilus facility (if you remember back to the old Nautilus equipment that came out of Florida). A friend of mine named Tommy Husted, a very elite wrestler at Lehigh University who worked out at that facility, introduced me to the health club's owner, Dave.

Dave starts to explain to me about this business that he and Tommy had gotten involved with called Herbalife. He explained to me that I could have my own business as well for $32. At that time, $32 was a lot of money for me. To put it in perspective, my vehicle at school was an old U.S. mail Jeep, like the ones they still use today.

I gave a check to Tommy and asked him to hold it for a couple of days so I could cover it. He graciously did. That night, I got home did my schoolwork, and finished up around 10 pm. I pulled out my new Herbalife Distributor Kit and looked through the magazine, *The Herbalife Journal*, that came with it. On the cover was Tish Rochin. She lived in a place called Plano, Texas. I didn't know who Tish Rochin was and I didn't know where Plano, Texas, was, but what I did know from reading the magazine was that Tish had earned $250,000 the previous year. For someone who had trouble covering a check for $32, this was inspiring.

I opened the career book, and inside were circles and diagrams. I started to look at the marketing plan and took out a yellow legal pad. I put some names in some circles; I stayed up until 4:00 am that morning, putting names in circles and making mathematical projections of what would happen with this Herbalife pay plan. By 4:00 am, I had made $1 Million on paper!

I thought, *This is a pretty simple business. This plan makes sense.* Whoever, whatever genius had put this business together, it was making total sense to me. Fast forward 30 days, I graduated from Seton Hall University. At that point in my life, I was very liberal thinking, a left-wing person. I believed that business was bad, and if you owned a business, you were probably getting one over on people.

At my graduation, I found out the commencement speaker was going to be President Ronald Wilson Reagan. I didn't like him for a variety of reasons, one of which was that he had fired the air traffic controllers. I felt like he was a union-buster, and I am from a very pro-union family. I didn't want to go, but my father who was still alive at that point said to me, you know what, we respect the office even though we don't like the guy. You need to go. You worked hard all these years to get this degree. You need to go. I'm glad he had that position on things. I ended up going begrudgingly, and I was one of those guys – I had my arms folded the whole session.

During the speech, President Reagan talked about some basic ideas, things like entrepreneurship and freedom. He discussed that when he was young, he met a wealthy man and asked him, "Can you help me find a job?"

The wealthy man replied, "Well, do you really want a job, or do you want a career?"

"I want a career."

"That's something you have to find."

That day, I began to understand that I already was being mentored a little by my upline in Herbalife. I'd been to several small meetings at local hotels, but there was going to be a much more extensive training the following month with the co-founder, Larry Thompson. I had heard so much about Larry; I felt it was an excellent time to take the next step and attend.

The problem was nobody in my upline had reliable transportation. I had my mail Jeep, but that wasn't going to make the four-hour drive from New Jersey to Hartford, Connecticut. My friend, Tommy, didn't have a car either, so he ended up asking his dad to borrow his old station wagon. Thankfully, his dad said yes, so Tommy, me, and three other people we had recruited drove up to Hartford and stayed overnight in a hotel. The next day, we got up and went to the training. I had never been to anything like that in my life. There were at least 2,000 people there from Boston to New York, and D.C., a vast area.

When Larry comes out on stage, it is a magical moment. There was a lot of outstanding leadership in the room and having Larry there in-person speaking was a huge deal. There were compelling things Larry said that day, that I still use in my business 36 years later. The number one being the mantra he had learned and passed on to us, "For things to change, you have to change. For things to get better, you have to get better."

It was the first time that I had heard those types of words articulated by someone. Larry's a stranger to me. He's an executive in this big company that I joined, and I'm just a total nobody. I'm just a kid out there in the audience, but that message was crucial not only for my career but for my life.

My upbringing was one where everything was the government's fault, or it was the politician's fault, or the union's fault, or the contractor's fault, or somebody else's fault. Failure was always somebody else's responsibility, not your own.

That day, I got "For things to change, you have to change. For things to get better, you have to get better." I can say it in my sleep. (And, I can even say that in Spanish and French, believe it or not!)

Larry was communicating a message related to him, and he was already hugely successful in his professional life as a result of that messaging. Hearing that one idea from Larry was incredibly eye-opening and it pointed me in the right direction mentally.

When I initially joined Herbalife, my distributor kit came with Larry's *The Millionaire Training* tapes, but I hadn't listened to them. My U.S. Mail Jeep didn't come with a cassette player, and I didn't own a cassette player at home, so I had no way to listen to the tapes. However, on the four-hour drive home from that training, we all listened to them in Tommy's dad's car. I couldn't believe how funny Larry was on these tapes. He could be a standup comedian with the stuff that's on there. But what was right, is that in all that humor, there was also so much wisdom. What also spoke to me when listening to those tapes, was the fact that conceptually anyone could do this business. Larry and the other people who spoke at the meeting that day illustrated that point, especially Tish Rochin, the lady truck driver, who was making $250,000 a year.

Mark Hughes and Larry Thompson created a brilliant business plan with Herbalife. Take ordinary people and get them successful. Show off every day common people having success.

When I joined Herbalife, the company was having a $140 million year. I understood this was a concept-driven business. Today, I listen to some of our colleagues in this industry who are trainers, and they're trying to teach technique instead of teaching concepts. I got from Larry that day in Hartford and listening to *The Millionaire Training* were concepts. For example, he didn't say, "Go down to the local bank and stand in the bank line at 10 am, talk to the first three ladies wearing dresses."

Larry said, "Talk to anyone who breathes." Now, that's a concept. Do they have to wear dresses? No. Could they wear shorts? Yeah. Could they be young? Yeah. Could they be old? Yeah. That's what I got from *The Millionaire Training* back in 1983: concepts vs. techniques. That is a big difference.

The Millionaire Training was straightforward because it was only two cassettes. It wasn't like you bought this big, huge 7-week training program and had to listen to 19 different tapes. It was simplified. You would listen, flip the tape over, and then listen to the other side. That was where we started. What Larry taught was simple enough. If you listened once, you got some, and if you listened a second time, you got a little more. If you listened a third time, you got a little more, but you metabolized it as you listened to it repeatedly.

The Millionaire Training had so many concepts that I needed to hear over and over; I say 9,000 times. (I'm not exaggerating how many times I listened. I actually wore the tapes out and had to buy a new set about every six months because I'd listen to them so often.) How you learn something is by repetition, where you continually listen to something until you get it, and then it becomes yours once you get it, but you still keep listening to it because you always miss something.

What I've found with the tapes is that there's so much information that you have to go back, listen again, go back, listen again, read again, however you are learning. To become professional at something, experts say you have to do it 10,000 times. When it comes to learning, part of that involves hearing the same thing repeatedly. Then, of course, the other part of that is applying what you've heard. It's one thing to listen to it, but if you don't apply it, you didn't learn. The best teacher in our business is the tell, show, try, do. And we all know the do part is the hard part, right?

I was fortunate enough to meet Larry's two mentors, Jim Rohn and Bobby Depew, who inspired Larry's training. I met Jim at a long lunch meeting in Dallas many years ago. I met Bobby through Larry back in the early 1990s. I would go out to California occasionally and visit Larry at his ranch. One time, when I was in New York he called and said, "Hey, Bobby's going to be out here when you're out here." I couldn't believe my luck. I was going to meet the famous Bobby Depew! I went out to California and spent an afternoon with Bobby. I don't know whether Larry had something else to do or he just figured, *Hey, you know what? Let me stay out of this. You talk to him directly.* I was skipping a generation. Larry was my mentor, I'm talking to his mentor, and Bobby and I sat on the back deck for five hours. I just listened to this guy and relished the fact that I was getting to talk with one of the original creators of this industry. He helped orchestrate many of the compensation models, pay plans, and training that Larry would often reference.

He passed shortly after that, but what an afternoon that was. As I look back on my 36 years now, getting to spend an afternoon with my mentor's mentor and pick his brain, just two guys, sitting on a back deck in California, chewing the fat. It was a great opportunity, and somewhere I've still got my notes from that day.

What we do affects so many people generationally; we don't even realize the lives we touch. I have a huge organization of Hispanic leaders in my company, and one of them last week said to me, "You're Tata."

I speak some Spanish, but I was like, *Tata?*

I know that's good. Because *tata* means *grandpa* in Spanish. To put it in perspective, if I'm the grandfather, then Larry is the great-grandfather. Even though my distributors don't know Larry, they know me. How many organizations are like that? Then Bobby and Jim Rohn as well. We have a responsibility to teach the right things to the next generation.

The last three years have been incredible, and currently I'm working as hard as I did when I was young. Maybe not that hard but working pretty hard, traveling a lot, and seeing new parts of the world. After the recent passing of my insurance mentor, it caused me to reflect on the people in my life that helped me along the way, and Larry is one of them.

I look back on that day Larry came to Hartford to speak. He didn't know there'd be a guy in the audience who got it. He probably hoped there were a lot of guys in that audience that likely did get it, but one got it at least. My oldest daughter is starting to do some public speaking on a situation that came into her life that was a very negative situation, and she's trying to turn it into a positive.

A couple of weeks ago, she was asked to speak to some people who are on the same road that she's on. Before her speech, I called her and told her something that Larry had taught me. That is, if there's one who gets it, you did your job. If there's one who changes something, you did your job. Yes, you want them all to get it, but they're all not going to get it. They're going to be distracted. There are days when they are going to be on their cell phone. They're going to be thinking of something else, whatever. If there's one person, one person's life you impact that day, you did your job. You can put your head on the pillow that night and know you did do what you're supposed to do.

I'm going to tie in another concept of Larry's as well. When my daughter had her challenge, and we were leaving the institution that she was treated at, I said to her, "You know what begins now?"

She said, "I know, dad. One day at a time, a brick at a time, process by process." The funny thing is that's construction talk, that's not multilevel. I tell that to my kids and distributors all the time. It's a phrase that applies to everything. So once again, how do you take all the stuff that we've done in our business and use them in your life? How do you apply those things when things are dire? Well, one day at a time, a brick at a time, process by process. My daughter got it, and she's working at it, and it's a struggle, but she's doing great.

Larry has a legacy that has done so much for so many. When I think back on the influence he has had on me, I think of several things. Number one is being a good student. I would say that is something many people wrestle with because we all want to be authoritative in our field and be good students. That takes a continual application of listening, reading, taking notes, and asking questions. Secondly, though, by being a good student, this is an applied science. In my other non-multilevel life, of course, I've coached many different sports, and I tell people, the only way to figure out what you're doing is to get out there and get your nose bloodied. Nobody likes to get their nose bloodied, but that's just the reality of sports, the reality of business, and the reality of life. Your nose gets bloodied sometimes, and it doesn't feel good, but that's how you're going to learn.

To build on that, even if you listen to everything, you read everything, and you've got a million notebooks filled with notes, if you don't go out and talk to somebody, I guarantee your business won't work. If you don't speak to your next-door neighbor this afternoon when you see him getting his mail and mention it to him, whatever it is that you're marketing, all the information you learned is for not. It's an applied science.

You have to know how to work with people, and these are things I learned from Larry and from other men who were serious about discipline as well. If you said you were going to do this, you better do this. Hold them not because you're trying to be nasty, but because you want them to succeed, and if they succeed once, they can succeed again and again and again. That's another concept I learned from Larry. If one can do it, all can do it.

Dan McCormick
Top Global Distributor, Nu Skin

 I'm here in my home in Coto de Caza, California. When I first started network marketing, I was a 19-year-old young man. At only 12 year's old, I got my first job at the Seattle Supersonics Racket and Health Club for $2.35 per hour. Every day, I went to that club because it felt like home, warmer than home actually. I took my pay as credit, so that I could hang out and play tennis. It was $20 an hour for court time; I washed the towels, did the laundry, and vacuumed the tennis courts. It was indoors, because of the rain in Seattle.

I watched people have a life that I never saw growing up in a single parent home. People had time freedom in the middle of the day to come and play tennis, and I remember their names even to this day. I remember the airline pilot, I remember the salesman, I remember the people who were in the military, I remember the world-class athletes. Some of the greatest athletes that ever lived came there to either work out, played for the Sonics, or were playing tennis. They had what I didn't have and that was money, but they loved what they did. I loved tennis, but I really wanted more than I had.

My mom was brilliant because every time I would ask for money, she said, "Son, you better make a lot of money because when you get older, you're going to need it. You're always asking me for money." A lot of times parents would say,

"What do you think, money grows on trees?" My mom said something different.

I met a man there who built tennis courts. He owned his own company and his partner and he were two of the top tennis players in the northwest. They asked me to work for them to build tennis courts.

At the time, I was a spoiled rotten, young, arrogant, cocky, no self-esteem, no self-worth individual, horrible in school, no people skills. I just loved tennis, and I went there every day to play tennis.

This guy asked me to work for him and he said he would pay me $5 an hour. I learned what it was like to work. I mean, this guy really put me to work, taught me to work, corrected me when I was wrong, and it was just unbelievable.

I did that until I graduated from high school and went to Washington State University. I always tell people that I finished college in two weeks. The following summer after working in the tennis clubs again and building tennis courts, an ad in the newspaper showed up that said, "Are you making what you're worth? I live in Beverly Hills, California. I drive a Clenet, and I made $96,000 in the health and nutrition industry, supervisory positions available."

Here's what was weird – that ad showed up in the newspaper from a group of distributors from Canada. I was scared to call it because I had no background in supervision or business. I used to look at the ads every day because it was inspiring to see what opportunities would be out there. I didn't know what I was going to do besides build tennis courts or string tennis rackets and play tennis.

This ad came out on a Sunday and stayed in the paper four days in a row. Finally, I looked at my mom and said, "They must be desperate because that ad is still in the paper." I kid you not! I remember the phone call because it was a live answering service that said somebody would call me back. I remember sitting at my desk (in the office I set up because I wanted to be in business somehow). When that phone call came in, the guy asked me some questions (just like Larry trained them).

"Tell me about your business background," he said. I was nervous. I really did not want to tell them that I worked at a tennis club. I must have done okay because he invited me to the Greenwood Inn in Bellevue, Washington, Northeast Eighth for an opportunity meeting.

I said, "How am I going to recognize you?"

"I'm a really big guy with a wide part."

I had so much hair at the time, I had no idea what he was talking about with the wide part program. I found him, and he got his flip book out. He started going through the program with me. He talked about the company history, he told me about the products, he told me about the opportunity, and then he started telling me stories of people who were my age. Santo Roberto, Ron Touchard, people who were literally 22 to 23 years old. I was 19, and they were out there beating the streets, making sales in weight loss.

August 12th, 1982 was the day my life changed forever because that night, not only did my upline tell me about a book to read, but he gave me *The Millionaire Training* cassette tapes. Now, learning on cassette tapes back in the day was a novelty. I wasn't a good student, I wasn't a good learner, but I want people to appreciate what this meant to me.

I'm lying on my bed in my room, and I plug in *The Millionaire Training* Tape One, Side A. I I promise you, if I slept more than an hour straight for the next week, that would have been amazing. There was something that came over me that was so powerful; I had so much pure adrenaline. I found my life's calling.

You have to understand, I was in so much pain as a kid because I didn't know what there was in life for me outside of tennis. Here, I saw the dream. I saw the opportunity. I knew my skill level could grow into it. I was immature beyond belief. My mom came to the meeting with me. I had a couple thousand dollars saved away from building tennis courts at $5 an hour. There were only 30 or so people at the meeting.

"Here's my application," I told my sponsor. He invited me to go out to his car.

He opens the trunk and says, "How much product would you like to start with? This senior consultant package is a good way to start because it has the biggest discount available."

I wrote him a check for $296 right there, walked away with my products and a new lease on life.

About a month later, Larry came to Seattle, and it was the big training. Now I've got *The Millionaire Training* coursing through my veins; I'm riveted. My sponsor asked me, "What did you like about those cassette tapes?" I was so immature. I was so at a loss for how to communicate. And, I was too embarrassed to say, I just wanted the money.

That was at a time when I believed money would fix everything. I imagined how cool it would be if I could be *that* guy and be able to show my friends who laughed at me for dropping out of college, that I was right.

Two weeks into college, I dropped out. (I say I finished college in two weeks.) I didn't have the mental capacity to do it. My brain didn't function there in that environment.

"No, you've got to go to college, Dan," my friends insisted. I just knew it wasn't for me. Instead, I'm inviting everyone I can to a three-hour training with Mark and Larry. I'm standing in my tennis club recruiting men 15 years older than me who came there to work out, play tennis or play racquetball. I remember this businessman who I invited to come with me. He showed up. There are hundreds and hundreds of people there.

I'm all fired up.

I've listened to *The Millionaire Training* tapes. I've got my sponsor, and I'm introduced to this 23-year old woman in my upline, Marilyn, who was the first distributor for Herbalife in Canada. Her sponsor lived in LA. I was so blown away at her composure, it was quite amazing.

I was young, raw, and hungry. I heard stories about people talking to people. They would wear this button that said, LOSE WEIGHT NOW, ASK ME HOW! They would do this thing called The 10 Pennies. I went to the mall with my sponsor, and I'm walking towards a Nordstrom's counter, and you know how all the people behind the cosmetics counters look amazing. I'm walking towards this lady who's really well put together, and I looked at my sponsor, and I looked at this lady, and I said, "This lady looks like somebody who would like to make $10,000 a month."

She leaned forward on the counter and said, "You bet your life I would. How would I do that?"

I looked at my sponsor and said, "Yeah, Dennis. How would she do that?" I didn't know how to do it! True story. She signs up, she buys her senior consultant kit just like I bought, 10 days go by and she's not communicating very well.

My mom says, "Hey, you got something in the mail from the bank." Her check bounced. I never got the money.

I'm talking to everyone I can as raw as I am. I'm talking to people off the newspaper ad. I call this guy named Joe, I remember his name to this day. "Hi, Joe. My name's Dan. You're looking for an opportunity? I can help you."

Long story short, I signed him up, he's absolutely fired up beyond belief, writes me a check, senior consultant kit, check bounces. I never got the money from either one of them. Tough start.

I didn't have a lot of money, but I went to another training class where Larry showed up at the Red Lion Inn in Bellevue. There were like 300 people there, and again, it was just the reaffirmation of the principles from *The Millionaire Training* cassettes as well as a real-life experience where I had guests in the room. My distributorship was starting. I can't remember if my mom was there, but I know my grandpa was there, my cousins, my uncles, strangers, you name it. I was just doing everything I could.

It was a riveting process. Larry will appreciate this because he'll know. He probably can remember how immature I was. It took me seven years before I got this stuff. Personal development is personal, and everybody comes in at a different level. I would've been diagnosed with ADD or ADHD or one of those things back in the day. I probably had a learning disorder, but I didn't know it. I just remember I was not smart when it came to books, but I loved people.

Larry likes to refer to these things as concepts, right? I always use the word principles. He and I have talked about this before. A principle is a strong channel that moves you forward. PRIN is strong channel, PLE moving you forward. When you think about the concepts that he taught in *The Millionaire Training*, they're universal principles that are timeless.

When I look at that period of time, I was just a young man. Larry was so good at every aspect of what his mentors taught him of breaking it down, simplifying it. The great thing is, I have done a training show for the last 18 years and I teach this stuff every day of my life.

When a distributor calls me today, and they want to talk about why they're not where they want to be, I point to those principles. There's nothing outside of it. There are new shiny objects, but there's only one shiny object that Larry taught me, and that is we get paid to recruit and sell. What do I do every day? I recruit and sell. In my company, with my product, my compensation plan, it has incentives on how you recruit and how you sell. Back in 1982, it was a little bit different, right? We had different retail markup, different product, different compensation plan. We didn't have the internet or a Zoom meeting like we do today, but every single day, 38 years later, I still teach the same thing.

February 1983, I received a compensation check for one penny. I've kept it all these years. Now, that was signed by our old friend Ed Williams, just after I started. Remember Marilyn? The first distributor in Canada? She and I were married only 10 months after meeting. I always tell people it's a good thing to marry your upline, especially three up.

Marilyn documented our career in a book several years ago about our journey in Herbalife. She documented everything, from her application, to her status of Supervisor, to her first $20,000 check, to the articles being written about her, letters from Larry and Mark, being invited to the first corporate school of all time.

When Canada was just blowing up, and she was pictured in the *Alberta Report*. They had Mark in there and they had my wife in there, being the first distributor in Alberta. Now, we go to Mark's house and we have parties, and we got Millionaire Team people, and we received one of the first small trips to Hawaii through a Western Union Mailgram congratulating us on your outstanding achievement. There's gold in them herbs!

I grew up driving a 1967 GS 400, a Buick convertible. I always loved cars, but I never knew they made cars like Larry was driving. Here's a picture of Larry and me and Larry Shine, we all had the same car in 1984. It was all because of what Larry did, and this is a 1984 SEC, and there's Larry right outside the Sheraton La Reina. Larry, Larry, and me, all with the same car.

I remember him taking me for a drive in his, and he gunned it a little bit going between one of the roads there at Century Boulevard, and he kind of hit the front end, it was so low to the ground, it was unbelievable. Here I am, 22 years old, driving a 1984AMG SEC. It's one of the coolest cars I ever had.

I might have, yeah. Needless to say, when you learn the principles and they become part of you, and you accept the fact that you are a network marketer, and I recruit and sell everyday everywhere I go. There's been people here at my house this week who I'm recruiting. There's been people here at my house this week that I'm selling product to. There's people in the community that I talk to. I do this every day, this is what I do, it's what I believe in, and it's what I know how to do. It's fun for me.

After the Herbalife fiasco with the FTC and the FDA, it was a rough time for a lot of people. I had a friend of mine who had a direct mail business. I said, "Why don't we try this?" It was another network marketing company. I was able to take all of these principles, these concepts, and wrap it around leading an organization, and teaching other people how to make recruiting and selling the most important part of what you get paid to do.

In only three years, I became the number one distributor for that company which was based in southern California. In 2002, I decided to launch a new technology with a billion-dollar player that's a New York Stock Exchange company, which company I'm with today, Nu Skin Enterprises. We launched a biophotonic scanner, and again, the same concepts. I got started in 2002 and 90 days in, I was teaching *The Millionaire Training* to the entire globe. Back then, it was all on a conference call bridge, and then it went to blog talk radio, and now I do everything on Facebook. Facebook Live is how I do my trainings every Saturday now, at 8:00 AM Pacific time every single Saturday for 18 years now.

It never leaves me. I think about it all the time. How do I better communicate the art that Larry and Jim were so masterful at?

There was a magic when Mark, Larry and Jim Rohn were together. They grew up together; when Larry said something, Jim could finish the sentence. Jim could say something, Larry could finish the sentence. We were at a meeting in Bermuda.

There was a magic at this meeting, and it was transforming for me. I knew I wasn't very good at many things, but I knew I was good enough not to quit, and I knew I was good enough that I could keep dialing every single day. I was a madman on the phones, and Jim said something that I will never forget that I still teach to this day. I still gauge my downline on how they do this to this day, and where Jim and Larry came up with this, I don't know.

Every month we had printouts that were hundreds of pages long with our Supervisors and their phone numbers that were mailed to us. Jim said something sitting in Bermuda, "What would happen to your life and your downline if all you did was call five people a day in your group that you had not met?"

I will never forget a year or two later, when Larry Shine (who my wife sponsored off an ad in the newspaper) was number one in the company in 90 days. Larry Shine called me because he was the man. I called him, The Goat. Larry Shine was the fastest growing distributor ever when he started. One day he called me, and he said, "How do you do that? How is it that I just talk to someone on my downline and they feel so good because you've already called them?"

Larry Thompson taught us. You call with two points: first, make them feel good about you, and second, make them feel good about Herbalife. How do you do that? By telling stories. I could be good at that. I just knew that if I called and called and called, and I told them about me, and I said two things, "How can I help you? How can Herbalife help you?" and by telling stories that would make a tremendous difference in my business. To me, that was a really significant Millionaire Training moment in Bermuda.

Larry learned his strategy from Bobby DePew and he learned his philosophical approach from Jim Rohn. Recently, I was talking to one of the women I sponsored, and I said, "Look, you deserve to be making X amount of dollars a month," and it blew her away. I said, "You just need to be at the right place at the right time with the right people."

Literally last month, I remember asking her, and I said, "How did you find them?" She said, "Well, I was just doing a Dan McCormick." I said, "What's that?" She said, "Well, you always used to say, you just keep calling and make them feel good about you and make them feel good about your company. I found a distributor who found a distributor who found a distributor, and I did a Dan McCormick. I found them that way, because I called five people a day that I don't know."

Obviously, I let her know where I learned that. I always give credit to all of those inspirational voices from the day I listened to *The Millionaire Training* forward. I still talk about it all the time. How can you not? First of all, I think that Larry has shared with me the entire lineage of who taught who and what they taught. All the way back into the '60's. I love history, and I like to study great people. It's just part of the journey of recognizing that great people figure things out, and they're humble enough to share it.

These principles that I've learned are life skills. My wife and I have been married 37 years. At the end of the day, one of my great mentors who was an iconic insurance agent from 1928 to 1968, and he wrote 33 books in his life, and he chronicled every aspect of how he trained his insurance team. One day while he was on stage, somebody asked, "How do I have a better year next year?"

His answer was, "Be a better person." At the end of the day, if you're going to be proactive in your business, hopefully those translate to your relationships.

I want to say this as candidly as I can. My relationships are real. I have thousands of people in my phone. To this day, when I'm driving down the road, I hit my contacts tab, I tap on a letter, and if I haven't talked to that person in a year or two, I call them, because that's what friendships are. If you're a friend and you're in my phone as a contact, and I don't talk to you, why are you in my phone?

The other day I called a guy, "Mike, how are you doing?" He was a huge success in my downline years ago. "Mike, how you doing? I got a rule, your name's in my phone, I haven't talked to you in a while. If you're going to be a friend in my phone, I got to reach out."

He said, "Wow. You're a better friend than I am."

We are fostering relationships with people who we have things in common. We want to make people's lives better every single day. What Larry taught me was this: We're looking for dissatisfied people. When I sponsored my daughter a couple years ago, because social media was easy for her, it worked for her. Nu Skin became okay for her. But to do it through the phone the Dan McCormick way or the Larry Thompson way, it wasn't okay.

It changed, and so that's why you're genuine and you're authentic and you're looking for dissatisfied people. When technologies change, when a new product shows up, it's always a reason to call somebody again. That's what genuine authentic friends do.

"How are you? How is your family? How is your job? How is your career? Oh, by the way, who do you know who might have an interest in social media?" What Larry and I do is not old school. We have got all the tools and even more some.

I personally don't like the side hustle terminology. I don't like the gig economy. I get it. Everybody tries to change terminology. I love Larry's terminology. In the '60's it was pyramid marketing. In the '70's it was multilevel marketing, and then it became network marketing. At the end of the day, I recruit and sell. I don't care how I recruit and sell; I recruit and sell. You want to recruit and sell online? Recruit and sell online. You want to recruit and sell in a meeting in a hotel room? Recruit and sell in a meeting in a hotel room. I just had 1,200 people at a meeting in Austria last month for one of my team members, all in one meeting room.

It's just different for everybody, but I recruit and sell. However, you want to word that, new school, old school, millennials, whatever, I recruit and sell.

There are so many people who are so busy doing so many other things that they're not doing the thing that they need to do the most. Recruit and sell. They're so busy trying to market and trying to figure out this and that and make it simple. They are asking themselves, *How can I do it faster, quicker, better?* They really are not doing the one thing that's going to build and grow their business – talking to people. I'm still doing it every single day.

I want to share another story about Larry that I will never forget. We're at this event, and we've got an upcoming event happening in LA. A distributor is arguing with Larry on whether he has time to come to the event. I'm a young 20-year-old kid sitting there. My wife and I have a grand team, we're doing just fine. I'm all in, and Larry's like, "You got to be at the event. You got to recruit and sell into the event."

What Larry taught me that night was the absolute clear importance that this is an event driven business. The cycles of that have never changed. We always are driving towards events, because leaders are born at events, and I always say in my company with our title, Blue Diamonds come in pairs, Team Elites come in triplets. You have got to be at the event.

I grasped early on that the cyclical nature of our business never stops. It's the pre-promotion, it's the event, it's the post follow-up, and I teach that vigorously every single day.

In this business you have got to have your why. For me, it was clear. I didn't have a great upbringing, I didn't have a family and I wanted one, so I knew what my why was – my wife. I wanted to be married young. I wanted a family. I didn't have a dad who wanted to be with his kids. I wanted to be a dad who wanted to be with his kids. I yearned for that.

Whatever your why is, it's genuine, authentic, real you. This book that you're reading, you're likely going to have read it many times. You're going to have dog eared corners, you're going to have highlights, you're going to have notes, and you're going to probably align yourself with your upline in your company because people from every company are going to read this book.

You've got to know what your system is, and you got to know what your recognition is, you have got to know what your event cycle is, and you got to know what the principles of your business are, and that's what you're going to learn.

You're going to learn the macro principles and concepts from Larry and the people in this book; they're going to be riveting, that'll never change for anybody and will work for you, even if you are brand new person or you've been in the business for years. No matter what the economy is doing, no matter your economy, where you're at, it will work. We've never had a bear market in the world of weight loss, nutrition, and anti-aging. There's never been a bear market for opportunity in innovation.

If you're reading this for the first time, you're going to take this book and you're going to see. You're not going to read this book, because that's what you do with a magazine. It's casual reading, it's garbage. You're going to study this book. There's a difference.

I didn't just listen to *The Millionaire Training*. I studied and dissected *The Millionaire Training*. I didn't try to be a network marketer; I had to become the person who was comfortable in every scenario, even to this day, sitting around the table with extremely affluent, iconic people, and they say, "What do you do?" I say my spiel (whatever my spiel is at the time). I love it, I live it, and just like the brand-new person can who is reading this book.

At the end of the day, here's what I'm most excited about (Jim Rohn taught me this with Larry on stage). What I'm most excited about is me, and how much more I can grow. I think about how many more people are out there on my path who I haven't even met yet, who I could teach these principles to, that'll be life changing generationally for them and their family.

If you are in this business to make a million dollars so you can set sail, then do that. I have made millions of dollars in network marketing. I do this because I love it. I love the people. I love the process. I love the journey. Doesn't mean it's easy. Doesn't mean there are not frustrations, setbacks, disappointments, and huge uh-oh's, right? But you bounce back and you realize, *Hey, you know what? Not everybody's going to see it my way, but I only need to find one new person this year who does.* This guy just out of the blue called me two months ago. He says, "I'm going to fly out there and meet with you, and you're going to be my sponsor at Nu Skin."

"Nah, nah, nah, you don't need to do that. Let's just get on a Zoom call, we'll chit chat, we'll figure this out." I can't find the guy on social media, I don't know who he is, we have one mutual friend. The mutual friend that we know didn't know him.

A couple weeks later he says, "Hey look, I got a ticket." This is a 56-year-old businessman in the Midwest who says I'm his sponsor, he picks me.

I'm like, "No, no, Ed, don't do this. That's a waste of money."

"I already bought my ticket. What time tomorrow? I'm buying dinner for you and me at The Pier in San Clemente."

"Okay, I'll see you at 5:00."

Long story short, he signed up. He's already producing, he's already got appointments, he's calling people every day. Look, how many more people are out there like that? He's looking to solve a problem. He's at the end of the runway for his career. He needs network marketing; he needs a residual income that'll pay him for a lifetime.

Dan Stammen
Co-owner WorldVentures Holdings

 I grew up in a large family with five sisters and no brothers. I was the kid in junior high and high school, who, when asked to give oral book report presentations, was too shy and nervous. I either managed a way to be "sick" on my day to speak or just took the zero. Even though I disliked speaking in front of people at that age, I was always a budding entrepreneur and did okay in one on one situations. *The lesson may be, find your strength and capitalize on it.* Because my parents had no money to give any of their six kids at age 10, I was selling hard candy at school to have a few dollars in my pocket. After that, I had a paper route for a few years. Then, starting in ninth grade, I had a full-time job working 40 hours a week stocking shelves and bagging groceries. I'd head straight from school to the grocery store where I worked four nights a week from 2-10 pm then all day Saturday. When other kids were home studying or at baseball practice, I was working.

I met Jeff Roberti, for the first time at Boy's Club when I was in fifth grade. We went on to become good friends after reconnecting in Jr High School. The two of us were always plotting ways to get rich. In high school, we both worked at the grocery store plus would host parties and charge money to attend. We also worked as security guards, did telemarketing etc. After high school, we both went to community college and stayed there for a couple of years.

However, I was frustrated with school and was always a C student. Things changed for me the day I walked into the local hardware store. I was working on my Ford Mustang and needed to buy some spray paint for the dashboard that was rusting out. Truth be told, I was also there to ask out the cashier who worked behind the counter.

Next thing I know, I'm standing in line, and there's a guy next to me named Stan wearing an Herbalife button that said, LOSE WEIGHT NOW, ASK ME HOW!

I looked at him and said, "What's that button? What are you selling?" He starts talking to me a hundred miles a minute and replies that he forgot he was even wearing it. His wife had made him put it on before he walked out the door. He explains that he doesn't know much about it, but that it's a new nutrition company in town. He was so excited that he followed me out to my car to keep chatting.

I finally said, "Well, here's my number. Have your wife call me." His wife ends up calling me and invites me to an opportunity meeting at a Holiday Inn Hotel in Sarasota, Florida.

I attend the presentation and end up meeting several notable people in the Herbalife world at the time, including one average guy with an above average income named Jim Fobair. He told me that prior to joining Herbalife, he was earning $1,000 a month selling mattresses in a furniture store and now because of the Herbalife opportunity he was earning over $13,000 per month after less than one year. And he attributed all his success because he was following Larry's duplicable system. After I signed up to be a distributor, I was invited to hear one of the vice presidents of Herbalife come to speak at the Van Wezel Performing Arts Hall. I was piddling around with Herbalife, but decided to attend, and brought my friend, Jeff Roberti, along with me to this big training.

Very few experiences in my life have measured up to that day of training with Larry. I had never been to a presentation with 600 people in one room. Maybe it was the way Larry taught on stage, but it sent a shockwave through me for whatever reason. Many of the points he made that night were from *The Millionaire Training* tapes. These were simple things, but they made an impact. Statements like, "Look at your life and see how it's going." "For things to get better, you've got to get better. For things to change, you've got to change." Those concepts just spoke to me.

The testimonials that night made a significant impact as well. I heard from people like Jeff Schlegel who was making over $15,000 a month and multiple others. It got me thinking, *these people put on their pants the same way I do.* The only difference is they've been in this business longer than Jeff and me. We both took to the idea of having a team of people that possessed more contacts, credibility, money, and knowledge than we had. And if we could get these people working for us in order to create leverage in the marketplace…we knew we hit a gold mind. Please know this for a fact that everyone at Sarasota High where Jeff and I went to school thought that Roberti and I were a couple of the two biggest knuckleheads to come out of the class of 1980. So, if we were going to make it big in anything it was going to be a big surprise to everyone.

Back to Larry. That same night he talked about the best way to get ahead was to build momentum. We saw his vision for momentum and went to work. I already knew how to work hard, so now it was just a matter of putting on my blinders, getting focused, eliminating any lame excuses and going after it. I worked for months straight, seven days a week, sometimes 18 hours a day. I didn't take time off to go to the beach or catch a movie. My goal was just to build, recruit, sponsor, train, and repeat. It's one thing to see an opportunity and a completely different thing to recognize it and be willing to roll up your sleeves and go to work. Jeff and I had hit Herbalife at the right time during their first wave of success. They had just hit $58 Million that year, and we got a glimpse of what could happen. We understood that we were leveraging the earning power of many, instead of only one person, and ended up with thousands of distributors in 38 states.

However, at this time, a lot of my friends and family still doubted me. I can remember a time right before I got to attend Herbalife's International Corporate School in Sydney Australia, where I was at my parent's house picking up my mail. My five sisters, Mom, Dad, and my Uncle Marv were all over there. My uncle was the president of three banks in Ohio and was making a respectable $63,000 a year back in 1985. My Dad was making $18,000 a year fixing pumps and motors. My Mom is flipping through the mail and tells me something had arrived for me from Herbalife. I ripped open the envelope, and it's was a check for over $10,000.00. Which I didn't exactly hide from plain sight being somewhat a confident young man at that point. My uncle looks at me and says, "Why's the check so big do they just pay you once a year?" I go on to inform him that, "Nope, that's for just this month." Then I said, "I hate to eat and run but I'm flying over to Sydney in the morning with about 500 of my best friends, so I need to pack."

That got all my non-believing family members thinking, "What the hell?" It was moments like that that made me realize I had learned a new skill set, just like Larry always talked about. Larry often taught that in this business, we were getting paid exactly what we're worth. If I wanted to get paid more, I needed to become more valuable to the marketplace. I didn't feel I was bringing much value, yet I had a team selling close to half a million dollars a month in nutrition products, which wasn't too bad for a 23-year-old.

After learning those skills from Larry, Jeff and I decided to dial things up a notch. We became good at recruiting. Everybody has the same 24 hours in a day, and you have to consider who would impact your business the most? The guy who manages a grocery store, or the guy who's in real estate and has 47 agents selling for him? If I get the real-estate guy going part-time, I'm probably going to get more results. So, we learned to recruit up, manage our time, and advertise in a big way. Don't get me wrong as I'm still going to recruit the store manager because you never know who's going to fire up your business. In addition, I got really good at recruiting top level talent. My philosophy was to recruit the best and they would enroll the rest.

At this time, Herbalife had two corporate schools. A basic corporate school and an international corporate school. To attend the basic school, you had to have a royalty override monthly check of $4,000 or more. At the peak of Corporate School, the company had about 1,100 people reach those levels. We had a lot of people making good money with this company. Once you qualified, Herbalife would pay for your airline ticket to fly out to the next big training event. Places like Chicago, Monterey, and Atlanta.

I learned from Larry that these corporate training events were a great time & place to recruit new people. I would sometimes fly out two weeks in advance, simultaneously running ads, hosting four to five opportunity meetings a day, and training as many people as possible. The thought being, was to get all my new enrollments recruiting and to have them bring guests to the big central meeting because all the corporate school leaders would be speaking. At those meetings, there were usually 2,000-4,000 people in attendance, and our sign-up rate would be almost 100% because the testimonials were so powerful causing everyone to enroll.

There was one time at the Arie Crown Theater in Chicago, where I had 23 guests sitting with me in the front row. After the testimonials, I looked at my guests and said to them (with a smile) and somewhat in joking manner the last thing you ever want to say to a new guest, "You don't want to do this, do you?" At that point because the meeting went so well all 23 of them said yes and the enrollment started. We learned to chase the momentum and go into areas before the big meetings to increase our odds of getting people enrolled with Herbalife.

The skills I learned during this time were invaluable, which served us greatly when Herbalife went through their challenges. The FDA and Herbalife had what ended up being unfounded legal battles which led to the business almost failing. It felt like a planned attack by the news media, FDA, and the Senate. Herbalife's sales had been soaring before the investigation. Prior to the investigation, sales went up from roughly $30 Million a month to $90 Million within six months. We were helping people get healthy and earn money; then all of a sudden, it felt like we were under attack.

My checks from Herbalife peaked out at $18,000 a month then went down to $2,000 a month fairly quickly after the attack. I ended up spending almost all the cash I had in the bank, trying to build my business back up. We were continually running ads and talking to people on the phone. I'd get 25 people to agree to appointments, then CNN or some other news network would run a negative story, and I'd have people calling to cancel or just not show up at all. Or I would manage to get someone to enroll, and then they would quit the next day because of too much negative publicity. During this time, I made a big mistake by leaving Herbalife and switching to another company called United Sciences of America. I came up with a long-term game plan and was able to have some people who were already planning on leaving Herbalife join my team. I went from zero enrollees to $15,000 per month in income in a fairly short time frame, but within nine months, that company had gone under.

After that, I bounced around for six or seven years working for other network marketing businesses. At one point, I even partnered up and owned part of a water filtration business called The Entrepreneur Network, but nothing seemed to stick. I was finally able to gain some traction with a consumer electronics company and able to build a large team over three-and-a-half years and earned over 2 million dollars. My sponsor that enrolled me was a good friend from Sarasota FL (a guy I actually introduced to network marketing previously) Mr. Harris Williams. And my number one sales rep by far in the electronics company was no other than Jay Bennett.

The one main thing I realize with all the ups and downs is that everything good and bad happens for a reason. Both the good and bad times gave me the experience and knowledge to grow mentally and emotionally. I learned my most valuable skills from Larry during my time at Herbalife and was able to take them with me everywhere I went and be successful, even if only for the short time each company was around. I appreciate the fact I was able to go to a new business and immediately knew exactly what to do, where to go and what to say to become successful. It's as if you could drop me (or any of Larry's top students) out of an airplane with a parachute & backpack and because the skills had become innate we would become successful.

Before founding my current enterprise, WorldVentures, I had built up my business at Prepaid Legal Services (now Legal Shield) to include 140,000 sales representatives and over 660,000 customers. Eventually, I was able to sell my distributorship to Paul J. Meyer, who is famous for starting the Success Motivation Institute. After selling to Paul, I semi-retired from network marketing but only for 6 months before my partner Wayne Nugent and I launched WorldVentures. WorldVentures the premiere travel club now has over $4.5 Billion in combined revenue, and is currently operating in 42 different countries. When I think of the success we've had and the leaders on our team it safe to say a lot of them either received their training directly or indirectly from the principles Larry taught years ago.

And when I think back even farther to my early Herbalife days and the long-term success they've had… the following story comes to mind. Just last year I was in New York doing a training with 500 leaders for WorldVentures. In the slide presentation, I shared my success long ago at Herbalife, plus it went into all the other businesses I had worked with whereby most of them had all gone by the wayside. In regard to Herbalife and even though they went through those tough years in the late eighties…they still had Larry Thompson's Millionaire Training fundamentals. And because of the fact that enough of their top leadership stayed intact they were able to regain their momentum by applying those fundamentals and today are a $5 Billion a year company. Some of my close friends stayed with the company during their tough times and they never gave up. And you know some of them are now earning between $50,000 and $100,000 and even up to $300,000 per month. And the best part is they've been at those very high pay levels since the mid 1990's. That's called legacy income. It often has me thinking what would have happened if I had stayed? And as I reflect back it seems that way too many network marketing beginners or professionals give up on their company way to soon when storms hit. Had I not folded my tent once the big FDA wind game blowing and left Herbalife I would have only been in one network marketing company my entire career. Wow!!!

All of these experiences have taught me many things, like keeping focused with your blinders on. Most people think the grass is greener on the other side when in reality if they would just water their own dam grass they'd be better off. Another big one is keeping your ego in check and being a constant student. Once you learn the basic skills, you then need to keep sharpening your ax. In other words, never stop learning, never stop growing. I've kept the concepts I learned from *The Millionaire Training* with me everywhere I've gone. They are timeless, and the beautiful part is you can teach those same skills to others, then those teachers become teachers. Over time, you build yourself a nice army that duplicates and turns into a large sales force.

When you first start in network marketing, it's easy to feel defeated and give up after a few failures. Most people don't understand in the beginning that success takes time and that everyone has to start from the bottom and work their way up. When you look back on some of the greats, people like Babe Ruth or Hank Aaron, for instance, you have to remember that they may have hit the most home runs, but they also struck out the most times as well.

Unfortunately, I think a lot of Millennials are given too much, too soon by their parents; they don't know how to work for what they want. Larry is always saying that if he could bottle up desire, he would be a Zillionaire because it's not something you can just put inside someone. It's only when you have a passion for something that you're willing to work for it. It creates a strong work ethic that serves your life in many areas.

For instance, if your son or daughter wants a $30,000 car, have them meet you halfway by matching them dollar for dollar with what they earn themselves. Otherwise, you're setting up your children for a system shock when they hit the real world and start a full-time job. I recently read a book that said 35% of Millennials are getting fired from their first job within 90 days. The number one reason is for repeatedly showing up late. The second reason is from being upset and constantly complaining about not getting a pay raise or promotion within those first 90 days.

I think if the younger generation could begin to find joy in setting big goals, working towards them and learn to enjoy the journey that they would be much happier & greatly rewarded. As you make your journey towards personal growth, you learn to realize that joy is in the process, not the destination. Looking back at my success, owning several homes and businesses is great, but the real fortune comes from personal development and growth. I've gotten to meet wonderful people along the way and have fun while doing it. There's a satisfaction in working hard, making mistakes, and learning from those experiences.

Having been in this business for over 37 years, I still listen to Larry's *The Millionaire Training* tapes time and time again. I often keep them on in the background as I go about my day while doing simple tasks. I love it, though, because it's almost like going back to my childhood. It feels good listening to it, and there's such a comforting familiarity, like talking with an old friend. But even though it's so familiar to me, I still take away new insights every time I listen. It's like watching a movie for the second time. There are always things you're going to pick up on the second time that you didn't catch the first time.

I love all of Larry's stories, but one of the best things I learned from Larry was the importance of your voice tone and voice fluctuation. I copied the way he talked to people, and from that, I learned how to influence people in a positive way. The way he presents is so convincing and positive. The way he delivered a message with his signature relaxed intensity you knew that he was going somewhere, and if you followed him, you're going to get what you wanted. I was able to learn that skill from him and transfer it to others. Sometimes, I'd be in a room with four or five hundred people delivering a talk or training, and most everybody after the meeting would take action. If I said, *here's a key point please write this down!* there was great comfort to watch most everyone focus their eyes down towards their paper and take copious notes on what I was saying. I learned that from Larry, the magic that draws people to you, and makes them want to follow you.

It's remarkable to think of all the companies that came out of that core group Larry taught. I could take up the next 20 pages listing top sales reps and companies that created tens of billions in revenue because of Larry. He always was delivering content at corporate school that you could write down, take to the marketplace, and make money with it. It was the notes I took from Larry that caused me to go out and build my business. Applicable concepts like employing yourself with the analogy of Larry 1 and Larry 2. Or his talk on overcoming procrastination. Or my favorite which was how to overcome all objections with the use of product & opportunity success stories. All those little things add up to make a huge difference.

Larry's teachings became especially invaluable to me after I had to become my team's trainer unexpectedly. Jeff and I would participate in the meetings and help guide them, but Jim Fobair was our head trainer who would lead our two- or four-hour Saturday sessions. He knew how to teach people where to go, what to do, and how to answer all the questions people would throw at us. He had it down to an art, but one day Jim said, "I'm out of here," and left us without a trainer. Jeff and I cancelled the next training session because we had no idea what we were doing at that point.

However, I took Jim's recording from a training session and listened to it over and over again. I actually wrote down 32 pages, word for word, front, and back. I locked myself in a friend's apartment for about 12 days and memorized the training Jim had learned from Larry. Then I got our team together and told them we were going to have a session like we usually did the next Saturday. I got up and presented this four-hour training word for word, and after that became the training guy. Jeff was great at recruiting & presenting the products and opportunity and I was doing most all the Saturday trainings. We had our system down and it worked. Jim leaving ended up being the best thing to happen to our small team because now I had the "magic talk," and my team and I were able to take our business to the next level. This incident forced us all to step up and fill his shoes to keep the business moving forward.

One of the biggest takeaways I would give someone in network marketing is to partner up with like-minded people. When I was at Prepaid Legal Services, (now Legal Shield) I was able to build 660,000 customers. I started that business initially with a company called The Peoples Network that was bought by Pre-Paid Legal. When we started, I only had a team of five representatives including myself. Our team would talk every morning, and every night we shared our trials, tribulations, and successes. We were our own little mastermind group. Within that group, some people were better at some things than others. Still, if you can develop a nucleus of just two or three committed people working the business in your city and learn to specialize in each of your skills, you're going to see more significant achievements than you would on your own.

I remember a colleague in the business, Rudolph Molnar who passed away a few years ago. Rudi was from Romania and was hard to understand because of his accent but he never let that stop him. He was never the presenter, or the guy at the front of the room during the meetings, or running the training sessions, but he always made sure to surround himself with a few people who *could* do those things. To his credit, though, what he excelled at was contacting and inviting people. He never met a stranger. He would go out on the street, to the mall or wherever and meet people. He would even test-drive automobiles just to talk with people. He got good at getting numbers and getting people excited enough so they would look at the products or business. He was able to get people to the opportunity meetings and then he let Jeff, me or a presenter do their part and get them enrolled. Rudolph was a prime example of specializing, because he understood that his domain was contacting and inviting people. Between his time at Herbalife and Juice Plus and investing funds he earned in real estate I watched him make over 5 million dollars.

If you were going to master one aspect of network marketing, it would be to know 10 different ways to contact and invite, and 10 different ways to get people to take a look at your presentation. Whether it's by phone, text message, email, social media direct messages to get someone to watch a 10-minute video or half-hour, in-person meeting, if you can get 50 people a week to look at your company vs. me only getting 10 a week, guess who is going to make more money?

Larry is always saying to "master the mundane." In network marketing, you have to remember that the money you're earning today is a direct result of what you did 90 days ago. If your check is not that much today, you didn't do much three months ago. Your pay is delayed gratification. It's all about exposure. You might think what you're doing isn't working, but next thing you know, you have someone who started two months ago somewhat slowly but all of a sudden, they bring in 30 people, and now you're reaping the profits.

If you had told me that I would be making up to $18,000 a month within my first three years at Herbalife before I turned 24 I would have told you no way, that's not going to happen to me. I didn't have the skills, money, and had very few contacts. But, I did have a burning desire and willingness to work. I was teachable and picked up quickly on how to leverage myself. You have to remember that in a way, we are overpaid grunts. I'm somewhat joking when I refer to network marketers doing grunt work. Which means to me just repeating for the most part the same presentation and activities over and over again. When you think about it you don't have to have a college degree to do this type work yet the rewards can be huge. I went to 2 years of jr. college and never got a degree. Who do you know that can contact and invite people and then press play on a video or drive somebody to a website link? All you have to do is show enough people as it's a total numbers game.

When you get sick and tired of contacting/inviting and explaining the plan and program, you keep doing it over and over again. When you don't want to talk to another person, or pick up a phone, or send a text, or meet up at Starbucks, guess what you need to do? Just keep doing it over and over and over again!

Think of it this way. If you talk to 10 people and only two join, and eight don't, but of those two people that joined you earn $300. If you divide the $300 by 10, you've still made $30 per person, whether each person bought anything or not. It's really about how fast you can present to 100 people. It allows me not to take each "no" I get to the heart. If I ask you to buy something and you turn me down, I just tell myself, *thank you for the $30*, and move on to the next person. It doesn't matter if you didn't buy anything, because due to the averages I get paid every time I share the story. And the mindset that Larry taught me got me excited about talking to strangers. I would pick up the phone and make 100 phone calls because it didn't matter whether they bought or not. Every no gets me that much closer to a yes and I never took one no personally.

When I'm presenting at a training, I ask people, "How many people here in this room are going to talk to 100 people about your product or opportunity within the next 12 months?" Everybody will raise their hand. Then I ask them, "Why wait? Why don't you contact 100 people in the next 12 days especially since you're going to do it anyway?" Collapse those time frames and do it faster, so you learn to master the mundane. Create your own mastermind group of three people – someone who can present, someone who can train, and someone good at making contacts. Then, set a goal to reach 1,000 people to look at your product and hear about your opportunity. Doing that will put your team and you on the path to results. You won't have to worry about if it's going to work or not, if you put that plan into motion.

On a similar note, let's talk about procrastination. I hear more about that than anything else in this industry. People tell me all the time how they are going to start working their business at 9:00 in the morning, or 7:00 at night, and the next thing you know, they're shuffling around papers, paying bills, reading through emails or wasting time on social media. Nothing was income producing and before you know it, an hour has gone by and it's been wasted.

Be honest with yourself. How many people did you actually talk to today about your products and opportunity? Stop putting off the real work and making excuses. Remember this important fact, this business is easier to build fast vs slow. By working hard and creating your personal momentum it will lead to team momentum, then group, area and regional momentum which is followed by large checks. Do your best to take massive action and try to replicate Larry's principles or at least what the top earners in your company are doing to get results.

I put notes all over my house with Larry's saying, "Keep the main thing, the main thing," to remind me that I needed to be presenting, recruiting, or training. Everything else was taking me off track. I knew only those three things were going to make me money. Go crank out 30 phone calls in the first two hours of your day, then load up your calendar for the afternoon or the next day. Do busy work at midnight when other people are sleeping. When I was working at Prepaid Legal Services, I had 32 people on my team who were part of the 100 calls per day club. We were making 100 outbound phone calls every day, setting up appointments for the next day or week. You don't just make a phone call and then set the phone down, then dial the next number in a half-paced fashion. It's you with a headset or ear buds on dialing number after number, without setting the phone down in between calls. Or better yet use an automatic dialing system that will dial 100 times per hour. And if you're prospecting another way whether its via social media, texting, internet ads make sure whatever you're doing... you go all in.

Most people can't keep up with that kind of intensity. My Herbalife business partner, Jeff, and I had an apartment together; I'd be in one room, and he would be in the other. We'd both be smiling and dialing all day long and all night setting up appointments and sending out packages to long-distance enrollees.

Back in the day, that meant putting together VHS tapes, product samples, with a bunch of brochures. We would send out a package to Seattle or wherever for $20 and then never knew if they got it, watched the video, or did anything with the products. Now it's so much easier. You can pick up the phone or email a link. I used to spend $20,000 a year to host one conference call a week with my team. Now anyone can use Zoom for free and host as many conference calls as they want. Things are so much easier.

When I think back on Larry's career, I'm so thankful he didn't quit even though there were several times he probably wanted to. If he had, my life would not be what it is today. Because Larry never gave up and kept learning, he's been able to affect so many people. Thanks to Larry's teaching, we've been able to put 4 million people in our business over the last 14 plus years and create over $4.5 Billion in revenue. If Larry had quit, I probably would be managing the Publix grocery store down the street. Instead, I found this business where I'm able to get paid every time hundreds of thousands of people buy or sell something. That's unfathomably awesome!

Dan Waldron
Chairman's Club,
Herbalife International

 My story starts when I was living in Houston and working a dead-end job making $7.50 an hour repairing furniture. I stumbled into Herbalife, by accident, but in reality, it wasn't an accident, but more a twist of fate. If I had walked into the library a couple of minutes later, I might not be where I am today.

One evening I was visiting the library researching possible new careers, and I look over and see a woman selling something to another woman. They exchanged money, and the customer went on her way. I've always been big on studying people and noticing things, so I went up to the woman selling and asked what she was doing. She told me she worked for Herbalife and invited me to an opportunity meeting. I go to the meeting and find out it costs $29.95 to join at the lowest level. I didn't have $29.95, so I had to wait two weeks to get some money together. At the time I was making so little money even with working full-time, I was desperate to earn some extra even if it was only $100 a month.

I save up my money and show up at the woman's house, who had invited me to the meeting and knocked on the door, ready to get my kit. I hand her my money, and she tells me it's $32.45, not $29.95 because of taxes. Honest truth, I went out to my car, got my ashtray and dumped out all the change, and counted out nickels, dimes, and pennies on that woman's kitchen table. She was just as broke as I was, so she needed the $30.45 right away. My kit arrives, and I got started on December 17, 1982. At first, I didn't do much with the package, but eventually I called my mom who lives in upstate New York and convinced my dad and her to try it. My mom ends up losing weight, and my fad loses weight, and now they're telling everyone in my big Italian family about how great this Herbalife stuff is. I'm sending them tons of products and making some great part-time money while I continuing to work at the furniture repair business.

When my kit first arrives, I was still living in Houston but was about to move to Austin to go to school. That's the real reason why I needed to earn the extra money so that I could attend community college. I had a buddy who lived in Austin who coached athletes, and I wanted to do the same thing, but I needed a degree for that. Herbalife felt like the perfect opportunity to make those dreams happen. I remember the kit came with a little button that said, LOSE WEIGHT NOW, ASK ME HOW! I called up Sandy, the woman who signed me up, and asked her, "What do I do with this?"

She told me, "Put it on, go walk around somewhere, and somebody will ask you about it." I was so naive and clueless. I put on the button, went into a grocery store, and started walking up and down the aisles just looking at people. I wasn't asking them anything.

I called Sandy back up and told her, "Nobody asked me about my button."

She said, "Did you say, 'Hi' or talk to anyone at all?"

"No."

It just goes to show you, I had no business mind at all during this time. Eventually, someone did ask me about the button – a girl in one of my college classes looked at my button and said, "How did you lose weight?" I had no idea what to tell her. I just started talking and showed her the little catalog, which at the time was only four pages. She looked through it and starts telling me all the things she'd like to order. I'm flipping out, and then I'm thinking, *I don't have any product to give her.* She circles everything she wants and then hands me a check for $109. I called Sandy again, and she tells me to go cash the check and then she sends me the products from a Greyhound bus in Houston. I pick up the order from the bus station in downtown Austin and bring it over to the girl. She ends up loving the products and tells her girlfriends all about it.

I was running these little bags of orders all over campus. One day, my anatomy and physiology professor asked me what I was doing. At this point, I had a plan, and I was starting to learn some stuff, so I tell her, "Oh, I'm helping people lose weight with these products." She ends up ordering $400 worth of items, and I'm so excited.

My parents continue to use the products, and friends and family are ordering so much, I eventually tell them they need to sign up themselves and become distributors because I'm in school. I can't keep shipping products up there all the time to New York. Things were getting out of control, so I told them they needed to order from Herbalife directly. Now things are rocking and rolling along. My royalties go from $2,000 a month to $5,000, and at the time, my expenses were minimal. I was rooming with a friend, and $500 a month was all I needed to pay my bills.

Larry and Mark would often tell us to bank our money and live off our retail and wholesale business, so I did just that. When I got those royalty checks, I put them in the bank. I would pay my taxes, but I wouldn't spend any of the money I earned. I never went out and bought a new car or new stuff. I just continued to live modestly. After graduating from college in 1986, I decided I didn't want to be a coach at that time and decided I wanted to keep going with Herbalife instead.

Unfortunately, that's around the time that Herbalife went through its controversy. I loved Herbalife and wanted to stay with it even though times were challenging. That's when Larry's *The Millionaire Training* saved me. It helped give me the basics and skills I needed. When I was in college, I was only able to attend a training here or there. I'd take a few notes, but I wasn't a student of network marketing because money was coming in so easily for me at first. I had a good team going with my family up in New York, and I was really coasting. Then 1986 begins, and it all starts going away.

Now, I was hearing *The Millionaire Training* differently. It's no longer that everybody wants the products and shows up to your meetings. Now, it's actual work. It was then that I began to understand the concept of employing yourself and how you can have diseases of attitude and procrastination. It's knowing you have to call and talk to 10 people every day, not eight. Ten.

If you've only spoken to eight people in a day, you have to get back out there that night and talk to two more people. You aren't going to sleep anyway, because you can't sleep because you just feel terrible that you didn't do your job. It was those messages from the tapes that helped me when adversity came.

Finally, around 1991, things began to turn around for Herbalife after launching a couple of new products. To think if I hadn't done what Mark and Larry said and put my money in the bank, I wouldn't have been able to stick it out with Herbalife and probably would have left as so many did in 1986. People then were so mad and dropped out because they couldn't make a living, but what they failed to mention was Larry telling them to save their money.

They went out and bought a new house or a new car, so when Herbalife wasn't paying as much, they had to find something else. So through those lean years, I was able to make it through by taking out a $100 or so if I was short one month on my expenses. At this time, I was still living on retail and wholesale, but I had that money in the bank to get me through when everybody else had to get a job. Thankfully, I lived modestly and didn't have any debt. I was driving the same car I had started with, which at that point had 150,000 miles on it. My royalty checks went down from $5,000 a month to $300 a month.

Because I lived within my means, I was able to keep going, and when things finally turned around in 1991, I qualified for the Global Expansion Team. Then in 1995, I made the President's Team. All this happened within three-and-a-half years. During this time, I was often reminded of Larry's analogy about our mind being a projector. He would often talk about that if the film in our projector is negative, failure is going to show up, so what are you thinking about? On the days when I was down and out, I would remind myself of that fact.

I knew this story so well from listening to his tapes over and over that I could recite it in my mind. I would tell myself I had a negative film projector going and I needed to change the film. I would snap myself out of it, and then go out to the marketplace or wherever with a smile on my face. I'd ask people how they were doing, and hand out catalogs in front of the H.E.B. grocery story in Austin. Some days it would be pouring rain, and I would still be out there talking to people, even if I got no response. I just knew I had to speak with 10 people each day, and I kept doing it.

There's no question that Larry's concept of talking with 10 people a day was vital. I was not going to let my team or myself have a negative film projector or a disease of attitude. Things are going to grow no matter what, so you have to eliminate what's bad. To take care of a rose bush, you have to water it, and you don't allow the weeds of negativity to grow. Those concepts have never left me, even 37 years later.

I relied so much on Larry's teachings during this time of transition at Herbalife. Larry would often come to Dallas to lead trainings, and if I knew he was coming, I would drive my old beat-up car three-and-a-half hours to listen to a two-hour training. I'd take my notes, drive back to Austin, and hold my own meeting where maybe three people would show up, but I would just go after it and teach those three people.

In August of 1991, I was still only making $300 a month, and I kept thinking, *When is it going to happen for me? I don't know how much longer I can go on like this.* That was my time of questioning, but I never applied for another job or went on any interviews. I never missed a meeting. I presented every Tuesday, Thursday, and Saturday. I even did a session on Christmas Eve because it fell on a Saturday. Everyone on my team was telling me we can't do a meeting then because it's Christmas Eve, and I simply said to them, "No, it's not

Christmas Eve. It's Saturday, and we do meetings Tuesday, Thursday, Saturday."

It was a huge turning point for me because I ended up recruiting a Supervisor from that meeting. He ended up qualifying with a volume of 7,500 in December, and we go to attend the annual party at Mark Hughes's house. It ended up being my biggest month of the year, where I had a personal volume of almost $15,000.

Finally, one year later, I make the Millionaire Team and a few years after that The President's Team.

Larry ended up leaving Herbalife in December of 1992, and I'll never forget his last training in Dallas. It was probably one of the greatest meetings he's ever done in his life. I still remember where it was. I have a picture from that day, walking across that stage. January 1993 was challenging for my team and me. Larry was our trainer, and it was challenging to lose him, but we kept moving forward just the way he would have wanted us to. Every time someone enrolled on my team, I would give them *The Millionaire Training* even though they weren't included in the distributor kits anymore.

Larry's legacy continues to live on even in my own family. My son is an Herbalife distributor as well and is currently working on his third diamond and has a massive organization underneath him. I taught him all of Larry's concepts because they are timeless and will never go away. Initially, my son didn't know what he wanted to do with his life. He tried different jobs, working as a waiter, folding shirts in a retail store, taking some college courses, that kind of thing. I didn't want to push him into Herbalife. Finally, he came to me and told me he wanted to do Herbalife and opened up his own nutrition club in February 2008 using the principles from

Larry that I taught him. Within three-and-a-half years he had made the President's Team.

I have compassion for those getting started in network marketing today. It's easy to get bombarded with social media and technology. It can be a tremendous blessing, but it can be a curse as well. It can be hard to stay focused when you're continually sending tweets or scrolling through pictures on your cell phone.

When I began in this industry, there wasn't as much confusion. We had to visit with 10 people and tell them about the products. We knew we needed to do an opportunity meeting every Tuesday, Thursday, Saturday, and run ads in the newspaper. It was a job where we knew we had to fulfill what's in this box to get the job done. It wasn't hard to do those things, but it was mentally taxing because you had to see people you didn't know and talk to people on the phone. It was a simpler life we led, and there wasn't as much confusion.

Today it's more challenging because there are so many things competing for your attention. There are so many things bombarding the minds of the youth, and I think they're stressed. I don't think they need to be on social media for three or four hours a day when they could go out and communicate with people in person. I would encourage young people that if they find something, they are passionate about, don't quit. Just stay with it.

If I had given up during the seven years of famine at Herbalife, where would I be today? You have to remain persistent and consistent, be relentless, and stay for the long haul. I think so many people today want fast results, but you have to be willing to endure the time because time brings wisdom. You're not going to get everything your first year, second year, or even third year. However, if you work with the same company for 30 years at the end of it, you'll have a chunk of change for your retirement if you can work hard, like what you're doing, and believe in the product you have.

I'm thankful for the principles and concepts Larry gave me because it would have been impossible for me to endure 1991 if it wasn't for him. My Dad was a laborer, he didn't have any wisdom about owning a business, and I didn't have any mentors. *The Millionaire Training* gave me strength. I needed somebody reliable with the belief to encourage me along, and Larry gave me that. Larry believed that all of us could do it and was relentless in his drive to go, go, go. I needed that because I have a strong personality. I can't have somebody up there on stage telling me to just kind of hang in there. I appreciate Larry's strength and power. I'm sure there were times during the 1980s when he went home and wondered what the crap was going on, but I never once saw him waver in his form or attitude. If he had, we would have smelt it and felt it.

During Herbalife's fights with the F.T.C. in 2016 and all the things we had to go through, I knew I needed to be a pillar of strength for my team. I was always checking in on my people asking how everybody was doing because that's what Larry did.

He always said, "Listen, you aren't going to find out who you are in times of greatness when everything is good." I knew during those hard times of adversity and problems I was showing my team either strength or insecurity, and I chose strength. I have such gratitude to Larry and the fortitude he showed us during his 13 years at Herbalife. It changed all our lives, and it still does. His principles have never left us.

Ray Higdon
Founder, Rank Makers

 If someone handed out badges for being Larry Thompson's number one fan, I'd be the first in line. I can't think of anyone else who has added as much value to this industry as Larry has. It's an honor to be a forever student of his, and that I'm able to call him a friend.

I was in real estate until the housing crisis hit, and I lost everything. I was a million dollars in debt. My house was in foreclosure, I was going through a divorce, and I was sleeping on my buddy's couch. I found my way into network marketing and went on to do very well.

At the time I met Larry and Taylor, to be honest, I hadn't been a great student of network marketing. I hadn't even heard of Jim Rohn. I know it probably sounds strange for long-time networkers to hear, but I hadn't. And, I was the #1 income earner and doing a lot of training for my company.

I remember going to Larry and I'm like, "Hey man, you know, have you seen any of my training?"

Larry's like, "Yeah, yeah."

So, I ask him, "Well, what do you think of it?"

He said, "You know what? It's really good for you and about 5% of your team."

I'm thinking, I don't know what he means. I was confused at first. Like, I don't understand. Is he saying it's too complicated?

That really messed me up because it was feedback I hadn't received before. But, let me tell you something. The most valuable thing that you can get as an entrepreneur (or as someone who wants to improve) is candid feedback. And, it's so hard to do, because everyone wants a pat on the back because that's a lot easier. It's a lot easier to say, "Good job up there."

You have to have some gumption to give someone candid feedback. And that's what Larry gave me, and that's such a precious gift.

One of the most significant pillars in network marketing training is Larry's 80-15-5 model, which is now referred to as The Thompson Rule. It goes like this…80% of people have a level of desire to earn $0 to $500 a month, 15% of people have a level of desire to earn between $2,000 and $3,000 a month, but only 5% have a level of desire to earn $25,000 or more a month.

When Larry and Taylor taught me this, it just made a lot of sense. It has got to be the largest pillar in your network marketing training. It is so important, and it's been so lost. If I look at other trainers and even top leaders, they don't get it.

They think it's about aggression. They think it's about intensity. They think it's about getting a check in the hand of every person as soon as humanly possible; that intensity is just chasing people away.

The essence of network marketing is having a good culture. It's about making people feel good regardless of the level of their desire or result. All of that I learned from Larry. The core essence of understanding the different levels of desire is the training that people need in network marketing because with that training, you can filter through everything else that you do.

I'll tell you, every time I listen to Larry and Taylor, I have a new takeaway. If I'm at an event and Larry and Taylor are speaking, I make a point to be in that room.

With Larry, I'm just so grateful. Through that understanding of 80-15-5 and the concepts he has taught over the last 50+ years, we've been able to help a lot of people. It's one of the core things I teach my people and if we are speaking at a company event, we are edifying Larry and Taylor and bringing that up.

After being in network marketing for over a decade now, as both a student and teacher, I've learned two big lessons. One is, despite the wisdom of Scarface, you can get high on your own supply. If you're a six-figure earner, you can feel like you're on top of the world and that you're the best there is.

The second lesson I've discovered is, understand the difference between hearing something and executing it. You hear something, and you think you know it, but you don't know something until you've actually gone out and implemented the thing you were told to do. Some people see being a student as an accumulation of knowledge. That mindset may help you win on *Jeopardy!*, but in reality, no one is quizzing you on facts. This is a doing, take action kind of business.

I'm not interested in the accumulation of knowledge. Most people get stuck in learn mode, but never do anything with it. They don't teach it, share it, implement it, or execute it, and that's a problem. That's not a problem for someone else, that's a problem for them.

Not everyone is a five-percenter and you should be ok with that. It's better to absorb and accept that fact. Larry always says, "The check doesn't make you a leader. A leader is determined by what you're doing TODAY."

I'm sure there have been many times over the last five decades when Larry didn't feel like sharing his knowledge or he felt like doing something else. There are lots of people who have vast expertise, but they go elsewhere and stop sharing. I'm grateful Larry kept giving of his wisdom. With his talent, he could do anything that he wants, but I'm thankful he's remained a mentor and a coach with a massively positive impact on all of us, whether it is directly or indirectly.

When it comes to network marketing, there is one person I've learned the most from and that is Larry Thompson, there is no question.

Taylor Thompson
Founder, The SheNetwork

 When I joined Herbalife International in 1993, I started as a stay-at-home mom of a brand-new baby. I basically was hoping to earn $800 a month, I wanted mom care versus daycare. Immediately, I was given a bootlegged copy of Larry Thompson's *The Millionaire Training.* I was also encouraged to listen to Jim Rohn as a part of my audio routine. At that time, he was a huge part of the Herbalife culture.

Tish, (Larry's sister) was my indirect upline, and I immediately admired her because she was so real and authentic. It was this kind of environment that allowed for a stay-at-home mom like me to thrive. I worked hard at making my business a success and as my business grew, I was fortunate to qualify for various meetings at Tish's ranch where I got to meet and get to know Jim Rohn personally. That is when I learned that it was Larry who brought Jim into the Herbalife family.

I was very proud of my success at Herbalife being a stay-at-home mom of three girls and ultimately a single mom. Shortly after Mark Hughes passed away in May of 2000, I qualified for the Presidential Summit in LA that August. As a bonus, Tish took a handful of top distributors in her group to go and meet her brother, Larry, at his estate in LA.

Riding up to Larry's mansion in a limo through the rolling hills, I had to pinch myself. I was just a West Texas girl. This was almost unimaginable…like a movie. We arrived in front of this sprawling estate and just as I was walking in the doorway, Larry was descending from this palatial staircase. I had never been star struck in my life, and I don't think I believed in love at first sight, until that minute. Little did I know that he felt the same way when he saw me for the first time, but it would be over a year before that was revealed. It was a year and a half later when we would finally have our first date.

I lived in Texas and he was in California; he had raised his girls, I had three little ones; we had a 20-year age difference and his closet was bigger than my entire house. It didn't make any sense to either of us. Well, true love with a higher purpose doesn't always make sense.

To describe Larry from my perspective and my experiences brings to mind the words: genius, wisdom beyond his years, insights, intuitiveness, empathy, humility, always a desire to help others belief in themselves, strong, passionate, and so giving of himself.

In 2005, the five of us, Larry, me and my three girls, went to Maui where we all got married on the beach. It was important to Larry to demonstrate to them how important they are. He has always put the girls first. He is a giver by nature. I brought him into a family lifestyle that he hadn't been able to experience with his own daughters. My girls were young, and we were going to sporting events, pep rallies and teacher's meetings.

When we decided to buy a house, we chose to live in a neighborhood in Prosper, Texas. Larry freaked out. His homes previously had gates. I wanted normal. I wanted our girls to have a neighborhood with kids and streets. It was meant to be temporary, but we live in the same home 16 years later.

Larry has told me, "I've lived in a lot of houses and I've lived in some mansions, but this is my first home." I moved a lot as a kid, so this has been my first home, too. It's been important for us to raise our girls around family. One of his daughters, Lari, and his granddaughters, live in Dallas and of course, his sister, Tish, and his nieces. We gather at Tish's for Thanksgiving at her ranch and always at our home for Christmas.

His daughters, Lari and Leah, seem grateful that Larry has been able to have this experience, because he didn't have this type of "normal" environment while raising them. We have our home, our family, our community, and our church. It's normal for us. We love it.

Preach what you practice. Larry is always teaching, always encouraging. He lives what he teaches every single day. His teaching is in the subtleties. It is in the way he treats me that my three daughters have witnessed day in and day out. He will ask, "What can I do for you today? How can I serve you today?"

Our girls have been indoctrinated into the philosophy of *The Millionaire Training* and all his teachings by how we live life each day, not by listening to the tapes. He has given me tools and philosophies for being a better parent. As the girls squabbled and fought over stuff like girls do, he would tell them, "It's not about what *they* did. What are *you* going to do about it?"

Today, we have three offices in our home. Two of our girls are entrepreneurs and know the concepts of Employ Yourself, Self-Discipline, and Self-Responsibility. They've picked up the lingo and basic fundamentals just by watching us and it's amazing to listen to them engage with clients. I believe more is caught than taught. When I started in Herbalife so many years ago, I had no idea the empowering and positive impact it would have on my three daughters and who they are in their lives.

When I was interviewing the people who shared their stories in this book, it became clear that just like in our family, their families and friends have also been impacted in many positive ways because they took the time to metabolize *The Millionaire Training* on a deep level. Trey Herron followed in his father's footsteps at Herbalife. Jeff Roberti and Dan Stammen, friends since high school, have both created network marketing legacies that impact people around the globe. The deep gratitude each of these people have for Larry and the difference he and *The Millionaire Training* have made in their life is profound.

As we were talking, I also witnessed a common thread – most of them listened to *The Millionaire Training* over and over and over. I think back to that time when they received *The Millionaire Training* in their Herbalife distributor packs, there was no internet. There weren't a million podcasts to choose from every morning. There were no shiny objects to distract them. They had this cassette training, and they listened to it, took notes and listened to it more until they knew every word.

All were students of *The Millionaire Training* and continue to be students to this day. That kind of deep understanding of the fundamentals of network marketing is missing in our industry right now.

We are in an era where we have all the information we could ever want at our fingertips, we have all the technology, we have all the tools, but we don't have the kind of results that the lady truck driver, Tish Rochin, and the waitress, Karla Ingolio, had in building legacy businesses. Why is that?

So much of the training today is based on *marketing* training, not *network marketing* training. Marketing training is evolving constantly, changing day-to-day and not the foundation. It changes on things that we have no control over like algorithms that come and go. The latest marketing techniques on social media change so fast; few of us keep up.

Network marketing training is timeless. It is about people and how people relate to each other through sharing stories and wanting to help each other. That never changes.

Most people are more comfortable hiding behind their computer gathering more information than getting out and talking to people. They want it all automated. There is nothing wrong with knowing how to do all the marketing stuff, but the stay-at-home mom, the waitress, the long-haired hippie construction worker would not be successful if they had to learn marketing BEFORE network marketing.

For those of you who love to do social media and are good at it, it is even more powerful when you can apply the solid network marketing fundamentals that I am talking about to what you do best.

There is no one alive today who understands the fundamental principles of network marketing better than Larry Thompson. Few people know that Larry did something similar with a reel-to-reel recording of Bobby DePew. In his third 90-days as a new distributor with Bestline, Larry was selected to take on a new territory in El Paso, Texas. As I think about this from a distributor perspective, I cannot even imagine how hard it must have been for him. He was there with no family, no friends, no conference calls, no zoom meetings, no downline and no upline.

Long-distance was too expensive to make phone calls back to family or his upline. I don't know that I would have made it, I truly believe most people would have quit.

It was during those long nights with tears on his pillow that Larry listened to Bobby over and over while focused on what he was putting into his own Mental Projector. He stayed focused on the basics, even when there were so many moments he wanted to quit and go back home to California. Larry lived these fundamental principles first-hand. It was there that he learned for himself, that the Daily Method of Operation, The 10 Pennies, and S.I.N.L.O.A. are real.

If Larry hadn't pressed through those challenges and fully understood these principles in his darkest hour, it is very likely he would have gone back to construction and never would have delivered *The Millionaire Training* that day. And, if that training had not been delivered, we would not have the network marketing industry as we know it today.

El Paso was a historical event in network marketing and one that also made Larry a great mentor to many distributors worldwide.

When you become a student of something timeless like *The Millionaire Training, The Thompson Rule 80-15-5*, and *The Six Pillars*, it changes your character. When you change your character, you change your life. When you learn the message, the psychology and understanding that people are people whether it is 1960, 1980 or 2020, however you go about delivering that message doesn't matter. You become that person with a briefcase full of skills that you can take with you anywhere and be successful.

Larry and I see new distributors overwhelmed by all this information, thinking that the more they know, the more success they will have. The problem is, they want to learn more to do more and they never learn enough and consequently never truly get started. You cannot allow yourself to get bogged down by information overload, you must get into, and stay in, purposeful activity. Activity is the only way you will achieve success in your personal growth.

If you want to become Arnold Schwarzenegger, you can read all the same books as Arnold will read. You can watch all the videos of him working out and you can study his techniques. You can read every bodybuilding article, listen to every podcast ever created on bodybuilding. Yet, until you go to the gym and lift the weights for yourself, nothing will happen. You have to lift the weights. You must do the activity. The same is true in our business and personal growth.

Be excited about the products/service/opportunity you represent and get into action. When I say action, I mean talk to people about what happened to you and what has happened to others. It doesn't matter what company you choose but choose the one that you feel passionate about and get to work. Quit scrolling. Stop looking for the magic dust. Quit getting ready to get ready. Get into the right activity, the income producing activity.

We have some trainers in our space who don't know and understand the fundamentals because they have never been taught. They don't understand the concepts on which this industry was built. They are trying to turn everyday people into marketers instead of network marketers.

Take the time to learn the fundamental concepts of network marketing. Network marketing is the average person's best chance. It is fun, simple and magical. I was always taught, *If they can do it, I can do it.* And, *If I can do it, they can do it.*

Just as Larry predicted 40 years ago during *The Millionaire Training,* women are truly a force in network marketing. Today, 70% of people in network marketing are women. We are searching for ways to provide more for our families without giving up our time away from home.

Women understand *The Six Pillars* instinctively because we love to tell stories. We take self-responsibility naturally as we care for our families and loved ones. We love to share and collaborate. It's all in network marketing. I know that as women, we still often take a backseat to men. Testosterone does not make one a better leader, especially now. Female leadership is vital to the next generation of network marketing.

Being able to take the stage and train these concepts with Larry has been an experience like no other. He gave me the right to be on stage with him long before I thought I deserved it. It gave me the opportunity to go to the gym and lift my own weights so speak. I have learned so much in the process of working side-by-side Larry. One example is, *You don't know it until you can't forget it.*

It is so powerful to be able to complement each other, finish each other's sentences and be congruent, succinct, and fluid. No notes. No PowerPoints. We pray together before every training that God may use our voices to speak what people need to hear. It's humbling to be used as a mouthpiece for the Lord and we both feel very strongly about that.

Larry has always believed in the possibilities of others. He has a way of inspiring and encouraging…it is his gift. He always answers the phone, no matter who is calling. He will invest hours of time and never have a concern.

Larry was a long-haired hippy construction worker whose potential was recognized by two people he never knew before – Bobby DePew and Jim Rohn. Bobby and Jim wrapped their arms around Larry, and he has never forgotten that someone else saw in him what he did not see in himself. Larry looks for the same in others; he looks for their strengths and instills possibilities.

There is so much to be grateful for in our marriage and our time together. He has taught me to be a giver at all levels without expectation. He gives without attachment, with no expected outcome or advantage. When I watch him with people, he gives. He teaches what he lives. He is one of the most forgiving human beings I've ever met. When you are a giver, it is easy for people to take advantage of you, and I have watched him overlook and forgive the unforgivable.

I am deeply grateful that God brought Larry into my life. I'm grateful for how he has loved me and cherished me as his wife. I'm grateful for the man and role model he has been for our family. I'm grateful for the joy and happiness he has brought to my life as my husband, best friend, business partner and my soulmate. I will never have the all the words I need to convey our incredible journey together and how much Larry means to me.

There is something I often think about and don't often bring up in conversation. I know there was no coincidence that when I met Larry for the first time that we felt the same way about each other even if we didn't say it. Personally, as a

Christian, I don't believe in such things as coincidence. There is no Hebrew translation for the word *coincidence*, which leads me to know there was no coincidence when I met Larry.

And, speaking of coincidence, I feel compelled to ask you...

Was it a coincidence in 1968 that Larry joined his first company on the same day, at the same meeting as Jim Rohn did?

Was it a coincidence that Jim spent more stage and personal time with Larry than anyone else in his career?

Was it a coincidence years later in 1978 that Larry Thompson and Mark Hughes joined Golden Youth Marketing at the same meeting? Where Larry became the Vice President of Sales and Mark the #1 Distributor?

Was it a coincidence that in 1979 Golden Youth closed its doors, the United States opened trade with the Republic of China which allowed them to bring in herbs for consumption, and Amway won the fight to legitimize multi-level marketing with the federal government?

Was it a coincidence in 1980 that Mark Hughes asked Larry to help him start a weight loss company from the trunk of his car that we now know as the multi-billion-dollar, global giant Herbalife International?

Was it a coincidence that Larry brought Jim Rohn to Herbalife where he touched thousands with his timeless business philosophies to become a global household name?

Was it a coincidence that at Larry's very first training for Herbalife International, Mark Hughes decided at the last minute to record that training?

Was it a coincidence that Mark Hughes decided to call that recording *The Millionaire Training?*

And, is it a coincidence that YOU are reading this book RIGHT NOW?

I think not.

Wealth Building with Larry and Taylor Thompson

Learning to Collaborate and Work Together to WIN

The concept of building wealth or becoming a Wealth Builder, as created by Larry Thompson and taught with his wife, Taylor, is to involve yourself in a learning rich environment that is stronger than wealth itself. With an exceptional curriculum of subjects and the background of those who serve as messengers of the Wealth Builder message, you'll discover that learning more knowledge must be supplemented with special insights that build the character, skills and effectiveness of the person seeking to build wealth that is truly the greater value.

The wisdom, experience and philosophies gathered by Larry during his 50+ years of experience and success in network marketing, has enabled him to create a set of values, principles, strategies and tactics that make it possible for success to be taught; and because it can be taught, it can be learned. Who else could we possibly learn from who would be more effective at teaching wealth building than the man *The Wall Street Journal* referred to as "The Original Architect of Wealth Building?"

Larry has proven that wealth building can be learned by people from all walks of life – truck drivers, schoolteachers, coaches, police and firefighters, mechanics, rocket scientists. The list of candidates has no limits.

The power inherent in Larry and Taylor's WealthBuilding Academy that can bring success within the reach of virtually anyone, is found in a very basic and profound truth – success and wealth are the result of the relentless execution of about a half-dozen simple disciplines, practiced every day. It is not complicated, but it does require focus.

The half-dozen purposeful activities are found in their acclaimed *The Six Pillars*, which is but one of the WealthBuilding major segments, another is the powerful and effective compilation of video subjects taught by Larry and Taylor in the LT WealthBuilding Academy.

Please realize, the ultimate wealth to be gained from becoming a Wealth Builder with Larry and Taylor Thompson is found not only in financial progress, but also in becoming a better person, a better parent, a happy and more effective leader, a more supportive and understanding spouse, a more productive and valued employee, and a better example for children and young people to emulate.

What would it feel like or look like for you (and your family) to finally get money out of the way as a source of daily preoccupation? That includes becoming free of the crushing, unintended consequences of personal debt.

Why not invest in your better future by designing it in advance so you and those around you may reach the natural, logical conclusion that it's best to have a life that's more on your terms than on the terms of someone else? This could be the last real chance you'll ever have to take a tangible step that can help assure that the years ahead of you will, perhaps, prove to be more rewarding and filled with happiness than those that are now behind you. Why not let Larry and Taylor show you that they believe in you until you're strong enough to believe in yourself.

The WealthBuilders
Exclusive Inner Circle

Join Larry and Taylor's Exclusive Inner Circle where you will be shown HOW TO APPLY the Success Fundamentals of *The Millionaire Training, The Thompson Rule 80-15-5, The Six Pillars* and *The Gig Economy for optimal results.* Plus, you'll receive:

LIVE, Monthly Hot Seat Training (4-6 hours per month) with Larry, Taylor and Inner Circle Members. PRICELESS.

DIRECT ACCESS to Larry, Taylor and Their Top Inner Circle as Your Needs May Require.

PRIVATE Facebook Group Interaction and Coaching with Elite Inner Circle Members

---

FULL ACCESS to the LT WealthBuilding Academy

FULL ACCESS to *The Fundamentals of Success*

FULL ACCESS to *The Gig Economy Success Fundamentals*

Plus, You Receive All the Benefits of *The WealthBuilder Membership (next page)*

Membership is limited. Application required.
Go to wealthbuilding.pro/application

The WealthBuilders Membership

Only $480

Annual Subscription

LIVE, Interactive Coaching (4-6 hours per month)
with Larry, Taylor and WealthBuilders Members.

PRIVATE Facebook Group Interaction and Coaching
with WealthBuilders Members.

FULL ACCESS to the LT WealthBuilding Academy Library
with More Than 80 Episodes | Building Leadership and
Concepts to Daily Method of Operation.

The Original Millionaire Training Audios

The Millionaire Training 2.0 (video and audio)
in English, Spanish and German

FULL ACCESS to the Highly Acclaimed Six Pillars
(Foundational to All Network Marketing Business)
with Larry, Taylor and Select Inner Circle Members

Join by going to www.WealthBuilding.pro to register.

Private Consulting with Larry and Taylor Thompson

If you are a distributor or a company who is committed to growing your organization exponentially or you are interested in having Larry and Taylor speak at your next big event, please contact them directly at www.WealthBuilding.pro/speaker for private consulting options and special requests.

THE
Millionaire
Training™

If you would like to order additional copies of *The Millionaire Training* or download the original audio of *The Millionaire Training,* go to TheMillionaireTraining.com. You will also receive special offers exclusive only to The Millionaire Training Book Club members.

Printed in Great Britain
by Amazon

67807839R00220